Java EE 7 with GlassFish 4 Application Server

A practical guide to install and configure the GlassFish 4 application server and develop Java EE 7 applications to be deployed to this server

David R. Heffelfinger

BIRMINGHAM - MUMBAI

Java EE 7 with GlassFish 4 Application Server

Copyright © 2014 Packt Publishing

All rights reserved. No part of this book may be reproduced, stored in a retrieval system, or transmitted in any form or by any means, without the prior written permission of the publisher, except in the case of brief quotations embedded in critical articles or reviews.

Every effort has been made in the preparation of this book to ensure the accuracy of the information presented. However, the information contained in this book is sold without warranty, either express or implied. Neither the author, nor Packt Publishing, and its dealers and distributors will be held liable for any damages caused or alleged to be caused directly or indirectly by this book.

Packt Publishing has endeavored to provide trademark information about all of the companies and products mentioned in this book by the appropriate use of capitals. However, Packt Publishing cannot guarantee the accuracy of this information.

First published: October 2007

Second Edition: July 2010

Third Edition: March 2014

Production Reference: 1200314

Published by Packt Publishing Ltd.
Livery Place
35 Livery Street
Birmingham B3 2PB, UK.

ISBN 978-1-78217-688-6

www.packtpub.com

Cover Image by Aniket Sawant (aniket_sawant_photography@hotmail.com)

Credits

Author
David R. Heffelfinger

Reviewers
Stefan Horochovec
Tim Pinet
Chirag Sangani

Acquisition Editors
Subho Gupta
Rubal Kaur

Content Development Editor
Akshay Nair

Technical Editors
Pratik More
Humera Shaikh
Rohit Kumar Singh
Pratish Soman

Copy Editors
Tanvi Gaitonde
Dipti Kapadia
Aditya Nair
Kirti Pai
Stuti Srivastava

Project Coordinator
Amey Sawant

Proofreaders
Maria Gould
Sandra Hopper
Linda Morris

Indexers
Mehreen Deshmukh
Rekha Nair

Graphics
Yuvraj Mannari

Production Coordinator
Aparna Bhagat

Cover Work
Aparna Bhagat

About the Author

David R. Heffelfinger is the Chief Technology Officer at Ensode Technology, LLC, a software consulting firm based in the Greater Washington DC area. He has been architecting, designing, and developing software professionally since 1995. He has been using Java as his primary programming language since 1996. He has worked on many large-scale projects for several clients including the U.S. Department of Homeland Security, Freddie Mac, Fannie Mae, and the U.S. Department of Defense. He has a master's degree in Software Engineering from Southern Methodist University. David is the Editor-in-chief of Ensode.net (http://www.ensode.net), a website on Java, Linux, and other technologies. David is a frequent speaker at Java conference such as JavaOne. You can follow David on Twitter, @ensode.

About the Reviewers

Stefan Horochovec is from Brazil. He has a graduate degree in Software Engineering and also in Project Management and currently works as a software architect.

Over the past 10 years, he has been dedicated to the development of Enterprise Applications using Java as the backend technology and application servers, such as GlassFish, JBoss, Weblogic, and WildFly.

With regards to frontend, Stefan has worked for 4 years with technologies such as Apache Flex (speaking for three consecutive years at FlexMania, the biggest event on Apache Flex in Latin America), Struts, and JSF. Today, his focus is on projects involving JSF 2 and JavaScript frameworks, with a strong focus on AngularJS.

He has worked with the mobile world for about 6 years, having extensive experience on the Android platform. He was one of the first Android instructors in Brazil and a speaker at the Android conference in Brazil. For about 2 years, he has been working with the HTML-based mobile development using frameworks such as PhoneGap to build enterprise applications.

In 2014, Stefan was invited to join the BlackBerry Elite Member program, which gathers around 100 people worldwide, emphasizing the importance of mobile development, technologies for their development, and using the operating system and BlackBerry devices on the mobile platform.

Stefan also teaches in University courses related to web and Mobile development and is an instructor of in-company courses related to Java, HTML/JS/CSS3, PhoneGap, Git, and Java application servers.

Tim Pinet is a practicing software engineer and web developer currently residing in Ottawa, Canada. From an early age, he was always fascinated with all electronic things and went on to graduate with a bachelor's degree in Engineering in the Software Engineering stream. As Ottawa is a large capital city with a technology sector rich with opportunity, Tim has had the fortune to practice software engineering and systems integration in both private (Computer Associates, Emergis, Telus, Nortel) and public (City of Ottawa) companies and in numerous industries such as transportation and road/weather information systems, healthcare recording, communications and telephony infrastructure, and municipal citizen-centric services and payment handling.

Tim's open source mantra helps him to focus on working for low cost, but high productivity in any environment and has him giving back to projects (such as Apache and SourceForge) and community knowledge bases (such as Stackoverflow and his personal blog). He has brought open source tools to his employers, saving them thousands of dollars and giving them best-practice accelerated development and testing capabilities without giving up dollars or quality.

Loving all things software and web, Tim constantly indulges himself in the newest technologies to better improve service to the end client. He has a vast experience in Java using enterprise technologies, web services, client GUI development, server backend development, database management integration, and SOA services integration. He is a very focused team player and works best in leading teams and architecting solutions.

Chirag Sangani is a computer scientist living in the Seattle area. He obtained his MS from Stanford University, CA, and his B. Tech. from IIT Kanpur, India. He currently works as a software development engineer for Microsoft.

www.PacktPub.com

Support files, eBooks, discount offers and more

You might want to visit `www.PacktPub.com` for support files and downloads related to your book.

Did you know that Packt offers eBook versions of every book published, with PDF and ePub files available? You can upgrade to the eBook version at `www.PacktPub.com` and as a print book customer, you are entitled to a discount on the eBook copy. Get in touch with us at `service@packtpub.com` for more details.

At `www.PacktPub.com`, you can also read a collection of free technical articles, sign up for a range of free newsletters and receive exclusive discounts and offers on Packt books and eBooks.

`http://PacktLib.PacktPub.com`

Do you need instant solutions to your IT questions? PacktLib is Packt's online digital book library. Here, you can access, read and search across Packt's entire library of books.

Why Subscribe?

- Fully searchable across every book published by Packt
- Copy and paste, print and bookmark content
- On demand and accessible via web browser

Free Access for Packt account holders

If you have an account with Packt at `www.PacktPub.com`, you can use this to access PacktLib today and view nine entirely free books. Simply use your login credentials for immediate access.

Instant Updates on New Packt Books

Get notified! Find out when new books are published by following `@PacktEnterprise` on Twitter, or the *Packt Enterprise* Facebook page.

Table of Contents

Preface	**1**
Chapter 1: Getting Started with GlassFish	**7**
An Overview of Java EE and GlassFish	**7**
What's new in Java EE 7?	8
JavaServer Faces (JSF) 2.2	8
Java Persistence API (JPA) 2.1	8
Java API for RESTful Web Services (JAX-RS) 2.0	9
Java Message Service (JMS) 2.0	9
Java API for JSON Processing (JSON-P) 1.0	10
Java API for WebSocket 1.0	10
GlassFish advantages	10
Obtaining GlassFish	**11**
Installing GlassFish	**13**
GlassFish dependencies	13
Performing the installation	13
Starting GlassFish	**14**
Deploying our first Java EE application	16
Deploying an application through the Web Console	16
Undeploying an application through the GlassFish Admin Console	19
Deploying an application through the command line	20
GlassFish domains	**23**
Creating Domains	23
Deleting domains	25
Stopping a domain	25
Setting up Database Connectivity	**26**
Setting up connection pools	26
Setting up the data sources	30
Summary	**31**

Chapter 2: JavaServer Faces — 33
Introduction to JSF — 33
Facelets — 33
Optional faces-config.xml — 34
Standard resource locations — 34
Developing our first JSF application — 35
Facelets — 35
Project stages — 41
Validation — 44
Grouping components — 45
Form submission — 46
Named beans — 46
Navigation — 48
Custom data validation — 50
Creating custom validators — 50
Validator methods — 53
Customizing JSF's default messages — 56
Customizing message styles — 57
Customizing message text — 59
Ajax-enabling JSF applications — 61
JSF 2.2 HTML5 support — 66
The HTML5-friendly markup — 66
Pass-through elements — 68
JSF 2.2 Faces Flows — 70
Additional JSF component libraries — 74
Summary — 74

Chapter 3: Object Relational Mapping with JPA — 75
The CustomerDB database — 75
Introducing the Java Persistence API — 77
Entity relationships — 82
One-to-one relationships — 83
One-to-many relationships — 89
Many-to-many relationships — 95
Composite primary keys — 102
Introducing the Java Persistence Query Language — 108
Introducing the Criteria API — 111
Updating data with the Criteria API — 115
Deleting data with the Criteria API — 117
Bean Validation support — 119
Final notes — 121
Summary — 122

Chapter 4: Enterprise JavaBeans — 123
Introduction to session beans — 124
- Developing a simple session bean — 124
- A more realistic example — 128
- Invoking session beans from web applications — 130
- Introduction to singleton session beans — 132
- Asynchronous method calls — 133

Message-driven beans — 136
Transactions in Enterprise JavaBeans — 137
- Container-managed transactions — 137
- Bean-managed transactions — 140

Enterprise JavaBean life cycles — 143
- The stateful session bean life cycle — 143
- The stateless session bean life cycle — 146
- Message-driven bean life cycle — 148

Introduction to the EJB Timer Service — 149
- Calendar-based EJB timer expressions — 152

EJB Security — 155
- Client authentication — 158

Summary — 159

Chapter 5: Contexts and Dependency Injection — 161
Named beans — 161
Dependency injection — 164
Working with CDI Qualifiers — 165
Named bean scopes — 169
Summary — 176

Chapter 6: JSON Processing with JSON-P — 177
The JSON-P Model API — 178
- Generating JSON data with the Model API — 178
- Parsing JSON data with the Model API — 181

The JSON-P Streaming API — 183
- Generating JSON data with the Streaming API — 183
- Parsing JSON data with the Streaming API — 185

Summary — 188

Chapter 7: WebSockets — 189
Developing a WebSocket server endpoint — 189
- Developing an annotated WebSocket server endpoint — 190

Developing WebSocket clients — 193
- Developing JavaScript client-side WebSocket code — 193
- Developing WebSocket clients in Java — 197

Additional information about the Java API for WebSocket	201
Summary	201
Chapter 8: The Java Message Service	**203**
Setting up GlassFish for JMS	203
Setting up a JMS connection factory	204
Setting up a JMS queue	207
Setting up a JMS topic	208
Working with message queues	209
Sending messages to a message queue	209
Retrieving messages from a message queue	212
Asynchronously receiving messages from a message queue	214
Browsing message queues	217
Working with message topics	219
Sending messages to a message topic	219
Receiving messages from a message topic	220
Creating durable subscribers	222
Summary	225
Chapter 9: Securing Java EE Applications	**227**
Security realms	227
Predefined security realms	228
The admin-realm	228
The file realm	231
The certificate realm	247
Defining additional realms	256
Defining additional file realms	256
Defining additional certificate realms	258
Defining an LDAP realm	260
Defining a Solaris realm	261
Defining a JDBC realm	262
Defining custom realms	267
Summary	273
Chapter 10: Web Services with JAX-WS	**275**
Developing web services with the JAX-WS API	275
Developing a web service client	281
Sending attachments to web services	287
Exposing EJBs as web services	290
EJB web service clients	291
Securing web services	292
Securing EJB web services	295
Summary	297

Chapter 11: Developing RESTful Web Services with JAX-RS — 299
Introducing RESTful web services and JAX-RS — 299
Developing a simple RESTful web service — 300
Configuring the REST resources path for our application — 303
Configuring via the @ApplicationPath annotation — 304
Testing our web service — 304
Converting data between Java and XML with JAXB — 307
Developing a RESTful web service client — 311
Working with query and path parameters — 312
Query parameters — 312
Sending query parameters via the JAX-RS client API — 315
Path parameters — 316
Sending path parameters via the JAX-RS Client API — 318
Summary — 320
Index — 321

Preface

Java Enterprise Edition 7, the latest version of Java EE, adds several new features to the specification. Several existing Java EE APIs have gone through major improvements in this version of the specification; additionally, some brand new APIs have been added to Java EE. This book includes coverage of the latest versions of the most popular Java EE specifications, including JavaServer Faces (JSF), Java Persistence API (JPA), Enterprise JavaBeans (EJB), Contexts and Dependency Injection (CDI), the new Java API for JSON Processing (JSON-P), WebSocket, the completely revamped Java Messaging Service (JMS) API 2.0, the Java API for XML Web Services (JAX-WS) and the Java API for RESTful Web Services (JAX-RS), as well as securing Java EE applications.

The GlassFish application server is the reference implementation for Java EE; it is the first Java EE application server in the market to support Java EE 7. This book covers GlassFish 4.0, the latest version of this powerful open source application server.

What this book covers

Chapter 1, *Getting Started with GlassFish*, explains how to install and configure GlassFish. Deploying Java EE applications through the GlassFish web console are also explained. Finally, basic GlassFish administration tasks such as setting up domains and database connectivity by adding connection pools and data sources are discussed.

Chapter 2, *JavaServer Faces*, covers development of web applications using JSF, including new features such as HTML5-friendly markup and Faces Flows. It also covers how to validate user input using JSF's standard validators and also by creating our own custom validators or by writing validator methods.

Chapter 3, *Object Relational Mapping with JPA*, discusses how to develop code that interacts with a Relational Database Management System (RDBMS) such as Oracle or MySQL through the Java Persistence API.

Chapter 4, *Enterprise JavaBeans*, explains how to develop applications using both session and message-driven beans. Major EJB features such as transaction management, the EJB timer service, and security are covered. The life cycle of the different types of Enterprise JavaBeans are covered, including an explanation of how to have EJB methods automatically invoked by the EJB container at certain points in the life cycle.

Chapter 5, *Contexts and Dependency Injection*, provides an introduction to Contexts and Dependency Injection (CDI). The chapter covers CDI named beans, dependency injection using CDI, and CDI qualifiers.

Chapter 6, *JSON Processing with JSON-P*, covers how to generate and parse JavaScript Object Notation (JSON) data using the new JSON-P API. It also covers both APIs for processing JSON: the Model API and the Streaming API.

Chapter 7, *WebSockets*, explains how to develop web-based applications that feature full duplex communication between the browser and the server as opposed to relying on the traditional HTTP request/response cycle.

Chapter 8, *The Java Message Service*, covers how to set up JMS connection factories, JMS message queues, and JMS message topics in GlassFish using the GlassFish web console. The chapter also discusses how to develop messaging applications using the completely revamped JMS 2.0 API.

Chapter 9, *Securing Java EE Applications*, covers how to secure Java EE applications through provided security realms as well as how to add custom security realms.

Chapter 10, *Web Services with JAX-WS*, covers how to develop web services and web service clients via the JAX-WS API. Web service client code generation using ANT or Maven as a build tool has been explained.

Chapter 11, *Developing RESTful Web Services with JAX-RS*, discusses how to develop RESTful Web services via the Java API for RESTful Web services as well as how to develop RESTful Web service clients via the brand new standard JAX-RS client API. It also explains how to automatically convert data between Java and XML by taking advantage of the Java API for XML Binding (JAXB).

What you need for this book

The following software needs to be installed to follow the material in this book:

- The Java Development Kit (JDK) 1.7 or newer
- GlassFish 4.0
- Maven 3 or newer is needed to build the examples
- A Java IDE such as NetBeans, Eclipse, or IntelliJ IDEA (optional, but recommended).

Who this book is for

This book assumes familiarity with the Java language. The target market for this book is the existing Java developers who wish to learn Java EE and the existing Java EE developers who wish to update their skills to the latest Java EE specification.

Conventions

In this book, you will find a number of styles of text that distinguish between different kinds of information. Here are some examples of these styles, and an explanation of their meaning.

Code words in text, database table names, folder names, filenames, file extensions, pathnames, dummy URLs, user input, and Twitter handles are shown as follows: "The `@Named` class annotation designates this bean as a CDI named bean."

A block of code is set as follows:

```
if (!emailValidator.isValid(email)) {
  FacesMessage facesMessage = new FacesMessage(htmlInputText.getLabel()
+ ": email format is not valid");
  throw new ValidatorException(facesMessage);
}
```

When we wish to draw your attention to a particular part of a code block, the relevant lines or items are set in bold:

```
<ejb>
    <ejb-name>CustomerDaoBean</ejb-name>
    <ior-security-config>
        <as-context>
            <auth-method>username_password</auth-method>
```

```
            <realm>file</realm>
            <required>true</required>
        </as-context>
    </ior-security-config>
</ejb>
```

Any command-line input or output is written as follows:

```
$ ~/GlassFish/glassfish4/bin $ ./asadmin start-domain
Waiting for domain1 to start ........
```

New terms and **important words** are shown in bold. Words that you see on the screen, in menus or dialog boxes for example, appear in the text like this: "Clicking on the **Next** button moves you to the next screen."

> Warnings or important notes appear in a box like this.

> Tips and tricks appear like this.

Reader feedback

Feedback from our readers is always welcome. Let us know what you think about this book—what you liked or may have disliked. Reader feedback is important for us to develop titles that you really get the most out of.

To send us general feedback, simply send an e-mail to `feedback@packtpub.com`, and mention the book title via the subject of your message.

If there is a topic that you have expertise in and you are interested in either writing or contributing to a book, see our author guide on `www.packtpub.com/authors`.

Customer support

Now that you are the proud owner of a Packt book, we have a number of things to help you to get the most from your purchase.

Downloading the example code

You can download the example code files for all Packt books you have purchased from your account at http://www.packtpub.com. If you purchased this book elsewhere, you can visit http://www.packtpub.com/support and register to have the files e-mailed directly to you.

Errata

Although we have taken every care to ensure the accuracy of our content, mistakes do happen. If you find a mistake in one of our books—maybe a mistake in the text or the code—we would be grateful if you would report this to us. By doing so, you can save other readers from frustration and help us improve subsequent versions of this book. If you find any errata, please report them by visiting http://www.packtpub.com/submit-errata, selecting your book, clicking on the **errata submission form** link, and entering the details of your errata. Once your errata are verified, your submission will be accepted and the errata will be uploaded on our website, or added to any list of existing errata, under the Errata section of that title. Any existing errata can be viewed by selecting your title from http://www.packtpub.com/support.

Piracy

Piracy of copyright material on the Internet is an ongoing problem across all media. At Packt, we take the protection of our copyright and licenses very seriously. If you come across any illegal copies of our works, in any form, on the Internet, please provide us with the location address or website name immediately so that we can pursue a remedy.

Please contact us at copyright@packtpub.com with a link to the suspected pirated material.

We appreciate your help in protecting our authors, and our ability to bring you valuable content.

Questions

You can contact us at questions@packtpub.com if you are having a problem with any aspect of the book, and we will do our best to address it.

1
Getting Started with GlassFish

In this chapter, we will discuss how to get started with GlassFish. The following are some of the topics discussed in this chapter:

- An overview of Java EE and GlassFish
- Obtaining GlassFish
- Installing and starting GlassFish
- Explaining the concept of GlassFish domains
- Deploying Java EE applications
- Setting up Database Connectivity

An Overview of Java EE and GlassFish

Java Enterprise Edition (Java EE, formerly called **J2EE** or **Java 2 Enterprise Edition)** is a standard set of technologies for server-side Java development. Java EE technologies include **JavaServer Faces (JSF)**, **Enterprise JavaBeans (EJBs)**, the **Java Messaging Service (JMS)**, the **Java Persistence API (JPA)**, the Java API for WebSocket, **Contexts and Dependency Injection (CDI)**, the **Java API for XML Web Services (JAX-WS)**, the **Java API for RESTful Web Services (JAX-RS)**, and the **Java API for JSON Processing (JSON-P)**, among others.

Several commercial and open source application servers exist. Java EE application servers allow developers to develop and deploy Java EE-compliant applications, GlassFish being one of them. Other open source Java EE application servers include Red Hat's WildFly (formerly JBoss), the Apache Software Foundation's Geronimo, and ObjectWeb's JOnAS. Commercial application servers include Oracle's WebLogic, IBM's WebSphere, and the Oracle Application Server.

GlassFish is the Java EE 7 reference implementation; as such, it implements the latest Java EE APIs before any other application server in the market. GlassFish is open source and freely available, and is licensed under the **Common Development and Distribution License (CDDL)**.

 You can find out more about the CDDL license at http://opensource.org/licenses/CDDL-1.0.

Like all Java EE-compliant application servers, GlassFish provides the necessary libraries to allow us to develop and deploy Java applications compliant with Java EE specifications.

What's new in Java EE 7?

Java EE 7, the latest version of the Java EE specification, includes several improvements and additions to the specification. The following sections list the major improvements to the specifications that are of interest to enterprise application developers:

JavaServer Faces (JSF) 2.2

Java EE 7 includes a new version of the **JavaServer Faces (JSF)** specification. JSF 2.2 includes the following notable new features:

- JSF 2.2 features the HTML5 friendly markup, that is, web pages can be written using the standard HTML 5 markup and using JSF-specific attributes on the HTML tags.
- JSF 2.2 also includes Faces Flows, which provides a way to encapsulate related pages with defined entry and exit points.
- Resource library contracts are the third major JSF feature introduced in JSF 2.2. Resource library contracts allow us to easily develop web applications that can have a different look and feel for different users using JSF.

Java Persistence API (JPA) 2.1

JPA was introduced as a standard part of Java EE in version 5 of the specification. JPA replaced entity beans as the standard object relational mapping framework for Java EE. JPA adopted ideas from third-party object relational frameworks such as Hibernate and JDO, and made them a part of the standard.

JPA 2.1 introduces the following new features:

- JPA 2.1 introduces the concept of **Converters**, which allows custom code conversions between values stored in the database and values stored in Java objects. For instance, a common problem when working with database data is that the desired value in Java code differs from the value stored in the database. For example, the values `1` and `0` are commonly stored in the database to denote `true` and `false` respectively. Java has a perfectly good boolean type, so `true` and `false` can be used directly.
- The JPA Criteria API can now perform bulk updates and deletes.
- JPA 2.1 now supports stored procedures.
- JPA 2.1 introduces the `@ConstructorResult` annotation, which allows returning standard Java classes (but not the JPA entities) from native SQL queries.

Java API for RESTful Web Services (JAX-RS) 2.0

JAX-RS is a Java API for developing RESTful web services. RESTful web services use the **Representational State Transfer** (**REST**) architecture. Java EE 6 adopted JAX-RS as an official part of the Java EE specification.

JAX-RS 2.0 includes the following new features:

- JAX-RS 2.0 introduces a new client-side API. While previous versions of JAX-RS made it easy to develop RESTful web services, each implementation defined its own proprietary client-side API.
- Extension points, method filters, and entity interceptors are also introduced in JAX-RS 2.0. These features allow **Aspect Oriented Programming** (**AOP**) when developing RESTful web services.
- JAX-RS 2.0 also introduces asynchronous processing both on the server side and as part of the client API.

Java Message Service (JMS) 2.0

The **Java Message Service** (**JMS**) API has been completely revamped in Java EE 7. Previous versions of JMS required lots of boilerplate code; with the new revamped JMS 2.0 API, this is no longer the case.

Java API for JSON Processing (JSON-P) 1.0

JSON-P is a brand new API introduced in Java EE 7. JSON-P allows us to parse and generate **JSON (JavaScript Object Notation)** strings.

Java API for WebSocket 1.0

Traditional web applications use a request-response model, that is, a client (typically a web browser) requests resources and the server provides a response. In this model, communication is always initiated by the client.

WebSockets were introduced as part of the HTML5 specification; they provide full-duplex communication between the client and the server.

GlassFish advantages

With so many options in Java EE application servers, why choose GlassFish? Besides the obvious advantage of GlassFish being available free of charge, it offers the following benefits:

- **Java EE reference implementation**: GlassFish is the Java EE reference implementation. What this means is that other application servers may use GlassFish to make sure their product complies with the specification. GlassFish could theoretically be used to debug other application servers. If an application deployed under another application server is not behaving properly, but it does behave properly when deployed under GlassFish, then more than likely the improper behavior is due to a bug in the other application server.

- **Supports the latest versions of the Java EE specification**: Since GlassFish is the reference Java EE specification, it tends to implement the latest specifications before any other application server in the market. As a matter of fact, at the time of writing, GlassFish is the only Java EE application server in the market that supports the complete Java EE 7 specification.

Chapter 1

Obtaining GlassFish

GlassFish can be downloaded at `https://glassfish.java.net`.

 GlassFish 4.0 is also bundled with the NetBeans IDE version 7.4 or newer.

Once there, you will see a window as shown in the following screenshot:

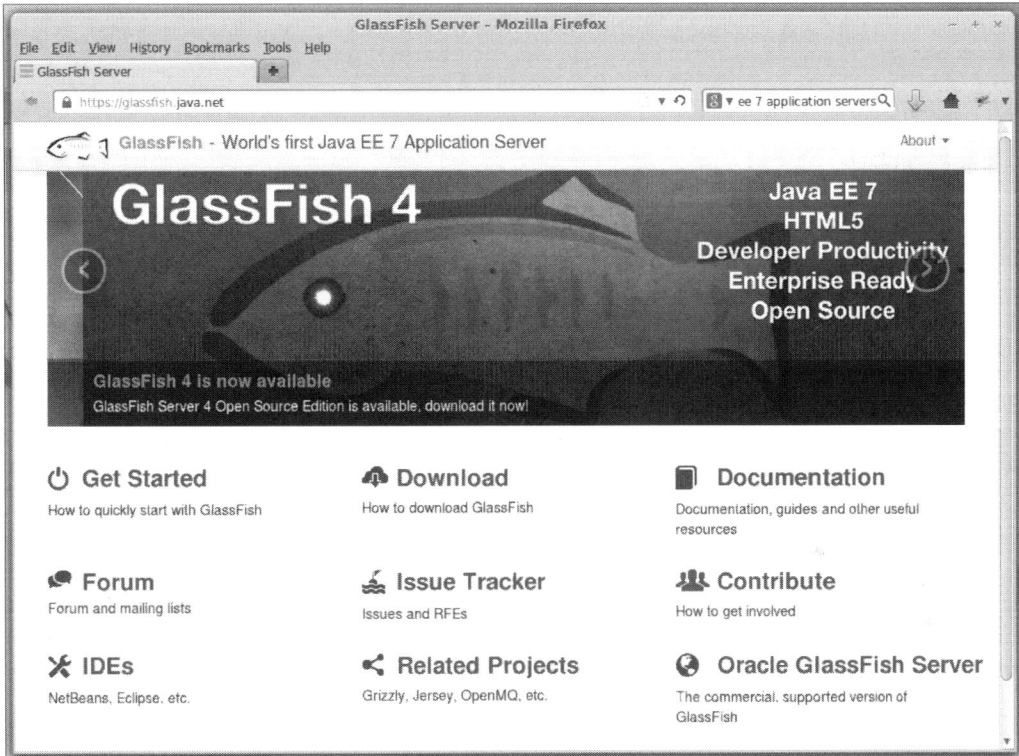

Getting Started with GlassFish

Clicking on the **Download** link takes us to a wizard page that provides several options to download GlassFish as shown in the following screenshot:

The download page has several options; we can get the full Java EE platform or the web profile. We can also download GlassFish as a compressed ZIP file or as a native installer for the operating system of our choice.

To be able to follow all of the examples in this book, we need to download the full Java EE platform version of GlassFish. We will download the compressed ZIP file version since the instructions to install it are very similar across any operating system; feel free to download a platform-specific installer if you prefer.

Installing GlassFish

We will use the ZIP installer to illustrate the installation process. This installation process works under all major operating systems.

Installing GlassFish is an easy process; however, GlassFish assumes that some dependencies are present in your system.

GlassFish dependencies

In order to install GlassFish 4, a recent version of the **Java Development Kit (JDK)** must be installed on your workstation (JDK 1.7 or newer required), and the Java executable file must be in your system PATH. The latest JDK can be downloaded at http://www.oracle.com/technetwork/java/javase/downloads/index.html. Please refer to the JDK installation instructions for your particular platform at http://docs.oracle.com/javase/7/docs/webnotes/install/index.html.

Performing the installation

Once JDK has been installed, the GlassFish installation can begin by simply extracting the download compressed file as shown in the following screenshot:

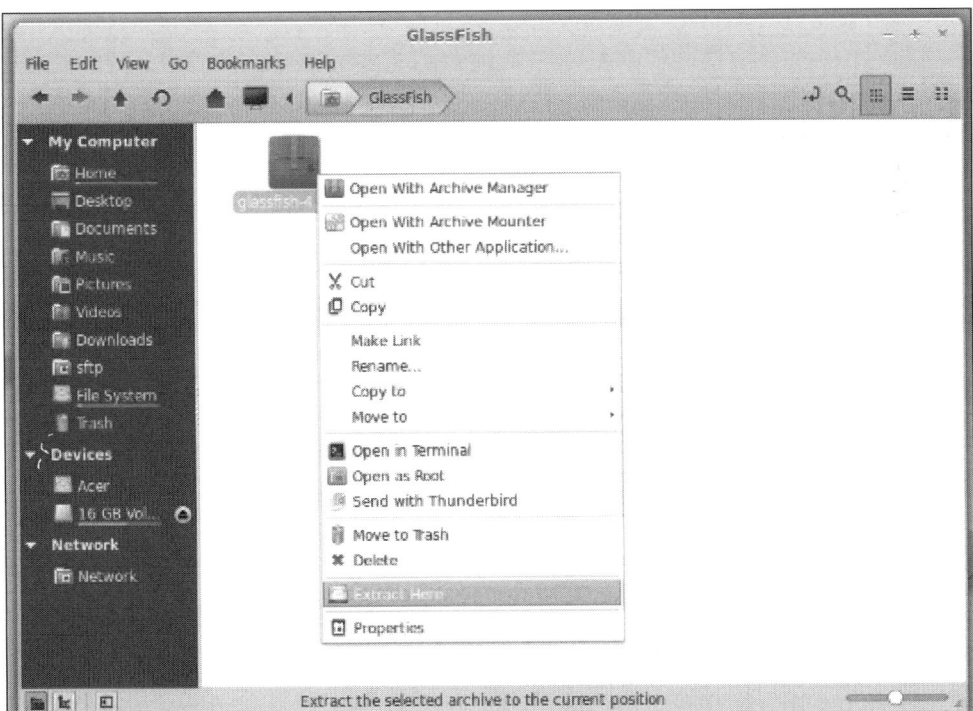

All modern operating systems including Linux, Windows, and Mac OS X include out-of-the-box support to extract compressed ZIP files; consult your operating system documentation for details.

After extracting the ZIP file, a new directory named `glassfish4` will be created. This new directory contains our GlassFish installation.

Starting GlassFish

To start GlassFish from the command line, change your directory to `[glassfish installation directory]/glassfish4/bin` and execute the following command:

`./asadmin start-domain domain1`

 The preceding command, and most commands shown in this chapter, assume a Unix or Unix-like operating system such as Linux or Mac OS. For Windows systems, the initial `./` is not necessary.

A few short seconds after executing the preceding command, we should see a message similar to the following at the bottom of the terminal:

```
$ ~/GlassFish/glassfish4/bin $ ./asadmin start-domain
Waiting for domain1 to start ........
Successfully started the domain : domain1
domain  Location: /home/heffel/GlassFish/glassfish4/glassfish/domains/domain1
Log File: /home/heffel/GlassFish/glassfish4/glassfish/domains/domain1/logs/server.log
Admin Port: 4848
Command start-domain executed successfully.
```

Downloading the example code

You can download the sample code files for all the Packt books that you have purchased from your account at http://www.packtpub.com. If you purchased this book elsewhere, you can visit http://www.packtpub.com/support and register to have the files e-mailed directly to you.

Chapter 1

We can then open a browser window and type the following URL in the browser's location text field:

```
http://localhost:8080
```

If everything goes well, we should see a page indicating that your GlassFish server is now running as shown in the following screenshot:

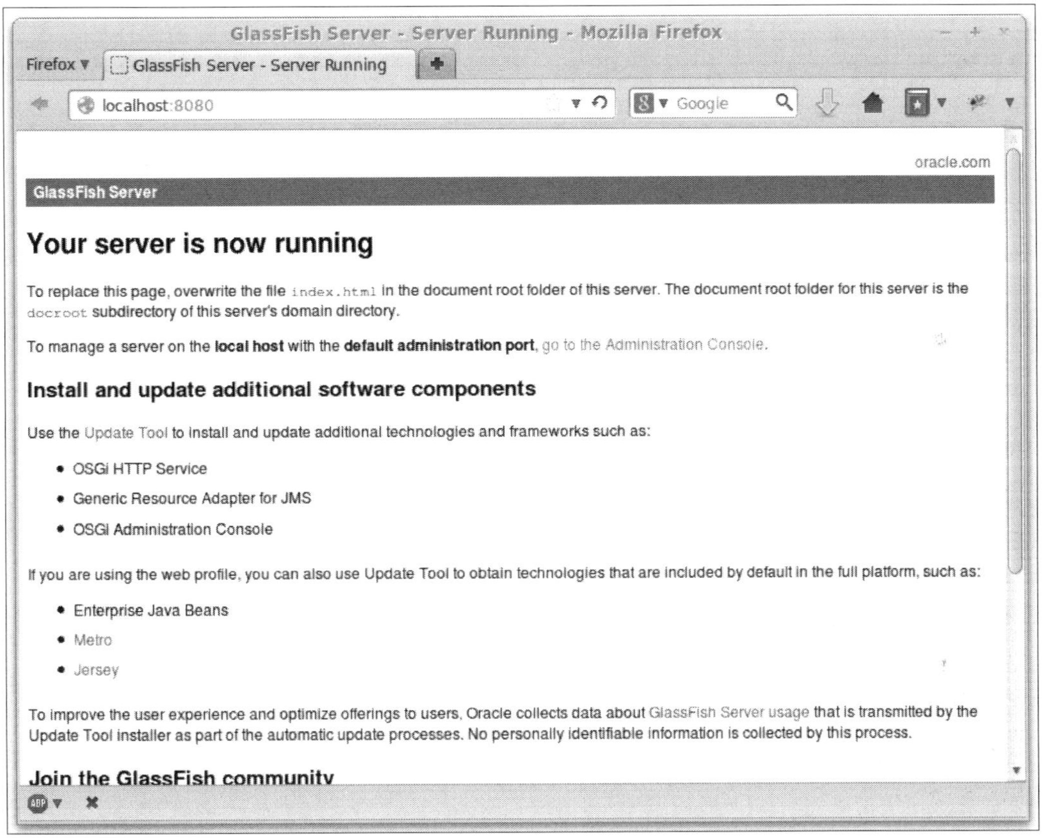

> **Getting Help**
>
> If any of the preceding steps fail or for help with GlassFish in general, a great resource is the GlassFish forum at https://www.java.net/forums/glassfish/glassfish.

Deploying our first Java EE application

To further confirm that our GlassFish installation is running properly, we will deploy a **WAR (Web ARchive)** file and make sure the file deploys and executes properly. Before moving on, please download the file `simpleapp.war` from this book's web site at www.packtpub.com.

Deploying an application through the Web Console

To deploy `simpleapp.war`, open a browser and navigate to `http://localhost:4848`. You should be greeted with the default GlassFish server administration page as shown in the following screenshot:

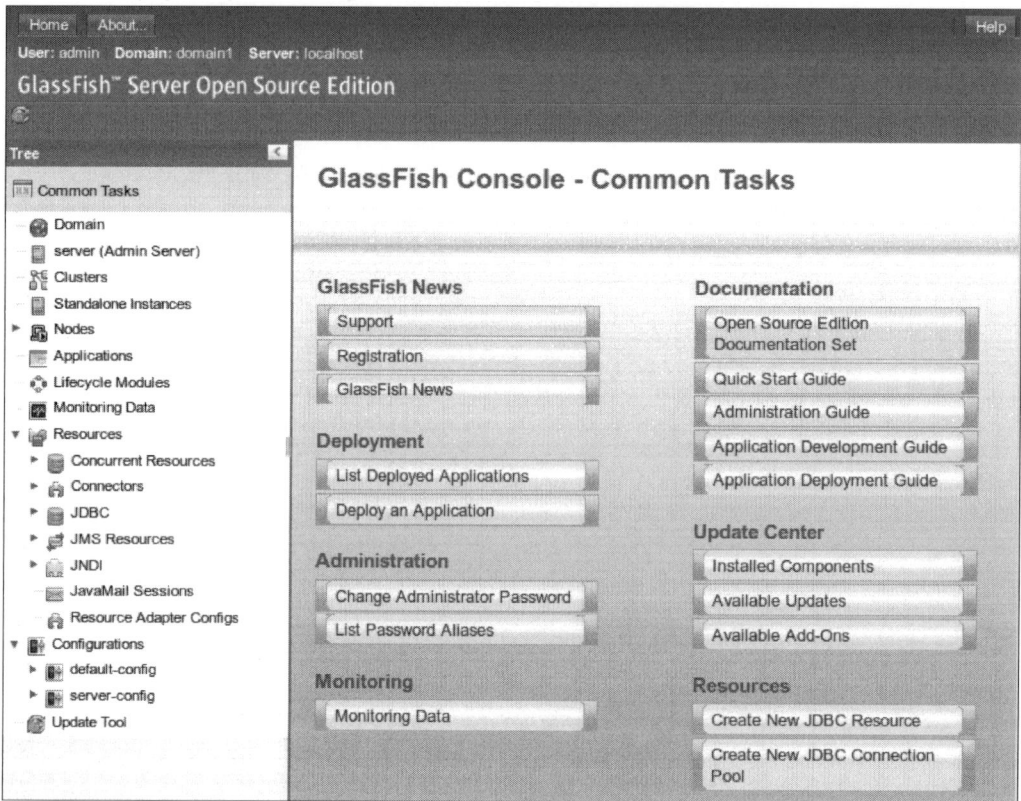

Chapter 1

By default, GlassFish is installed in development mode. In this mode, it is not necessary to enter a username and password to access the GlassFish web console. In production environments, it is highly advisable to configure the web console so that it is password protected.

At this point, we should click on the **Deploy an Application** item under the **Deployment** section on the main screen.

To deploy our application, we should select the **Local Packaged File or Directory That is Accessible from GlassFish Server** radio button and either type the path to our WAR file or select it by clicking on the **Browse Files...** button. Once this is done, you will see a window as shown in the following screenshot:

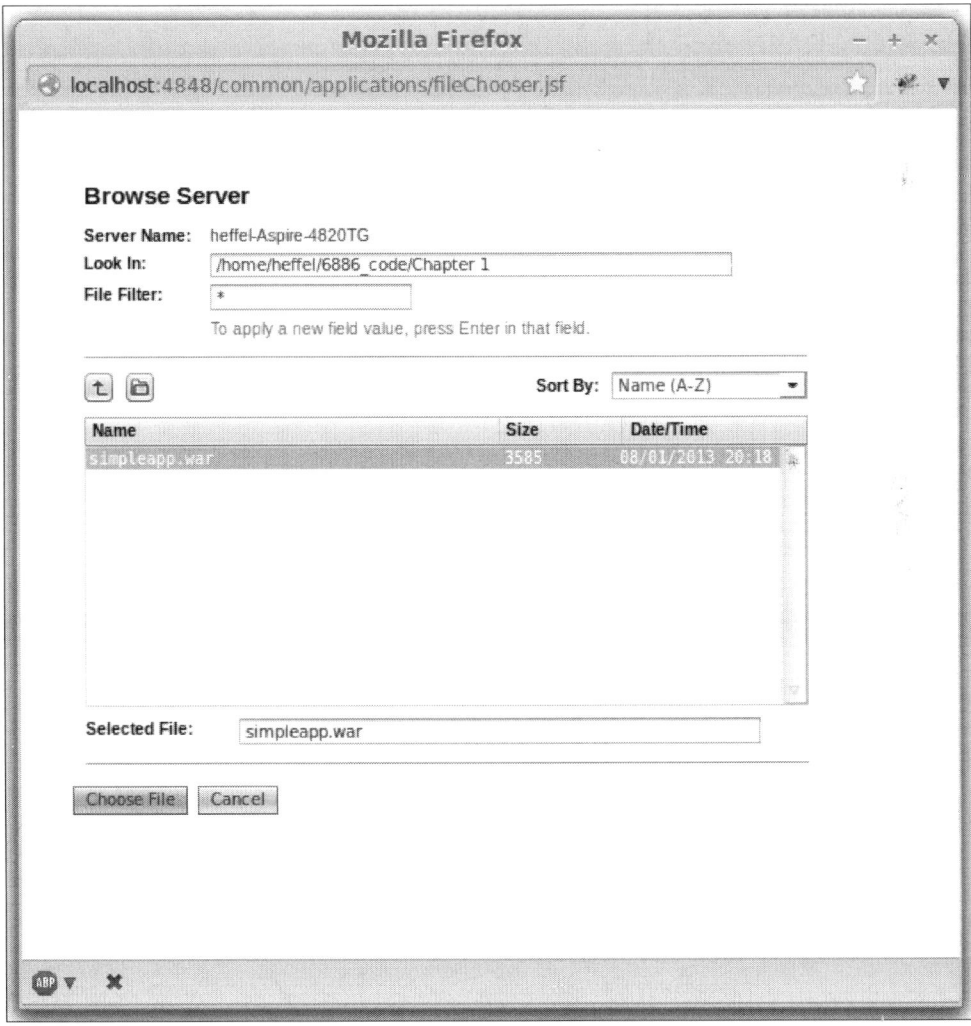

Getting Started with GlassFish

After we have selected our WAR file, a number of input fields that allow us to specify several options are shown. For our purposes, all defaults are fine. We can simply click on the **OK** button at the top right of the page as shown in the following screenshot:

Once we deploy our application, the GlassFish web console displays the **Applications** window, with our application listed as one of the deployed applications as shown in the following screenshot:

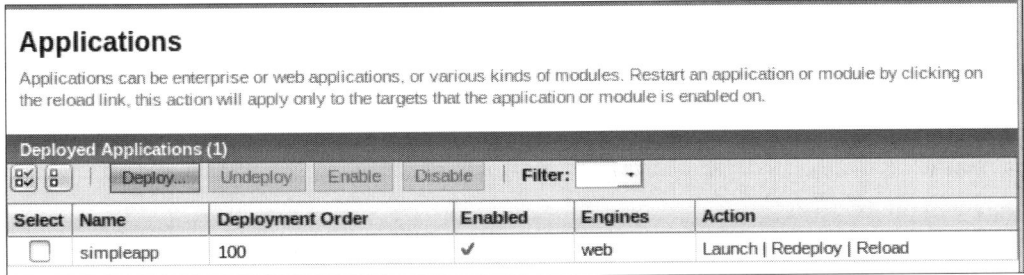

To execute the `simpleapp` application, type the following URL in the browser's location text field:

`http://localhost:8080/simpleapp/simpleservlet`

The resulting page should look like the following screenshot:

That's it! We have successfully deployed our first Java EE application.

Undeploying an application through the GlassFish Admin Console

To undeploy the application we just deployed, log in to the GlassFish Admin Console by typing the following URL in the browser:

`http://localhost:4848`

Then, either click on the **Applications** menu item in the navigation pane on the left, or click on the **List Deployed Applications** item on the administration console's home page.

Either way should take us to the application management page as shown in the following screenshot:

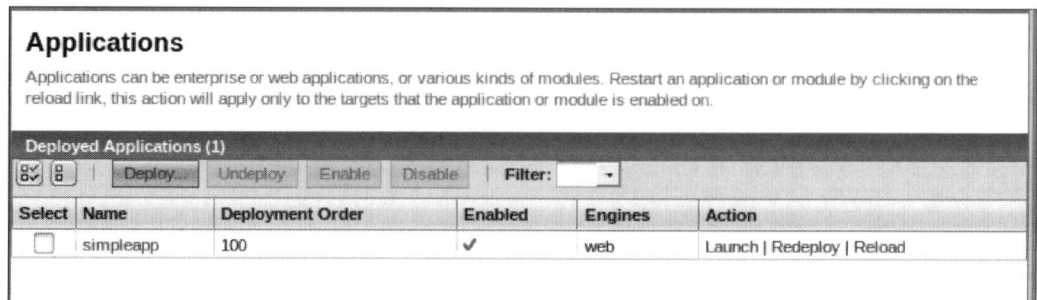

The application can be undeployed simply by selecting the checkbox next to the `simpleapp` name from the list of deployed applications and clicking on the **Undeploy** button above the list of deployed applications.

Once our application has been undeployed, it is no longer shown on the application management page as shown in the following screenshot:

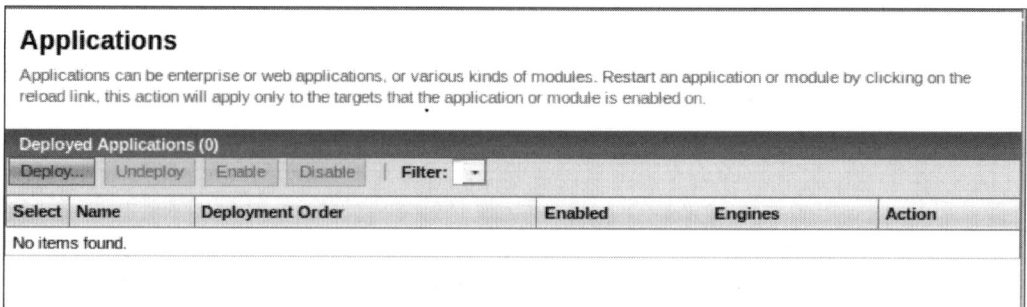

Deploying an application through the command line

There are two ways in which an application can be deployed through the command line—it can be done either by copying the artifact we want to deploy to an `autodeploy` directory, or by using GlassFish's `asadmin` command-line utility.

The autodeploy directory

Now that we have undeployed the `simpleapp` WAR file, we are ready to deploy it using the command line. To deploy the application in this manner, simply copy `simpleapp.war` to `[glassfish installation directory]/glassfish4/glassfish/domains/domain1/autodeploy`. The application will automatically be deployed just by copying it to this directory.

We can verify that the application has successfully been deployed by looking at the server log. The server log can be found by typing `[glassfish installation directory]/glassfish4/glassfish/domains/domain1/logs/server.log`. The last few lines on this file should look something like the following:

```
[2013-08-02T10:57:45.387-0400] [glassfish 4.0] [INFO] [NCLS-
DEPLOYMENT-00027] [javax.enterprise.system.tools.deployment.autodeploy]
[tid: _ThreadID=91 _ThreadName=AutoDeployer] [timeMillis: 1375455465387]
[levelValue: 800] [[

  Selecting file /home/heffel/GlassFish/glassfish4/glassfish/domains/
domain1/autodeploy/simpleapp.war for autodeployment]]

[2013-08-02T10:57:45.490-0400] [glassfish 4.0] [INFO] [] [javax.
enterprise.system.tools.deployment.common] [tid: _ThreadID=91 _
ThreadName=AutoDeployer] [timeMillis: 1375455465490] [levelValue: 800] [[

  visiting unvisited references]]

[2013-08-02T10:57:45.628-0400] [glassfish 4.0] [INFO] [AS-WEB-GLUE-00172]
[javax.enterprise.web] [tid: _ThreadID=91 _ThreadName=AutoDeployer]
[timeMillis: 1375455465628] [levelValue: 800] [[

  Loading application [simpleapp] at [/simpleapp]]]

[2013-08-02T10:57:45.714-0400] [glassfish 4.0] [INFO] [] [javax.
enterprise.system.core] [tid: _ThreadID=91 _ThreadName=AutoDeployer]
[timeMillis: 1375455465714] [levelValue: 800] [[

  simpleapp was successfully deployed in 302 milliseconds.]]

[2013-08-02T10:57:45.723-0400] [glassfish 4.0] [INFO] [NCLS-
DEPLOYMENT-00035] [javax.enterprise.system.tools.deployment.autodeploy]
[tid: _ThreadID=91 _ThreadName=AutoDeployer] [timeMillis: 1375455465723]
[levelValue: 800] [[

  [AutoDeploy] Successfully autodeployed : /home/heffel/GlassFish/
glassfish4/glassfish/domains/domain1/autodeploy/simpleapp.war.]]
```

Getting Started with GlassFish

We can, of course, also verify the deployment by navigating to the same URL for the application, which we used when deploying through the web console: `http://localhost:8080/simpleapp/simpleservlet`.

Once here, the application should execute properly.

An application deployed this way can be undeployed by simply deleting the artifact (WAR file, in our case) from the `autodeploy` directory. After deleting the file, we should see a message similar to the following in the server log:

```
[2013-08-02T11:01:57.410-0400] [glassfish 4.0] [INFO] [NCLS-
DEPLOYMENT-00026] [javax.enterprise.system.tools.deployment.autodeploy]
[tid: _ThreadID=91 _ThreadName=AutoDeployer] [timeMillis: 1375455717410]
[levelValue: 800] [[

  Autoundeploying application:   simpleapp]]


[2013-08-02T11:01:57.475-0400] [glassfish 4.0] [INFO] [NCLS-
DEPLOYMENT-00035] [javax.enterprise.system.tools.deployment.autodeploy]
[tid: _ThreadID=91 _ThreadName=AutoDeployer] [timeMillis: 1375455717475]
[levelValue: 800] [[

  [AutoDeploy] Successfully autoundeployed : /home/heffel/GlassFish/
glassfish4/glassfish/domains/domain1/autodeploy/simpleapp.war.]]
```

The asadmin command-line utility

An alternate way of deploying an application through the command line is to use the following command:

```
asadmin deploy [path to file]/simpleapp.war
```

 The preceding command must be executed from the `[glassfish installation directory]/glassfish4/bin` path.

We should see the following confirmation on the command line terminal letting us know that the file was deployed successfully:

```
Application deployed with name simpleapp.

Command deploy executed successfully.
```

The server logfile should show a message similar to the following:

```
[2013-08-02T11:05:34.583-0400] [glassfish 4.0] [INFO] [AS-WEB-GLUE-00172]
[javax.enterprise.web] [tid: _ThreadID=37 _ThreadName=admin-listener(5)]
[timeMillis: 1375455934583] [levelValue: 800] [[

  Loading application [simpleapp] at [/simpleapp]]]

[2013-08-02T11:05:34.608-0400] [glassfish 4.0] [INFO] [] [javax.
enterprise.system.core] [tid: _ThreadID=37 _ThreadName=admin-listener(5)]
[timeMillis: 1375455934608] [levelValue: 800] [[

  simpleapp was successfully deployed in 202 milliseconds.]]
```

The `asadmin` executable can be used to undeploy an application as well by issuing a command like the following:

`asadmin undeploy simpleapp`

The following message should be shown at the bottom of the terminal window:

`Command undeploy executed successfully.`

Please note that the file extension is not used to undeploy the application, the argument to `asadmin undeploy` should be the application name, which is, by default, the WAR file name (minus the extension).

GlassFish domains

Alert readers might have noticed that the `autodeploy` directory is under a `domains/domain1` subdirectory. GlassFish has a concept of domains. Domains allow a collection of related applications to be deployed together. Several domains can be started concurrently. GlassFish domains behave like individual GlassFish instances; a default domain called `domain1` is created when installing GlassFish.

Creating Domains

Additional domains can be created from the command line by issuing the following command:

`asadmin create-domain domainname`

Getting Started with GlassFish

The preceding command takes several parameters to specify ports where the domain will listen to for several services (HTTP, Admin, JMS, IIOP, Secure HTTP, and so on). Type the following command in the command line to see these parameters:

```
asadmin create-domain --help
```

If we want several domains to execute concurrently on the same server, these ports must be chosen carefully since specifying the same ports for different services (or even the same service across domains) will prevent one of the domains from working properly.

The default ports for the default `domain1` domain are listed in the following table:

Service	Port
Admin	4848
HTTP	8080
Java Messaging System (JMS)	7676
Internet Inter-ORB Protocol (IIOP)	3700
Secure HTTP (HTTPS)	8181
Secure IIOP	3820
Mutual Authorization IIOP	3920
Java Management Extensions (JMX) administration	8686

Please note that when creating a domain, the only port that needs to be specified is the admin port. If the other ports are not specified, the default ports listed in the preceding table will be used. Care must be taken when creating a domain, since, as explained above, two domains cannot run concurrently in the same server if any of their services listen for connections on the same port.

An alternate method of creating a domain, without having to specify ports for every service, is to issue the following command:

```
asadmin create-domain --portbase [port number] domainname
```

The value of the `--portbase` parameter dictates the base port for the domain; ports for the different services will be offsets of the given port number. The following table lists the ports assigned to all the different services:

Service	Port
Admin	portbase + 48
HTTP	portbase + 80
Java Messaging System (JMS)	portbase + 76

Service	Port
Internet Inter-ORB Protocol (IIOP)	portbase + 37
Secure HTTP (HTTPS)	portbase + 81
Secure IIOP	portbase + 38
Mutual Authorization IIOP	portbase + 39
Java Management Extensions (JMX) administration	portbase + 86

Of course, care must be taken when choosing the value for `--portbase`, making sure that none of the assigned ports collide with any other domain.

> As a rule of thumb, creating domains using a portbase number greater than 8000 and divisible by 1000 should create domains that don't conflict with each other. For example, it should be safe to create a domain using a portbase of 9000, another one using a portbase of 10000, so on and so forth.

Deleting domains

Deleting a domain is very simple. It can be accomplished by issuing the following command in the command line:

`asadmin delete-domain domainname`

We should see the following message on the terminal window:

`Command delete-domain executed successfully.`

> Please use the preceding command with care. Once a domain is deleted, it cannot be easily recreated (all deployed applications as well as any connection pools, data sources, and so on will be gone).

Stopping a domain

A domain that is running can be stopped by issuing the following command:

`asadmin stop-domain domainname`

The preceding command will stop the domain named `domainname`.

Getting Started with GlassFish

If only one domain is running, the `domainname` argument is optional, that is, we can simply stop the running domain by issuing the following command:

`asadmin stop-domain`

 This book will assume that the reader is working with the default domain called `domain1` and the default ports. If this is not the case, instructions given need to be modified to match the appropriate domain and port.

Setting up Database Connectivity

Any nontrivial Java EE application will connect to a **Relational Database Management System (RDBMS)**. Supported RDBMS systems include Java DB, Oracle, Derby, Sybase, DB2, PointBase, MySQL, PostgreSQL, Informix, Cloudscape, and SQL Server. In this section, we will demonstrate how to set up GlassFish to communicate with a MySQL database. The procedure is similar for other RDBMS systems.

 GlassFish comes bundled with an RDBMS called JavaDB. This RDBMS is based on Apache Derby. To limit the download and configuration needed to follow this book's code, all examples needing an RDBMS will use the bundled JavaDB RDBMS. The instructions in this section are to illustrate how to connect GlassFish to a third-party RDBMS.

Setting up connection pools

Opening and closing the database connections is a relatively slow operation. For performance reasons, GlassFish and other Java EE application servers keep a pool of open database connections; when a deployed application requires a database connection, one is provided from the pool; when the application no longer needs the database connection, the said connection is returned to the pool.

The first step to follow when setting up a connection pool is to copy the JAR file containing the JDBC driver for our RDBMS in the `lib` directory of the domain (consult your RDBMS documentation for information on where to obtain this JAR file). If the GlassFish domain where we want to add the connection pool is running when copying the JDBC driver, it must be restarted for the change to take effect. The domain can be restarted by executing the following command:

`asadmin restart-domain domainname`

Once the JDBC driver has been copied to the appropriate location and the application server has been restarted, log in to the admin console by pointing the browser to `http://localhost:4848`.

Then, navigate to **Resources | JDBC | JDBC Connection Pools**. The browser should now look something like what is shown in the following screenshot:

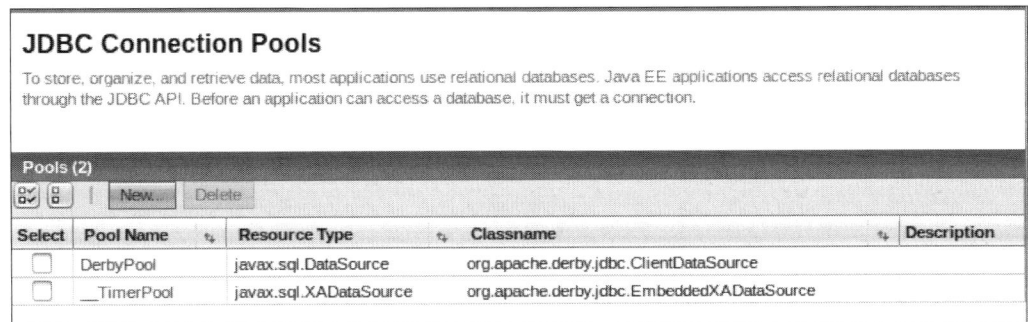

Click on the **New...** button. After entering the appropriate values for our RDBMS, the main area of the page should look something like the following screenshot:

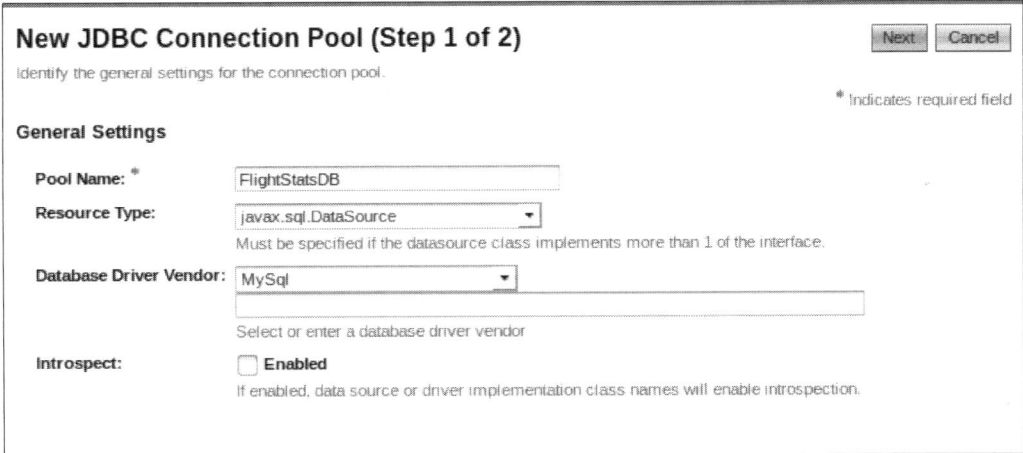

After clicking on the **Next** button, we should see a page similar to the one shown in the following screenshot:

Most of the default values on the top portion of the page shown in the preceding screenshot are sensible. Scroll all the way down and enter the appropriate property values for our RDBMS (at a minimum, username, password, and URL). Then, click on the **Finish** button at the top right of the screen.

Property names vary depending on the RDBMS we are using, but usually there is a URL property where we should enter the JDBC URL for our database, plus username and password properties where we should enter authentication credentials for our database.

Our newly created connection pool should now be visible in the list of connection pools as shown in the following screenshot:

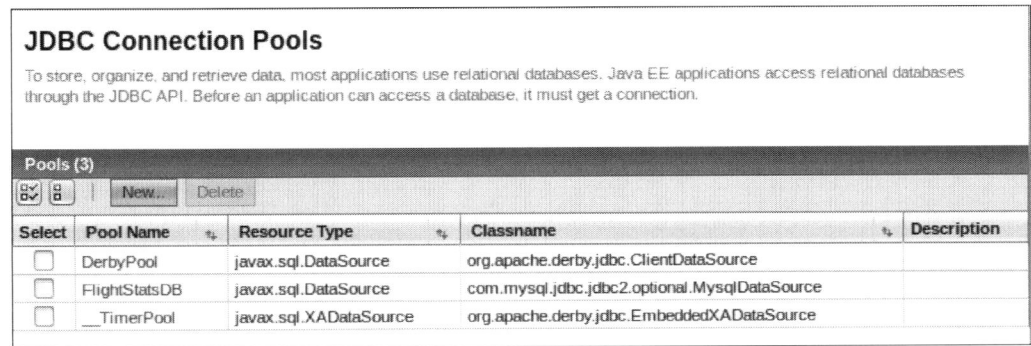

In some cases, the GlassFish domain may need to be restarted after setting up a new connection pool.

We can verify that our connection pool was successfully set up by clicking on its pool name and then enabling the **Ping** button on the resulting page as shown in the following screenshot:

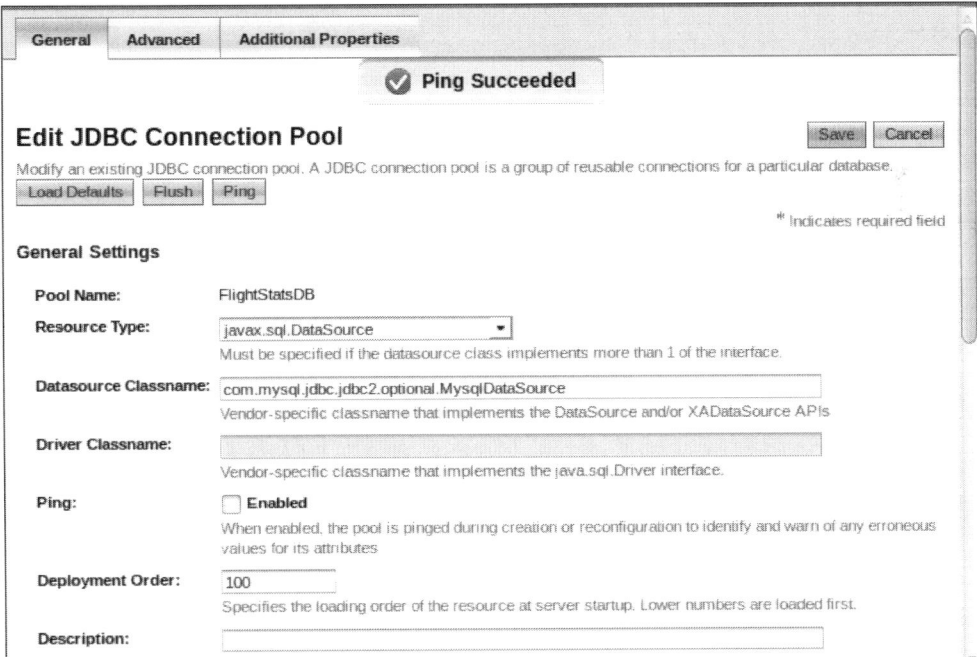

Our connection pool is now ready to be used by our applications.

Setting up the data sources

Java EE applications don't access connection pools directly; they access a data source instead, which points to a connection pool. To set up a new data source, click on the **JDBC** icon under the **Resources** menu item on the left-hand side of the web console, then click on the **JDBC Connection Pools** tab, and then click on the **New...** button. After filling out the appropriate information for our new data source, the main area of the web console should look something like what is shown in the following screenshot:

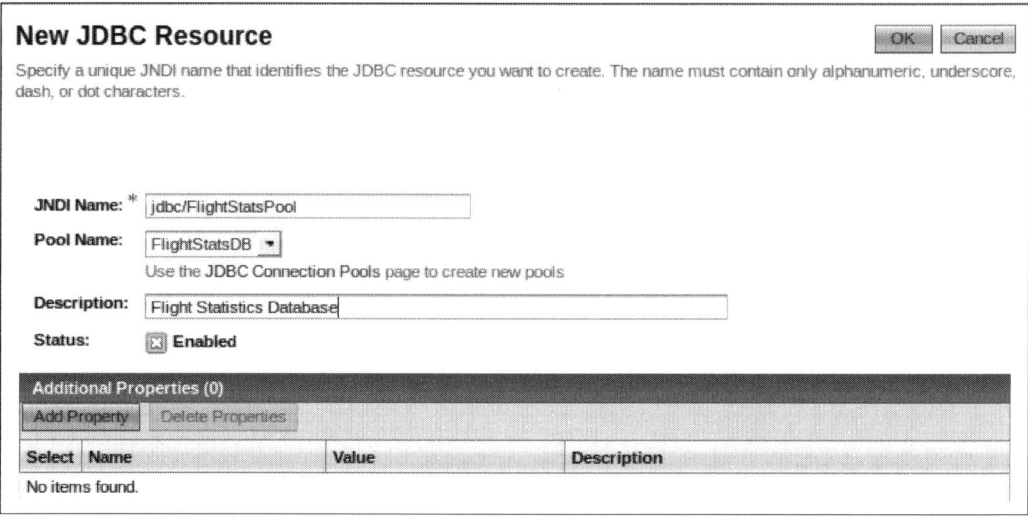

After clicking on the **OK** button, we can see our newly created data source as shown in the following screenshot:

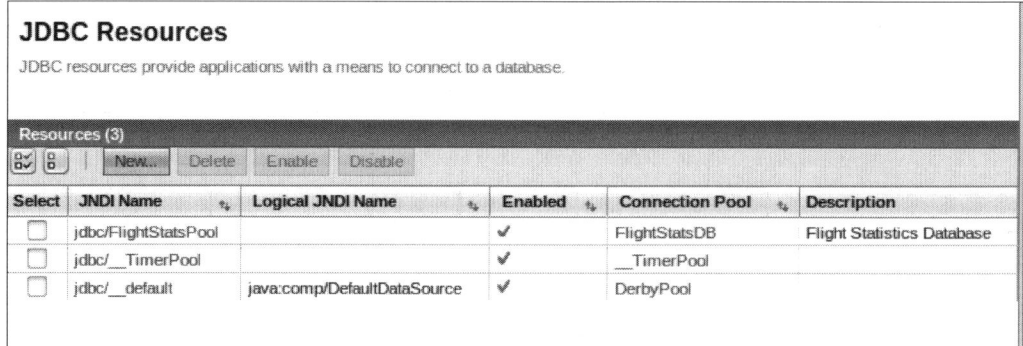

Summary

In this chapter, we discussed how to download and install GlassFish. We also discussed several methods of deploying the Java EE application through the GlassFish web console, through the `asadmin` command, and by copying the file to the `autodeploy` directory. We also discussed basic GlassFish administration tasks like setting up domains and setting up Database Connectivity by adding connection pools and data sources. In the next chapter, we will cover how to develop web applications using JSF.

2
JavaServer Faces

In this chapter, we will cover **JavaServer Faces (JSF)**, the standard component framework of the Java EE platform. Java EE 7 includes JSF 2.2, the latest version of JSF. JSF relies a lot on convention over configuration. If we follow JSF conventions, then we don't need to write a lot of configuration. In most cases, we don't need to write any configuration at all. This fact, combined with the fact that web.xml has been optional since Java EE 6, means that in many cases, we can write complete web applications without having to write a single line of XML configuration.

Introduction to JSF

JSF 2.0 introduced a number of enhancements to make JSF application development easier. In the following few sections, we will explain some of these features.

> Readers unfamiliar with the earlier versions of JSF may not understand the following few sections completely. Don't worry, everything will be perfectly clear by the end of this chapter.

Facelets

One notable difference between the modern versions of JSF and the earlier versions is that Facelets is now the preferred view technology. The earlier versions of JSF used JSP as their default view technology. Since JSP technology predates JSF, sometimes using JSP with JSF felt unnatural or created problems. For example, the lifecycle of JSPs is different from the lifecycle of JSFs; this mismatch introduced some problems for JSF 1.x application developers.

JSF was designed from the beginning to support multiple view technologies. To take advantage of this capability, Jacob Hookom wrote a view technology specifically for JSF. He named his view technology **Facelets**. Facelets was so successful that it became a de facto standard for JSF. The JSF expert group recognized Facelets' popularity and made it the official view technology for JSF in Version 2.0 of the JSF specification.

Optional faces-config.xml

Legacy J2EE applications suffered what some would have considered being excessive XML configuration.

Java EE 5 took some measures to reduce the XML configuration considerably. Java EE 6 reduced the required configuration even further, making the `faces-config.xml` JSF configuration file optional in JSF 2.0.

In JSF 2.0 and newer, JSF managed beans can be configured via the `@ManagedBean` annotation, obviating the need to configure them in `faces-config.xml`. Java EE 6 introduced the **Contexts and Dependency Injection** (**CDI**) API, which provides an alternative way to implement the functionality that was typically implemented with JSF managed beans. As of JSF 2.2, CDI named beans are preferred over JSF managed beans.

Additionally, there is a convention for JSF navigation. If the value of the `action` attribute of a JSF 2 command link or command button matches the name of a facelet (minus the XHTML extension), then by convention, the application will navigate to the facelet that matches the action name. This convention allows us to avoid having to configure an application's navigation in `faces-config.xml`.

For many modern JSF applications, `faces-config.xml` is completely unnecessary as long as the established JSF conventions are followed.

Standard resource locations

JSF 2.0 introduced standard resource locations. Resources are the artifacts that a page or JSF component needs to render properly, such as CSS style sheets, JavaScript files, and images.

In JSF 2.0 and newer, resources can be placed in a subdirectory under a folder called `resources` either at the root of the WAR file or under `META-INF`. By convention, JSF components know that they can retrieve resources from one of these two locations.

In order to avoid cluttering the resources directory, resources are typically placed in a subdirectory. This subdirectory is referred to from the `library` attribute of JSF components.

For example, we could place a CSS style sheet called `styles.css` under /resources/css/.

In our JSF pages, we can retrieve this CSS file using the `<h:outputStylesheet>` tag as follows:

```
<h:outputStylesheet library="css" name="styles.css"/>
```

The value of the `library` attribute must match the subdirectory where our style sheet is located.

Similarly, we can have a JavaScript file, `somescript.js`, under /resources/scripts/ and we can access it using the following code:

```
<h:outputScript library="scripts" name="somescript.js"/>
```

We can have an image, `logo.png`, under /resources/images/ and we can access this resource with the following code:

```
<h:graphicImage library="images" name="logo.png"/>
```

Note that in each case, the value of the `library` attribute matches the corresponding subdirectory name under the `resources` directory and the value of the `name` attribute matches the resource's filename.

Developing our first JSF application

To illustrate basic JSF concepts, we will develop a simple application consisting of two Facelets pages and a single CDI named bean.

Facelets

As we mentioned in this chapter's introduction, the default view technology for JSF 2 is Facelets. Facelets need to be written using standard XML. The most popular way of developing Facelets pages is to use XHTML in conjunction with JSF-specific XML namespaces. The following example shows how a typical Facelets page looks:

```
<?xml version='1.0' encoding='UTF-8' ?>
<!DOCTYPE html PUBLIC "-//W3C//DTD XHTML 1.0 Transitional//EN"
    "http://www.w3.org/TR/xhtml1/DTD/xhtml1-transitional.dtd">
<html xmlns="http://www.w3.org/1999/xhtml"
    xmlns:h="http://java.sun.com/jsf/html"
```

```xml
      xmlns:f="http://java.sun.com/jsf/core">
<h:head>
    <title>Enter Customer Data</title>
</h:head>
<h:body>
    <h:outputStylesheet library="css" name="styles.css"/>
    <h:form id="customerForm">
        <h:messages></h:messages>
        <h:panelGrid columns="2"
                    columnClasses="rightAlign,leftAlign">
            <h:outputLabel for="firstName" value="First
                                    Name:">
            </h:outputLabel>
            <h:inputText id="firstName"
                         label="First Name"
                         value="#{customer.firstName}"
                         required="true">
                <f:validateLength minimum="2" maximum="30">
                </f:validateLength>
            </h:inputText>
            <h:outputLabel for="lastName" value="Last Name:">
            </h:outputLabel>
            <h:inputText id="lastName"
                         label="Last Name"
                         value="#{customer.lastName}"
                         required="true">
                <f:validateLength minimum="2" maximum="30">
                </f:validateLength>
            </h:inputText>
            <h:outputLabel for="email" value="Email:">
            </h:outputLabel>
            <h:inputText id="email"
                         label="Email"
                         value="#{customer.email}">
                <f:validateLength minimum="3" maximum="30">
                </f:validateLength>
            </h:inputText>
            <h:panelGroup></h:panelGroup>
            <h:commandButton action="confirmation"
                                        value="Save">
            </h:commandButton>
        </h:panelGrid>
    </h:form>
</h:body>
</html>
```

The following screenshot illustrates how our example page is rendered in the browser:

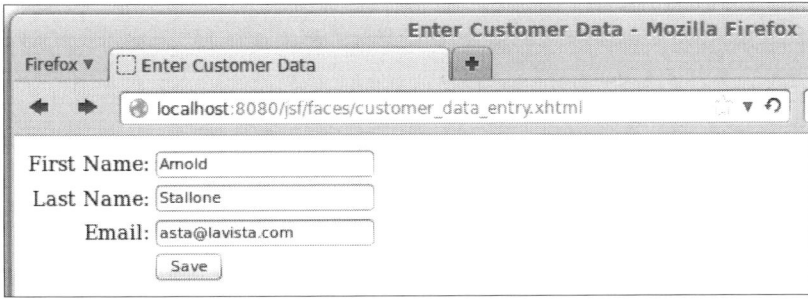

The preceding screenshot, of course, was taken after entering some data in every text field; originally, each text field was blank.

Pretty much any Facelets JSF page will include the two namespaces illustrated in the example. The first namespace (xmlns:h="http://java.sun.com/jsf/html") is for the tags that render HTML components; by convention, the prefix h (for HTML) is used when using this tag library.

The second namespace (xmlns:f="http://java.sun.com/jsf/core") is the core JSF tag library; by convention, the prefix f (for faces) is used when using this tag library.

The first JSF-specific tags we see in our example are the <h:head> and the <h:body> tags. These tags are analogous to the standard HTML <head> and <body> tags and are rendered as such when the page is displayed in the browser.

The <h:outputStylesheet> tag is used to load a CSS style sheet from a well-known location. (JSF standardizes the locations of resources such as CSS style sheets and JavaScript files; this will be discussed in detail later in the chapter.) The value of the library attribute must correspond to the directory where the CSS file resides (this directory must be under a resources directory). The name attribute must correspond to the name of the CSS style sheet we wish to load.

The next tag that we see is the <h:form> tag. This tag generates an HTML form when the page is rendered. As can be seen in the example, there is no need to specify an action or a method attribute for this tag; as a matter of fact, there is neither an action attribute nor a method attribute for this tag. The action attribute for the rendered HTML form will be generated automatically, and the method attribute will always be "post". The id attribute of <h:form> is optional; however, it is a good idea to always add it since it makes debugging JSF applications easier.

JavaServer Faces

The next tag we see is the `<h:messages>` tag. As its name implies, this tag is used to display any messages. As we will see shortly, JSF can automatically generate validation messages. These will be displayed inside this tag. Additionally, arbitrary messages can be added programmatically via the `addMessage()` method defined in `javax.faces.context.FacesContext`.

The next JSF tag we see is `<h:panelGrid>`. This tag is roughly equivalent to an HTML table, but it works a bit differently. Instead of declaring rows and columns, the `<h:panelGrid>` tag has a `columns` attribute; the value of this attribute indicates the number of columns in the table rendered by this tag. As we place components inside this tag, they will be placed in a row until the number of columns defined in the `columns` attribute is reached, and then the next component will be placed in the next row. In the example, the value of the `columns` attribute is two. Therefore, the first two tags will be placed in the first row, the next two will be placed in the second row, and so forth.

Another interesting attribute of `<h:panelGrid>` is the `columnClasses` attribute. This attribute assigns a CSS class to each column in the rendered table. In the example, two CSS classes (separated by a comma) are used as the value for this attribute. This has the effect of assigning the first CSS class to the first column and the second one to the second column. Had there been three or more columns, the third one would have gotten the first CSS class, the fourth one would have gotten the second one, and so on, alternating between the first one and the second one. To clarify how this works, the next code snippet illustrates a portion of the source of the HTML markup generated by our example page:

```
<table>
    <tbody>
        <tr>
            <td class="rightAlign">
                <label for="customerForm:firstName">
                    First Name:
                </label>
            </td>
            <td class="leftAlign">
                <input id="customerForm:firstName" type="text"
                    name="customerForm:firstName" />
            </td>
        </tr>
        <tr>
            <td class="rightAlign">
                <label for="customerForm:lastName">
                    Last Name:
                </label>
```

```
                    </td>
                    <td class="leftAlign">
                        <input id="customerForm:lastName" type="text"
                                name="customerForm:lastName" />
                    </td>
                </tr>
                <tr>
                    <td class="rightAlign">
                        <label for="customerForm:lastName">
                            Email:
                        </label>
                    </td>
                    <td class="leftAlign">
                        <input id="customerForm:email" type="text"
                                name="customerForm:email" />
                    </td>
                </tr>
                <tr>
                    <td class="rightAlign"></td>
                    <td class="leftAlign">
                        <input type="submit" name="customerForm:j_idt12"
                            value="Save" />
                    </td>
                </tr>
            </tbody>
        </table>
```

Note how each `<td>` tag has an alternating CSS tag of "`rightAlign`" or "`leftAlign`". We achieved this by assigning the value "`rightAlign,leftAlign`" to the `columnClasses` attribute of `<h:panelGrid>`. The CSS classes we have used in our example are defined in the CSS style sheet we loaded via the `<h:outputStylesheet>` tag we discussed earlier. The IDs of the generated markup are a combination of the ID we gave to the `<h:form>` component plus the ID of each individual component. We didn't assign an ID to the `<h:commandButton>` component near the end of the page, so the JSF runtime assigned one automatically.

At this point in the example, we start adding components inside `<h:panelGrid>`. These components will be rendered inside the table rendered by `<h:panelGrid>`. As we have mentioned before, the number of columns in the rendered table is defined by the columns attribute of `<h:panelGrid>`. Therefore, we don't need to worry about columns (or rows); we have to just start adding components, and they will be inserted in the right place.

JavaServer Faces

The next tag we see is the `<h:outputLabel>` tag. This tag renders an HTML `label` element. Labels are associated with other components via the `for` attribute, whose value must match the ID of the component that the label is for.

Next, we see the `<h:inputText>` tag. This tag generates a text field in the rendered page; its `label` attribute is used for any validation messages. It lets the user know which field the message refers to.

> Although it is not required for the value of the `label` attribute of `<h:inputText>` to match the label displayed on the page, it is highly recommended to use this value. In case of an error, this will let the user know exactly which field the message is referring to.

Of particular interest is the tag's `value` attribute. What we see as the value for this attribute is a **value-binding expression**. This means that this value is tied to a property of one of the application's named beans. In the example, this particular text field is tied to a property called `firstName` in a named bean called `customer`. When a user enters a value for this text field and submits the form, the corresponding property in the named bean is updated with this value. The tag's `required` attribute is optional, and valid values for it are `true` and `false`. If this attribute is set to `true`, the container will not let the user submit the form until the user enters some data in the text field. If the user attempts to submit the form without entering a required value, the page will be reloaded and an error message will be displayed inside the `<h:messages>` tag. The following screenshot shows the error message:

The preceding screenshot illustrates the default error message shown when the user attempts to save the form in the example without entering a value for the customer's first name. The first part of the message (**First Name**) is taken from the value of the `label` attribute of the corresponding `<h:inputTextField>` tag. You can customize the text as well as the style of the message (font, color, and so on). We will cover how to do this later in this chapter.

Project stages

Having an `<h:messages>` tag on every JSF page is a good idea; without it, the user might not see the validation messages and will have no idea why the form submission is not going through. By default, JSF validation messages do not generate any output in the GlassFish log. A common mistake new JSF developers make is that they fail to add an `<h:messages>` tag to their pages. Without the tag, if the validation fails, then the navigation seems to fail for no reason. (The same page is rendered if the navigation fails, and without an `<h:messages>` tag, no error messages are displayed in the browser.)

To avoid the situation described in the previous paragraph, JSF 2.0 introduced the concept of **project stages**.

The following project stages are defined in JSF 2:

- Production
- Development
- UnitTest
- SystemTest

We can define the project stage as an initialization parameter to the faces servlet in the `web.xml` file or as a custom JNDI resource. Since `web.xml` is now optional and altering it makes it relatively easy to use the wrong project stage if we forget to modify it when we move our code from one environment to another, the preferred way of setting the project stage is through a custom JNDI resource.

With GlassFish, we can do this by logging in to the web console, navigating to **JNDI | Custom Resources**, and then clicking on the **New...** button. The page that appears looks as shown in the following screenshot:

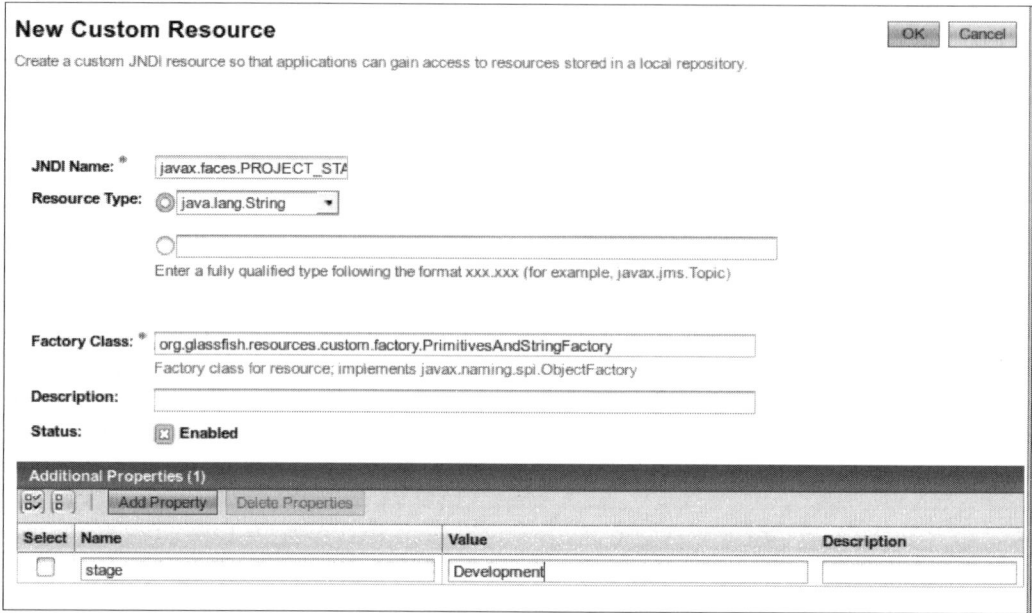

In the resulting page, we need to enter the following information:

JNDI Name	`javax.faces.PROJECT_STAGE`
Resource Type	`java.lang.String`

After you enter the preceding two values, the **Factory Class** field will be automatically populated with the value `org.glassfish.resources.custom.factory.PrimitivesAndStringFactory`.

After entering the values, we need to add a new property with a name of the stage and a value corresponding to the project stage we wish to use.

Setting the project stage allows us to perform some logic only if we are running the program in a specific stage. For instance, in one of our named beans, we could have code that looks as follows:

```
FacesContext facesContext =
    FacesContext.getCurrentInstance();
Application application = facesContext.getApplication();
```

```
      if (application.getProjectStage().equals(
         ProjectStage.Production)) {
        //do production stuff
      } else if (application.getProjectStage().equals(
         ProjectStage.Development)) {
        //do development stuff
      } else if (application.getProjectStage().equals(
         ProjectStage.UnitTest)) {
        //do unit test stuff
      } else if (application.getProjectStage().equals(
         ProjectStage.SystemTest)) {
        //do system test stuff
      }
```

As we can see, project stages allow us to modify our code's behavior for different environments. More importantly, setting the project stage allows the JSF engine to behave a bit differently based on the project stage setting. Relevant to our discussion, setting the project stage to Development results in additional logging statements in the application server log. Therefore, if we forget to add an <h:messages> tag to our page—our project stage is Development—and validation fails, a validation error will be displayed on the page even if we omit the <h:messages> component. The following screenshot shows the validation error message:

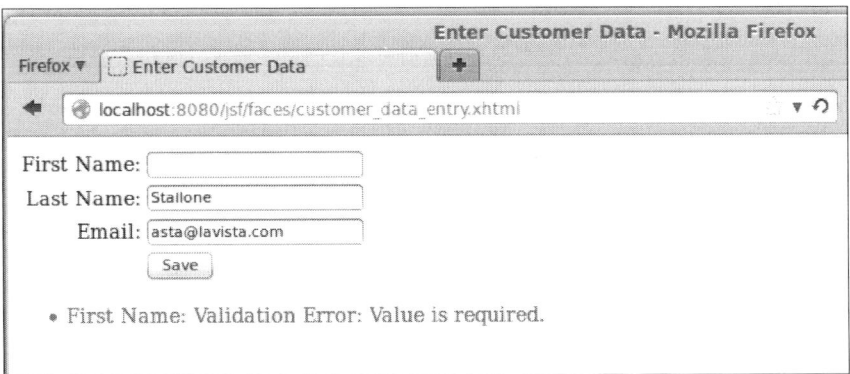

In the default Production stage, this error message is not displayed on the page, leaving us confused as to why our page navigation doesn't seem to work.

Validation

JSF provides built-in input validation capabilities.

In the previous section's example, note that each `<h:inputField>` tag has a nested `<f:validateLength>` tag. As its name implies, this tag validates that the entered value for the text field is between a minimum and maximum length. The minimum and maximum values are defined by the tag's `minimum` and `maximum` attributes. `<f:validateLength>` is one of the standard validators included in JSF. Just like with the `required` attribute of `<h:inputText>`, JSF will automatically display a default error message when a user attempts to submit a form with a value that does not validate.

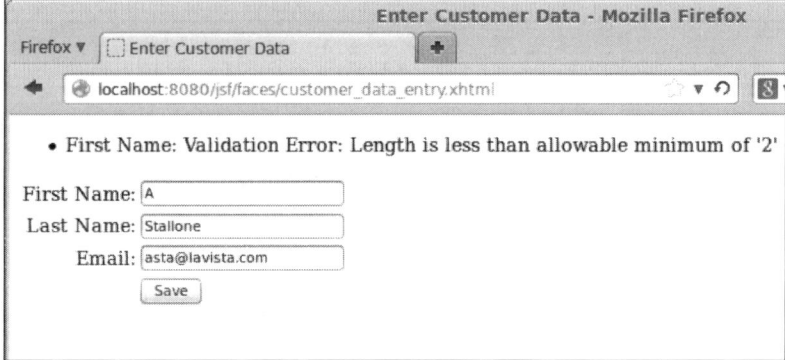

Again, the default message and style can be overridden; we will cover how to do this later in this chapter in the *Customizing JSF's default messages* section.

In addition to `<f:validateLength>`, JSF includes other standard validators, which are listed in the following table:

Validation tag	Description
`<f:validateBean>`	Bean validation allows us to validate named bean values using annotations in our named beans without having to add validators to our JSF tags. These tags allow us to fine-tune Bean Validation if necessary.
`<f:validateDoubleRange>`	This tag validates that the input is a valid `Double` value between the two values specified by the tag's `minimum` and `maximum` attributes, inclusive.
`<f:validateLength>`	This tag validates that the input's length is between the values specified by the tag's `minimum` and `maximum` values, inclusive.

Validation tag	Description
`<f:validateLongRange>`	This tag validates that the input is a valid `Long` value between the values specified by the tag's `minimum` and `maximum` attributes, inclusive.
`<f:validateRegex>`	This tag validates that the input matches a regular expression pattern specified in the tag's `pattern` attribute.
`<f:validateRequired>`	This tag validates that the input is not empty. This tag is equivalent to setting the `required` attribute to `true` in the parent input field.

Note that in the description for `<f:validateBean>`, we briefly mentioned Bean Validation. The Bean Validation JSR aims to standardize JavaBean validation. JavaBeans are used across several other API's that, up until recently, had to implement their own validation logic. JSF 2.0 adopted the Bean Validation standard to help validate named bean properties.

If we wish to take advantage of Bean Validation, all we need to do is annotate the desired field with the appropriate Bean Validation annotation, without having to explicitly use a JSF validator.

For the complete list of Bean Validation annotations, refer to the `javax.validation.constraints` package in the Java EE 7 API at http://docs.oracle.com/javaee/7/api/.

Grouping components

`<h:panelGroup>` is the next new tag in the example. Typically, `<h:panelGroup>` is used to group several components together so that they occupy a single cell in a `<h:panelGrid>` tag. This can be accomplished by adding components inside `<h:panelGroup>` and adding `<h:panelGroup>` to `<h:panelGrid>`. As can be seen in the example, this particular instance of `<h:panelGroup>` has no child components. In this particular case, the purpose of `<h:panelGroup>` is to have an "empty" cell and have the next component, `<h:commandButton>`, align with all other input fields in the form.

Form submission

`<h:commandButton>` renders an HTML submit button in the browser. Just like with standard HTML, its purpose is to submit the form. Its `value` attribute simply sets the button's label. This tag's `action` attribute is used for navigation. The next page shown is based on the value of this attribute. The `action` attribute can have a `String` constant or a **method binding expression**, meaning that it can point to a method in a named bean that returns a `String` value.

If the base name of a page in our application matches the value of the `action` attribute of an `<h:commandButton>` tag, then we navigate to this page when clicking on the button. This JSF feature frees us from having to define navigation rules, as we used to do in the older versions of JSF. In our example, our confirmation page is called `confirmation.xhtml`; therefore, by convention, this page will be shown when the button is clicked since the value of its `action` attribute (`"confirmation"`) matches the base name of the page.

 Even though the label for the button reads **Save**, in our simple example clicking on the button won't actually save any data.

Named beans

There are two types of JavaBeans that can interact with JSF pages: JSF managed beans and CDI named beans. JSF managed beans have been around since the first version of the JSF specification and can be used only in a JSF context. CDI named beans were introduced in Java EE 6 and can interoperate with other Java EE APIs such as Enterprise JavaBeans. For these reasons, CDI named beans are preferred over JSF managed beans.

To make a Java class a CDI named bean, all we need to do is make sure that the class has a public, no-argument constructor (one is created implicitly if there are no other constructors declared, which is the case in our example), and add the `@Named` annotation at the class level. The following code snippet is the managed bean for our example:

```
package net.ensode.glassfishbook.jsf;
import javax.enterprise.context.RequestScoped;
import javax.inject.Named;

@Named
@RequestScoped
public class Customer {
```

```java
    private String firstName;
    private String lastName;
    private String email;

    public String getEmail() {
      return email;
    }

    public void setEmail(String email) {
      this.email = email;
    }

    public String getFirstName() {
      return firstName;
    }

    public void setFirstName(String firstName) {
      this.firstName = firstName;
    }

    public String getLastName() {
      return lastName;
    }

    public void setLastName(String lastName) {
      this.lastName = lastName;
    }
}
```

The `@Named` class annotation designates this bean as a CDI named bean. This annotation has an optional `value` attribute that we can use to give our bean a logical name to use in our JSF pages. However, by convention, the value of this attribute is the same as the class name (`Customer`, in our case) with its first character switched to lowercase. In our example, we retain this default behavior; therefore, we access our bean's properties via the `customer` logical name. Notice the `value` attribute of any of the input fields in our example page to see this logical name in action.

Notice that other than the `@Named` and `@RequestScoped` annotations, there is nothing special about this bean. It is a standard JavaBean with private properties and corresponding getter and setter methods. The `@RequestScoped` annotation specifies that the bean should live through a single request.

Named beans always have a scope. A named bean scope defines the lifespan of the bean, and it is defined by a class-level annotation. The following table lists all valid named bean scopes:

Named bean scope annotation	Description
`@ApplicationScoped`	The same instance of the application scoped named beans are available to all of our application's clients. If one client modifies the value of an application scoped managed bean, the change is reflected across all clients.
`@SessionScoped`	An instance of each session scoped named bean is assigned to each of our application's clients. A session scoped named bean can be used to hold client-specific data across requests.
`@RequestScoped`	Request scoped named beans only live through a single request.
`@Dependent`	Dependent scoped named beans are assigned the same scope as the bean they are injected into. This is the default scope if none is specified.
`@ConversationScoped`	The conversation scope can span multiple requests and is typically shorter than the session scope.

Navigation

As can be seen on our input page, when we click on the **Save** button in the `customer_data_entry.xhtml` page, our application will navigate to a page called `confirmation.xhtml`. This happens because we are taking advantage of the JSF's convention over configuration feature, in which if the value of the `action` attribute of a command button or link matches the base name of another page, then the navigation takes us to this page.

Does the same page reload when you click on a button or link that should navigate to another page?

When JSF does not recognize the value of the `action` attribute of a command button or command link, it will, by default, navigate to the same page that was displayed in the browser when the user clicked on a button or link that was meant to navigate to another page.

If navigation does not seem to be working properly, chances are there is a typo in the value of this attribute. Remember that by convention, JSF will look for a page whose base name matches the value of the `action` attribute of a command button or link.

The source for confirmation.xhtml looks as follows:

```xml
<?xml version='1.0' encoding='UTF-8' ?>
<!DOCTYPE html PUBLIC "-//W3C//DTD XHTML 1.0 Transitional//EN"
"http://www.w3.org/TR/xhtml1/DTD/xhtml1-transitional.dtd">
<html xmlns="http://www.w3.org/1999/xhtml"
      xmlns:h="http://java.sun.com/jsf/html">
  <h:head>
    <title>Customer Data Entered</title>
  </h:head>
  <h:body>
    <h:panelGrid columns="2" columnClasses="rightAlign,leftAlign">
      <h:outputText value="First Name:"></h:outputText>
      <h:outputText value="#{customer.firstName}"></h:outputText>
      <h:outputText value="Last Name:"></h:outputText>
      <h:outputText value="#{customer.lastName}"></h:outputText>
      <h:outputText value="Email:"></h:outputText>
      <h:outputText value="#{customer.email}"></h:outputText>
    </h:panelGrid>
  </h:body>
</html>
```

The `<h:outputText>` tag is the only tag on this page that we haven't covered before. This tag simply displays the value of its `value` attribute to the rendered page; its `value` attribute can be a simple string or a value binding expression. Since the value binding expressions in our `<h:outputText>` tags are the same expressions that were used in the previous page for the `<h:inputText>` tags, their values will correspond to the data that the user entered.

In traditional (that is, non-JSF) Java web applications, we defined URL patterns to be processed by specific servlets. Specifically for JSF, the suffixes `.jsf` or `.faces` were commonly used; another commonly used URL mapping for JSF was the `/faces` prefix. By default, GlassFish automatically adds the `/faces` prefix to the faces servlet; therefore, we don't have to specify any URL mappings at all. If, for any reason, we need to specify a different mapping, then we need to add a `web.xml` configuration file to our application. However, the default will suffice in most cases.

The URL we used for the pages in our application was the name of our Facelets page, prefixed by /faces. This takes advantage of the default URL mapping.

Custom data validation

In addition to providing standard validators, JSF allows us to create custom validators. This can be done in two ways: by creating a custom validator class or by adding validation methods to our named beans.

Creating custom validators

In addition to the standard validators, JSF allows us to create custom validators by creating a Java class that implements the `javax.faces.validator.Validator` interface.

The following class implements an e-mail validator, which we will use to validate the e-mail text input field in our customer data entry screen.

```
package net.ensode.glassfishbook.jsfcustomval;

import javax.faces.application.FacesMessage;
import javax.faces.component.UIComponent;
import javax.faces.component.html.HtmlInputText;
import javax.faces.context.FacesContext;
import javax.faces.validator.FacesValidator;
import javax.faces.validator.Validator;
import javax.faces.validator.ValidatorException;
import org.apache.commons.lang.StringUtils;

@FacesValidator(value = "emailValidator")
public class EmailValidator implements Validator {

  @Override
  public void validate(FacesContext facesContext,
      UIComponent uiComponent,
      Object value) throws ValidatorException {
    org.apache.commons.validator.EmailValidator emailValidator =
        org.apache.commons.validator.EmailValidator.getInstance();
    HtmlInputText htmlInputText = (HtmlInputText) uiComponent;

    String email = (String) value;
```

```
        if (!StringUtils.isEmpty(email)) {
          if (!emailValidator.isValid(email)) {
            FacesMessage facesMessage = new
                FacesMessage(htmlInputText.
                getLabel()
                + ": email format is not valid");
            throw new ValidatorException(facesMessage);
          }
        }
      }
    }
```

The `@FacesValidator` annotation registers our class as a JSF custom validator class. The value of its `value` attribute is the logical name that JSF pages can use for reference.

As can be seen in the example, the only method we need to implement when implementing the `Validator` interface is a method called `validate()`. This method takes three parameters: an instance of `javax.faces.context.FacesContext`, an instance of `javax.faces.component.UIComponent`, and an object. Typically, application developers only need to be concerned with the last two. The second parameter is the component whose data we are validating, and the third parameter is the actual value. In the example, we cast `uiComponent` to `javax.faces.component.html.HtmlInputText`; in this way, we get access to its `getLabel()` method, which we can use as part of the error message.

If the entered value is not in a valid e-mail address format, a new instance of `javax.faces.application.FacesMessage` is created, passing the error message to be displayed in the browser as its constructor parameter. We then throw a new exception as `javax.faces.validator.ValidatorException`. The error message is then displayed in the browser.

Apache Commons Validator

Our custom JSF validator uses the Apache Commons Validator to do the actual validation. This library includes many common validations such as dates, credit card numbers, ISBN numbers, and e-mails. When implementing a custom validator, it is worth investigating if this library already has a validator that we can use.

JavaServer Faces

In order to use our validator in our page, we need to use the `<f:validator>` JSF tag. The following Facelets page is a modified version of the customer data entry screen. This version uses the `<f:validator>` tag to validate e-mails.

```xml
<?xml version='1.0' encoding='UTF-8' ?>
<!DOCTYPE html PUBLIC "-//W3C//DTD XHTML 1.0 Transitional//EN"
  "http://www.w3.org/TR/xhtml1/DTD/xhtml1-transitional.dtd">
<html xmlns="http://www.w3.org/1999/xhtml"
      xmlns:h="http://java.sun.com/jsf/html"
      xmlns:f="http://java.sun.com/jsf/core">
  <h:head>
    <title>Enter Customer Data</title>
  </h:head>
  <h:body>
    <h:outputStylesheet library="css" name="styles.css"/>
    <h:form>
      <h:messages></h:messages>
      <h:panelGrid columns="2"
                   columnClasses="rightAlign,leftAlign">
        <h:outputText value="First Name:">
        </h:outputText>
        <h:inputText label="First Name"
                     value="#{customer.firstName}"
                     required="true">
          <f:validateLength minimum="2" maximum="30">
          </f:validateLength>
        </h:inputText>
        <h:outputText value="Last Name:"></h:outputText>
        <h:inputText label="Last Name"
                     value="#{customer.lastName}"
                     required="true">
          <f:validateLength minimum="2" maximum="30">
          </f:validateLength>
        </h:inputText>
        <h:outputText value="Email:">
        </h:outputText>
        <h:inputText label="Email" value="#{customer.email}">
          <f:validator validatorId="emailValidator" />
        </h:inputText>
        <h:panelGroup></h:panelGroup>
        <h:commandButton action="confirmation" value="Save">
        </h:commandButton>
      </h:panelGrid>
    </h:form>
  </h:body>
</html>
```

Notice that the value of the `validatorId` attribute of `<f:validator>` matches the `value` attribute of the `@FacesValidator` annotation in our custom validator.

After writing our custom validator and modifying our page to take advantage of it, we can see our validator in action as shown in the following screenshot:

Validator methods

Another way we can implement custom validation is by adding validation methods to one or more of the application's named beans. The following Java class illustrates the use of validator methods for JSF validation:

```
package net.ensode.glassfishbook.jsfcustomval;

import javax.enterprise.context.RequestScoped;
import javax.faces.application.FacesMessage;
import javax.faces.component.UIComponent;
import javax.faces.component.html.HtmlInputText;
import javax.faces.context.FacesContext;
import javax.faces.validator.ValidatorException;
import javax.inject.Named;

import org.apache.commons.lang.StringUtils;

@Named
@RequestScoped
public class AlphaValidator {

  public void validateAlpha(FacesContext facesContext,
      UIComponent uiComponent,
      Object value) throws ValidatorException {
    if (!StringUtils.isAlphaSpace((String) value)) {
      HtmlInputText htmlInputText = (HtmlInputText) uiComponent;
```

```
        FacesMessage facesMessage = new FacesMessage(htmlInputText.
          getLabel()
          + ": only alphabetic characters are allowed.");
        throw new ValidatorException(facesMessage);
      }
    }
  }
```

In this example, the class contains only the validator method. We can give our validator method any name we want; however, its return value must be void, and it must take the three parameters illustrated in the example, in that order. In other words, except for the method name, the signature of a validator method must be identical to the signature of the `validate()` method defined in the `javax.faces.validator.Validator` interface.

As we can see, the body of our validator method is nearly identical to the body of our custom validator's `validate()` method. We check the value entered by the user to make sure that it contains only alphabetic characters and/or spaces. If it does not, then we throw `ValidatorException`, passing an instance of `FacesMessage` containing an appropriate `String` error message.

StringUtils

In the example, we used `org.apache.commons.lang.StringUtils` to perform the actual validation logic. In addition to the method used in the example, this class contains several methods to verify whether a string is numeric or alphanumeric. This class, part of the Apache `commons-lang` library, is very useful when writing custom validators.

Since every validator method must be in a named bean, we need to make sure that the class containing our validator method is annotated with the `@Named` annotation, as illustrated in our example.

The last thing we need to do in order to use our validator method is to bind it to our component via the tag's `validator` attribute. The code to do so is as follows:

```
<?xml version='1.0' encoding='UTF-8' ?>
<!DOCTYPE html PUBLIC "-//W3C//DTD XHTML 1.0 Transitional//EN"
   "http://www.w3.org/TR/xhtml1/DTD/xhtml1-transitional.dtd">
<html xmlns="http://www.w3.org/1999/xhtml"
      xmlns:h="http://java.sun.com/jsf/html"
      xmlns:f="http://java.sun.com/jsf/core">
  <h:head>
    <title>Enter Customer Data</title>
  </h:head>
```

```xml
<h:body>
  <h:outputStylesheet library="css" name="styles.css"/>
  <h:form>
    <h:messages></h:messages>
    <h:panelGrid columns="2"
                 columnClasses="rightAlign,leftAlign">
      <h:outputText value="First Name:">
      </h:outputText>
      <h:inputText label="First Name"
                   value="#{customer.firstName}"
                   required="true"
                   validator="#{alphaValidator.validateAlpha}">
        <f:validateLength minimum="2" maximum="30">
        </f:validateLength>
      </h:inputText>
      <h:outputText value="Last Name:"></h:outputText>
      <h:inputText label="Last Name"
                   value="#{customer.lastName}"
                   required="true"
                   validator="#{alphaValidator.validateAlpha}">
        <f:validateLength minimum="2" maximum="30">
        </f:validateLength>
      </h:inputText>
      <h:outputText value="Email:">
      </h:outputText>
      <h:inputText label="Email" value="#{customer.email}">
        <f:validateLength minimum="3" maximum="30">
        </f:validateLength>
        <f:validator validatorId="emailValidator" />
      </h:inputText>
      <h:panelGroup></h:panelGroup>
      <h:commandButton action="confirmation" value="Save">
      </h:commandButton>
    </h:panelGrid>
  </h:form>
</h:body>
</html>
```

Since neither the first name nor the last name fields would accept anything other than alphabetic characters or spaces, we added our custom validator method to both of these fields.

Notice that the value of the `validator` attribute of the `<h:inputText>` tag is a JSF expression language expression that uses the default name for the bean containing our validation method. `alphaValidator` is the name of our bean, and `validateAlpha` is the name of our validator method.

After modifying our page to use our custom validator, we can now see it in action as follows:

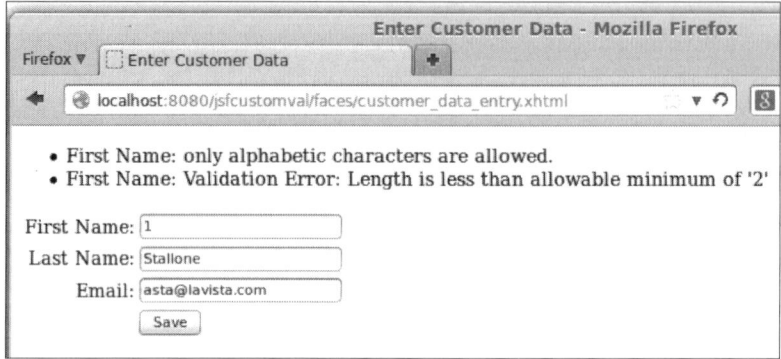

Note how for the **First Name** field both our custom validator message and the standard length validator were executed.

The advantage of implementing validator methods is that you do not need the overhead of creating a whole class just for a single validator method. (Our example does just that, but in many cases, validator methods are added to an existing named bean containing other methods.) The disadvantage of validator methods is that each component can only be validated by a single validator method. When using validator classes, several `<f:validator>` tags can be nested inside the tag to be validated; therefore, multiple validations, both custom and standard, can be done to the field.

Customizing JSF's default messages

As we mentioned earlier, it is possible to customize the style (font, color, text, and so on) of JSF default validation messages. Additionally, it is possible to modify the text of the default JSF validation messages. In the following sections, we will explain how to modify error message formatting and text.

Customizing message styles

Customizing message styles can be done via **Cascading Style Sheets (CSS)**. This can be accomplished using the `<h:message>` style or the `styleClass` attributes. The `style` attribute is used when we want to declare the CSS style inline. The `styleClass` attribute is used when we want to use a predefined style in a CSS style sheet or inside a `<style>` tag in our page.

The following markup illustrates the use of the `styleClass` attribute to alter the style of error messages. It is a modified version of the input page that we saw in the previous section.

```xml
<?xml version='1.0' encoding='UTF-8' ?>
<!DOCTYPE html PUBLIC "-//W3C//DTD XHTML 1.0 Transitional//EN"
   "http://www.w3.org/TR/xhtml1/DTD/xhtml1-transitional.dtd">
<html xmlns="http://www.w3.org/1999/xhtml"
      xmlns:h="http://java.sun.com/jsf/html"
      xmlns:f="http://java.sun.com/jsf/core">
  <h:head>
    <title>Enter Customer Data</title>
  </h:head>
  <h:body>
    <h:outputStylesheet library="css" name="styles.css" />
    <h:form>
      <h:messages styleClass="errorMsg"></h:messages>
      <h:panelGrid columns="2"
                  columnClasses="rightAlign,leftAlign">
        <h:outputText value="First Name:">
        </h:outputText>
        <h:inputText label="First Name"
                     value="#{customer.firstName}"
                     required="true"
                     validator="#{alphaValidator.validateAlpha}">
          <f:validateLength minimum="2" maximum="30">
          </f:validateLength>
        </h:inputText>
        <h:outputText value="Last Name:"></h:outputText>
        <h:inputText label="Last Name"
                     value="#{customer.lastName}"
                     required="true"
                     validator="#{alphaValidator.validateAlpha}">
          <f:validateLength minimum="2" maximum="30">
          </f:validateLength>
        </h:inputText>
        <h:outputText value="Email:">
```

```
          </h:outputText>
          <h:inputText label="Email" value="#{customer.email}">
            <f:validator validatorId="emailValidator" />
          </h:inputText>
          <h:panelGroup></h:panelGroup>
          <h:commandButton action="confirmation" value="Save">
          </h:commandButton>
        </h:panelGrid>
      </h:form>
    </h:body>
</html>
```

The only difference between this page and the previous one is the use of the styleClass attribute of the <h:messages> tag. As mentioned earlier, the value of the styleClass attribute must match the name of a CSS style defined in a cascading style sheet that our page can access.

In our case, we defined a CSS style in style.css for messages as follows:

```
.errorMsg {
  color: red;
}
```

We then used this style as the value of the styleClass attribute of our <h:messages> tag.

The following screenshot illustrates how the validation error messages look after we have implemented this change:

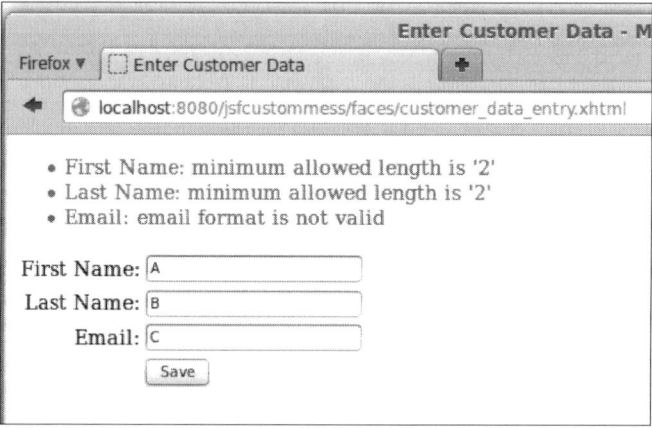

In this particular case, we just set the color of the error message text to red, but we are only limited by CSS capabilities in setting the style of the error messages.

Customizing message text

Sometimes it is desirable to override JSF's default validation errors. Default validation errors are defined in a resource bundle called Messages.properties. This file can be found inside the javax.faces.jar file under [glassfish installation directory]/glassfish/modules. It can be found under the javax/faces folder inside the JAR file. The file contains several messages, but we are only interested in validation errors at this point. The default validation error messages are defined as follows:

```
javax.faces.validator.DoubleRangeValidator.MAXIMUM={1}: Validation
    Error: Value is greater than allowable maximum of "{0}"
javax.faces.validator.DoubleRangeValidator.MINIMUM={1}: Validation
    Error: Value is less than allowable minimum of ''{0}''
javax.faces.validator.DoubleRangeValidator.NOT_IN_RANGE={2}:
    Validation Error: Specified attribute is not between the
    expected values of {0} and {1}.
javax.faces.validator.DoubleRangeValidator.TYPE={0}: Validation
    Error: Value is not of the correct type
javax.faces.validator.LengthValidator.MAXIMUM={1}: Validation
    Error: Value is greater than allowable maximum of ''{0}''
javax.faces.validator.LengthValidator.MINIMUM={1}: Validation
    Error: Value is less than allowable minimum of ''{0}''
javax.faces.validator.LongRangeValidator.MAXIMUM={1}: Validation
    Error: Value is greater than allowable maximum of ''{0}''
javax.faces.validator.LongRangeValidator.MINIMUM={1}: Validation
    Error: Value is less than allowable minimum of ''{0}''
javax.faces.validator.LongRangeValidator.NOT_IN_RANGE={2}:
    Validation Error: Specified attribute is not between the
    expected values of {0} and {1}.
javax.faces.validator.LongRangeValidator.TYPE={0}: Validation
    Error: Value is not of the correct type.
javax.faces.validator.NOT_IN_RANGE=Validation Error: Specified
    attribute is not between the expected values of {0} and {1}.
javax.faces.validator.RegexValidator.PATTERN_NOT_SET=Regex pattern
    must be set.
javax.faces.validator.RegexValidator.PATTERN_NOT_SET_detail=Regex
    pattern must be set to non-empty value.
javax.faces.validator.RegexValidator.NOT_MATCHED=Regex Pattern not
    matched
javax.faces.validator.RegexValidator.NOT_MATCHED_detail=Regex
    pattern of ''{0}'' not matched
javax.faces.validator.RegexValidator.MATCH_EXCEPTION=Error in
    regular expression.
```

```
javax.faces.validator.RegexValidator.MATCH_EXCEPTION_detail=Error
    in regular expression, ''{0}''
javax.faces.validator.BeanValidator.MESSAGE={0}
```

In order to override the default error messages, we need to create our own resource bundle using the same keys used in the default one, but altering the values to suit our needs. The following is a very simple customized resource bundle for our application:

```
javax.faces.validator.LengthValidator.MINIMUM={1}: minimum allowed
    length is ''{0}''
```

In this resource bundle, we override the error message for when the value entered for a field validated by the `<f:validateLength>` tag is less than the allowed minimum. In order to let our application know that we have a custom resource bundle for message properties, we need to modify the application's `faces-config.xml` file as follows:

```
<?xml version='1.0' encoding='UTF-8'?>
<faces-config version="2.0"
     xmlns="http://java.sun.com/xml/ns/javaee"
     xmlns:xsi="http://www.w3.org/2001/XMLSchema-instance"
     xsi:schemaLocation="http://java.sun.com/xml/ns/javaee
     http://java.sun.com/xml/ns/javaee/web-facesconfig_2_0.xsd">
  <application>
    <message-bundle>net.ensode.Messages</message-bundle>
  </application>
</faces-config>
```

As we can see, the only thing we need to do to the application's `faces-config.xml` file is to add a `<message-bundle>` element indicating the name and location of the resource bundle containing our custom messages.

> A custom error message text definition is one of the few cases in which we still need to define a `faces-config.xml` file for modern JSF applications. However, note how simple our `faces-config.xml` file is; it is a far cry from a typical `faces-config.xml` file for JSF 1.x, which typically contains named bean definitions, navigation rules, JSF validator definitions, and so on.

After adding our custom message resource bundle and modifying the application's `faces-config.xml` file, we can see our custom validation message in action, as shown in the following screenshot:

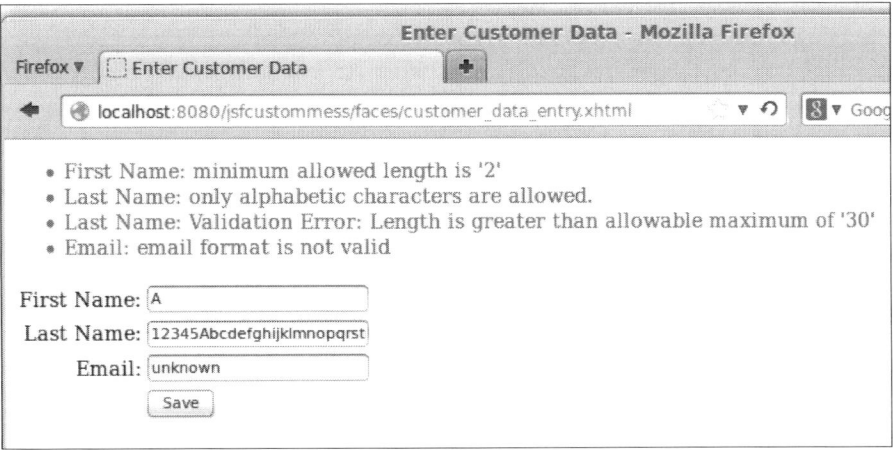

As can be seen in the screenshot, if we haven't overridden a validation message, the default will still be displayed. In our resource bundle, we only overrode the minimum length validation error message; therefore, our custom error message is shown for the **First Name** text field. Since we didn't override the error messages for the other standard JSF validators, the default error message is shown for each one of them. The e-mail validator is the custom validator we developed previously in this chapter. Since it is a custom validator, its error message is not affected.

Ajax-enabling JSF applications

Early versions of JSF did not include native Ajax support. Custom JSF library vendors were forced to implement Ajax in their own way. Unfortunately, this state of events introduced incompatibilities between JSF component libraries. JSF 2.0 standardized Ajax support by introducing the `<f:ajax>` tag.

The following page illustrates the typical usage of the `<f:ajax>` tag:

```
<?xml version='1.0' encoding='UTF-8' ?>
<!DOCTYPE html PUBLIC "-//W3C//DTD XHTML 1.0 Transitional//EN"
  "http://www.w3.org/TR/xhtml1/DTD/xhtml1-transitional.dtd">
<html xmlns="http://www.w3.org/1999/xhtml"
      xmlns:h="http://java.sun.com/jsf/html"
      xmlns:f="http://java.sun.com/jsf/core">
  <h:head>
```

```
        <title>JSF Ajax Demo</title>
      </h:head>
      <h:body>
        <h2>JSF Ajax Demo</h2>
        <h:form>
          <h:messages/>
          <h:panelGrid columns="2">

            <h:outputText value="Echo input:"/>
            <h:inputText id="textInput" value="#{controller.text}">
              <f:ajax render="textVal" event="keyup"/>
            </h:inputText>

            <h:outputText value="Echo output:"/>
            <h:outputText id="textVal" value="#{controller.text}"/>
          </h:panelGrid>
          <hr/>
          <h:panelGrid columns="2">
            <h:panelGroup/>
            <h:panelGroup/>
            <h:outputText value="First Operand:"/>
            <h:inputText id="first" value="#{controller.firstOperand}"
                         size="3"/>
            <h:outputText value="Second Operand:"/>
            <h:inputText id="second"
                         value="#{controller.secondOperand}"
                         size="3"/>
            <h:outputText value="Total:"/>
            <h:outputText id="sum" value="#{controller.total}"/>
            <h:commandButton
                actionListener="#{controller.calculateTotal}"
                         value="Calculate Sum">
              <f:ajax execute="first second" render="sum"/>
            </h:commandButton>
          </h:panelGrid>
        </h:form>
      </h:body>
    </html>
```

After deploying our application, our page renders as illustrated in the following screenshot:

This example page illustrates two uses of the `<f:ajax>` tag. At the top of the page, we have used this tag for implementing a typical Ajax Echo example, in which we have an `<h:outputText>` component updating itself with the value of an input text component. Any time a character is entered into the input field, the value of the `<h:outputText>` component is automatically updated.

To implement the functionality described in the previous paragraph, we put an `<f:ajax>` tag inside an `<h:inputText>` tag. The value of the `render` attribute of the `<f:ajax>` tag must correspond to the ID of a component we wish to update after the Ajax request finishes. In our example, we wish to update the `<h:outputText>` component with an ID of "textVal"; therefore, we will use this value for the `render` attribute of our `<f:ajax>` tag.

>  In some cases, we may need to render more than one JSF component after an Ajax event finishes; in order to accommodate this, we can add several IDs as the value of the `render` attribute, and we simply need to separate them by spaces.

The other `<f:ajax>` attribute we used in this instance is the `event` attribute. This attribute indicates the JavaScript event that triggers the Ajax event. In this particular case, we need to trigger the event any time a key is released while a user is typing into the input field; therefore, the appropriate event to use is `keyup`.

The following table lists all supported JavaScript events:

Event	Description
blur	The component loses focus.
change	The component loses focus, and its value is modified.
click	The component is clicked on.
dblclick	The component is double-clicked on.
focus	The component gains focus.
keydown	A key is depressed while the component has focus.
keypress	A key is pressed or held down while the component has focus.
keyup	A key is released while the component has focus.
mousedown	The mouse button is depressed while the component has focus.
mousemove	The mouse pointer is moved over the component.
mouseout	The mouse pointer leaves the component.
mouseover	The mouse pointer is placed over the component.
mouseup	The mouse button is released while the component has focus.
select	The component's text is selected.
valueChange	Equivalent to change; the component loses focus and its value has been modified.

We use the `<f:ajax>` tag once again farther down in the page to Ajax-enable a command button component. In this instance, we want to recalculate a value based on the value of two input components. In order to have the values on the server updated with the latest user input, we used the `execute` attribute of `<f:ajax>`; this attribute takes a space-separated list of component IDs to use as input. We then use the `render` attribute just as before to specify which components need to be re-rendered after the Ajax request finishes.

Notice that we used the `actionListener` attribute of `<h:commandButton>`. This attribute is typically used when we don't need to navigate to another page after clicking on the button. The value for this attribute is an action listener method we wrote in one of our named beans. Action listener methods must return void and take an instance of `javax.faces.event.ActionEvent` as their sole parameter.

The named bean for our application looks as follows:

```
package net.ensode.glassfishbook.jsfajax;

import javax.faces.event.ActionEvent;
import javax.faces.view.ViewScoped;
import javax.inject.Named;
```

```java
@Named
@ViewScoped
public class Controller {

  private String text;
  private int firstOperand;
  private int secondOperand;
  private int total;

  public Controller() {
  }

  public void calculateTotal(ActionEvent actionEvent) {
    total = firstOperand + secondOperand;
  }

  public String getText() {
    return text;
  }

  public void setText(String text) {
    this.text = text;
  }

  public int getFirstOperand() {
    return firstOperand;
  }

  public void setFirstOperand(int firstOperand) {
    this.firstOperand = firstOperand;
  }

  public int getSecondOperand() {
    return secondOperand;
  }

  public void setSecondOperand(int secondOperand) {
    this.secondOperand = secondOperand;
  }

  public int getTotal() {
    return total;
  }

  public void setTotal(int total) {
    this.total = total;
  }
}
```

Notice that we didn't have to do anything special in our named bean to enable Ajax in our application. It is all controlled by the `<f:ajax>` tag on the page.

As we can see from this example, Ajax-enabling JSF applications is very simple. We simply need to use a single tag to Ajax-enable our page, without having to write a single line of JavaScript, JSON, or XML.

JSF 2.2 HTML5 support

HTML 5 is the latest version of the HTML specification. It includes several improvements over the previous version of HTML. JSF 2.2 includes several updates to make JSF pages work nicely with HTML5.

The HTML5-friendly markup

Through the use of pass-through elements, we can develop our pages using HTML 5 tags and also treat them as JSF components. To do this, we need to specify at least one of the `element` attributes using the `http://xmlns.jcp.org/jsf` namespace. The following example demonstrates this approach in action:

```
<!DOCTYPE html>
<html xmlns="http://www.w3.org/1999/xhtml"
      xmlns:jsf="http://xmlns.jcp.org/jsf">
    <head jsf:id="head">
        <title>JSF Page with HTML5 Markup</title>
        <link jsf:library="css" jsf:name="styles.css"
            rel="stylesheet"
            type="text/css"
            href="resources/css/styles.css"/>
    </head>
    <body jsf:id="body">
        <form jsf:prependId="false">
            <table style="border-spacing: 0; border-collapse:
                collapse">
                <tr>
                    <td class="rightAlign">
                        <label jsf:for="firstName">First
                            Name</label>
                    </td>
                    <td class="leftAlign">
                        <input type="text" jsf:id="firstName"
                            jsf:value="#{customer.firstName}"/>
                    </td>
```

```
                </tr>
                <tr>
                    <td class="rightAlign">
                        <label jsf:for="lastName">Last Name</label>
                    </td>
                    <td class="leftAlign">
                        <input type="text" jsf:id="lastName"
                                jsf:value="#{customer.lastName}"/>
                    </td>
                </tr>
                <tr>
                    <td class="rightAlign">
                        <label jsf:for="email">Email
                            Address</label>
                    </td>
                    <td class="leftAlign">
                        <input type="email" jsf:id="email"
                                jsf:value="#{customer.email}"/></td>
                </tr>
                <tr>
                    <td></td>
                    <td>
                        <input type="submit"
                            jsf:action="confirmation"
                                value="Submit"/>
                    </td>
                </tr>
            </table>
        </form>
    </body>
</html>
```

The first thing we should notice about this example is the XML namespace prefixed by `jsf` near the top of the page. This namespace allows us to add JSF-specific attributes to HTML 5 pages. When the JSF runtime encounters attributes prefixed by `jsf` in any of the tags on the page, it automatically converts the HTML5 tag to the equivalent JSF component. JSF-specific tags are the same as in regular JSF pages, except that they are prefixed with `jsf`. Therefore, at this point, they should be self-explanatory and will not be discussed in detail. Our example will render and behave just like the first example in this chapter.

The technique described in this section is useful if you have experienced HTML web designers in your team who prefer to have full control over the look of the page. The pages are developed using standard HTML5 with JSF-specific attributes so that the JSF runtime can manage user input.

If your team consists primarily of Java developers with limited CSS/HTML knowledge, then it is preferable to develop the web pages for your web application using JSF components. HTML 5 introduced several new attributes that didn't exist in the previous versions of HTML. For this reason, JSF 2.2 introduces the ability to add arbitrary attributes to JSF components. This JSF/HTML5 integration technique is discussed in the next section.

Pass-through elements

JSF 2.2 allows the definition of any arbitrary attributes (not processed by the JSF engine). These attributes are simply rendered as is on the generated HTML displayed in the browser. The following example is a new version of an earlier example in this chapter, which has been modified to take advantage of the HTML5 pass-through elements:

```
<?xml version='1.0' encoding='UTF-8' ?>
<!DOCTYPE html PUBLIC "-//W3C//DTD XHTML 1.0 Transitional//EN"
    "http://www.w3.org/TR/xhtml1/DTD/xhtml1-transitional.dtd">
<html xmlns="http://www.w3.org/1999/xhtml"
    xmlns:h="http://java.sun.com/jsf/html"
    xmlns:f="http://java.sun.com/jsf/core"
    xmlns:p="http://xmlns.jcp.org/jsf/passthrough">
<h:head>
    <title>Enter Customer Data</title>
</h:head>
<h:body>
    <h:outputStylesheet library="css" name="styles.css"/>
    <h:form id="customerForm">
        <h:messages/>
        <h:panelGrid columns="2"
                columnClasses="rightAlign,leftAlign">
            <h:outputLabel for="firstName" value="First Name:">
            </h:outputLabel>
            <h:inputText id="firstName"
                    label="First Name"
                    value="#{customer.firstName}"
                    required="true"
                    p:placeholder="First Name">
```

```
                            <f:validateLength minimum="2" maximum="30">
                            </f:validateLength>
                </h:inputText>
                <h:outputLabel for="lastName" value="Last Name:">
                </h:outputLabel>
                <h:inputText id="lastName"
                            label="Last Name"
                            value="#{customer.lastName}"
                            required="true"
                            p:placeholder="Last Name">
                            <f:validateLength minimum="2" maximum="30">
                            </f:validateLength>
                </h:inputText>
                <h:outputLabel for="email" value="Email:">
                </h:outputLabel>
                <h:inputText id="email"
                            label="Email"
                            value="#{customer.email}"
                            p:placeholder="Email Address">
                            <f:validateLength minimum="3" maximum="30">
                            </f:validateLength>
                </h:inputText>
                <h:panelGroup></h:panelGroup>
                <h:commandButton action="confirmation" value="Save">
                </h:commandButton>
            </h:panelGrid>
        </h:form>
    </h:body>
</html>
```

The first thing we should notice about this example is the addition of the `xmlns:p="http://xmlns.jcp.org/jsf/passthrough` namespace; this namespace allows us to add any arbitrary attributes to our JSF components.

In our example, we added the HTML5 placeholder attribute to all input text fields in our page; as we can see, it needs to be prefixed by the defined prefix for the namespace at the top of the application (p, in our case). The placeholder HTML attribute simply adds some placeholder text to the input fields, which is automatically deleted once the user starts typing in the input field (this technique was commonly implemented "by hand" using JavaScript before HTML5).

The following screenshot shows our updated page in action:

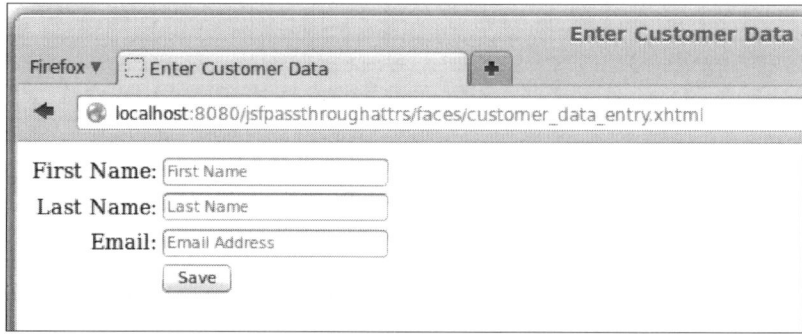

JSF 2.2 Faces Flows

Faces Flows is a new JSF 2.2 feature that defines a scope that can span several pages. Flow scoped beans are created when the user enters a flow (a set of web pages) and are destroyed when the user leaves the flow.

Faces Flows adopts the convention over configuration principle of JSF. The following conventions are typically used when developing applications employing Faces Flows:

- All pages in the flow must be placed in a directory with a name that defines the name of the flow
- An XML configuration file named after the directory name and suffixed with `-flow` must exist inside the directory that contains the pages in the flow (the file may be empty, but it must exist)
- The first page in the flow must be named after the directory name that contains the flow
- The last page in the flow must not be located inside the directory containing the flow and must be named after the directory name and suffixed with `-return`

The following screenshot illustrates these conventions:

In this example, we define a flow named customerinfo; by convention, these files are inside a directory named customerinfo, and the first page of the flow is named customerinfo.xhtml (there are no restrictions on the names of other pages in the flow). When we exit the flow, we navigate to customerinfo-return.xhtml, which follows the naming convention and takes us out of the flow.

The markup for the pages doesn't illustrate anything we haven't seen before, so we will not show it. All example code is available as part of this book's code download bundle.

All the pages in our example store data in a named bean called Customer, which has a scope of flow.

```
@Named
@FlowScoped("customerinfo")
public class Customer implements Serializable {
    //class body omitted
}
```

The @FlowScoped annotation has a value attribute that must match the name of the flow that the bean is meant to work with (customerinfo in this example).

This example creates a wizard-style set of pages in which data for a user is entered across several pages in the flow.

On the first page, we enter information about the name.

On the second page, we enter address information as shown in the following screenshot:

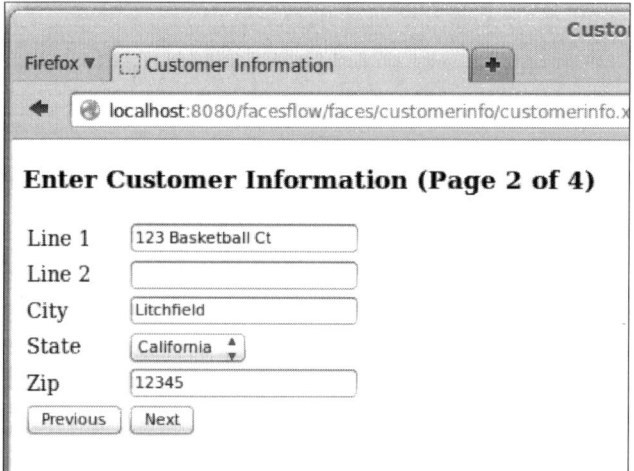

On the next page, we enter phone number information as shown in the following screenshot:

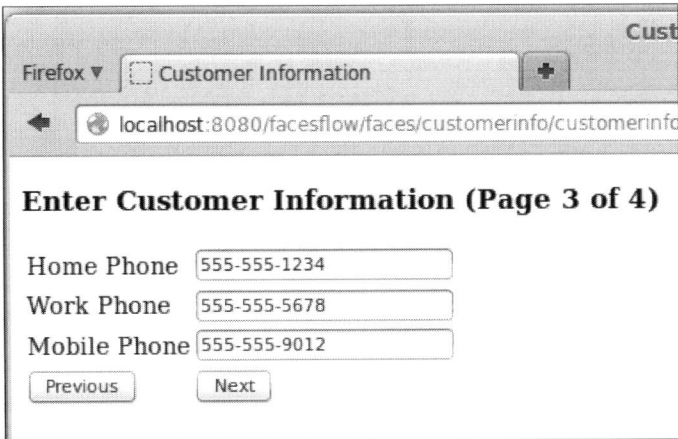

Finally, we display a confirmation page as shown in the following screenshot:

If the user verifies that the information is correct, we navigate outside the flow to `customerinfo-return.xhtml`; otherwise, we go back to the first page in the flow to allow the user to make any necessary corrections.

Additional JSF component libraries

In addition to the standard JSF component libraries, there are a number of third-party JSF tag libraries available. The following table lists some of the most popular ones:

Tag library	Distributor	License	URL
ICEfaces	ICEsoft	MPL 1.1	`http://www.icefaces.org`
RichFaces	Red Hat/JBoss	LGPL	`http://www.jboss.org/richfaces`
Primefaces	Prime Technology	Apache 2.0	`http://www.primefaces.org`

Summary

In this chapter, we covered how to develop web-based applications using JavaServer Faces, the standard component framework for the Java EE platform. We covered how to write a simple application by creating pages using Facelets as the view technology and CDI named beans. We also covered how to validate user input by using JSF's standard validators and by creating our own custom validators or by writing validator methods. Additionally, we covered how to customize standard JSF error messages, both the message text and the message style (font, color, and so on). Also, we covered how to develop Ajax-enabled JSF pages as well as how to integrate JSF and HTML5.

In the next chapter, we will cover how to interact with relational databases via the Java Persistence API.

3
Object Relational Mapping with JPA

Any non-trivial Java EE application will persist data to a relational database. In this chapter, we will cover how to connect to a database and perform **CRUD** operations (**Create**, **Read**, **Update**, **Delete**).

The **Java Persistence API (JPA)** is the standard Java EE **Object Relational Mapping (ORM)** tool. We will discuss this API in detail in this chapter.

Some of the topics covered in this chapter include:

- Retrieving data from a database through JPA
- Inserting data into a database through JPA
- Updating data in a database through JPA
- Deleting data in a database through JPA
- Building queries programmatically through the JPA Criteria API
- Automating data validation through JPA 2.0's Bean Validation support

The CustomerDB database

Examples in this chapter will use a database called CUSTOMERDB. This database contains tables to track customer and order information for a fictitious store. The database uses JavaDB for its **Relational Database Management System (RDBMS)** since it comes bundled with GlassFish.

Object Relational Mapping with JPA

A script is included with this book's code download to create this database and prepopulate some of its tables. Instructions on how to execute the script and add a connection pool and datasource to access it are included in the download as well. The schema for the CUSTOMERDB database is depicted in the following diagram:

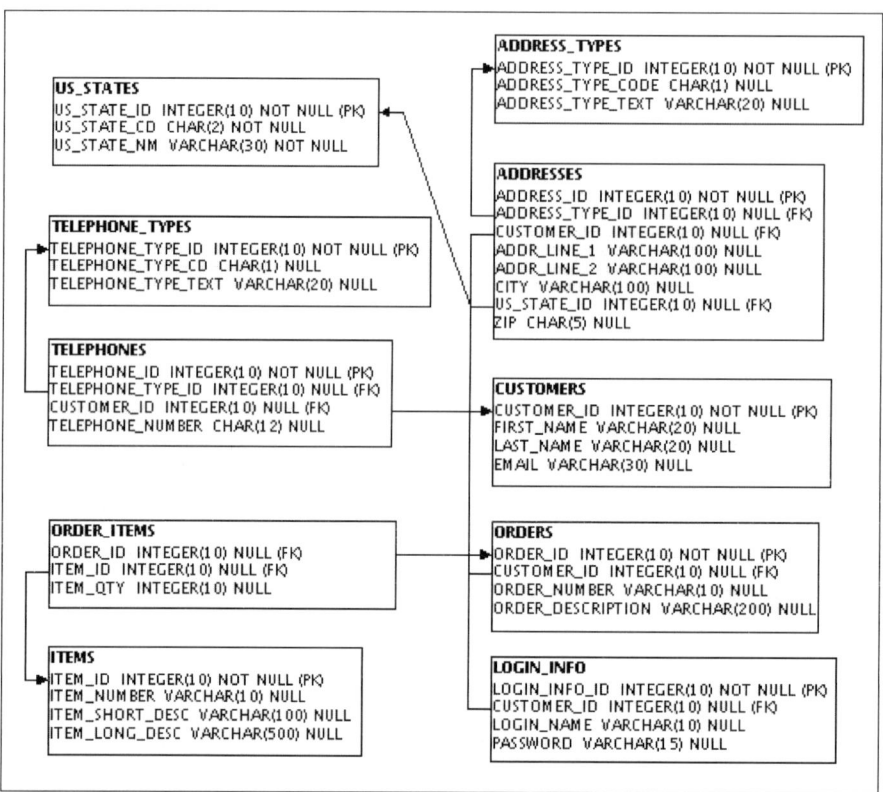

As can be seen in the preceding diagram, the database contains tables to store customer information such as name, address, and e-mail address. It also contains tables to store order and item information.

The ADDRESS_TYPES table will store values such as "Home", "Mailing", and "Shipping" to distinguish the type of address in the ADDRESSES table; similarly, the TELEPHONE_TYPES table stores the values "Cell", "Home", and "Work". These two tables are prepopulated when creating the database as well as the US_STATES table.

 For simplicity, our database only deals with US addresses.

Introducing the Java Persistence API

JPA was introduced to Java EE in Version 5 of the specification. As its name implies, it is used to persist data to an RDBMS. JPA is a replacement for Entity Beans that were used in J2EE. JPA Entities are regular Java classes; the Java EE container recognizes these classes as JPA entities. Let's look at an Entity mapping to the CUSTOMER table in the CUSTOMERDB database, shown in the following code:

```java
package net.ensode.glassfishbook.jpaintro.entity;

import java.io.Serializable;

import javax.persistence.Column;
import javax.persistence.Entity;
import javax.persistence.Id;
import javax.persistence.Table;

@Entity
@Table(name = "CUSTOMERS")
public class Customer implements Serializable
{
  @Id
  @Column(name = "CUSTOMER_ID")
  private Long customerId;

  @Column(name = "FIRST_NAME")
  private String firstName;

  @Column(name = "LAST_NAME")
  private String lastName;

  private String email;

  public Long getCustomerId()
  {
    return customerId;
  }
  public void setCustomerId(Long customerId)
  {
    this.customerId = customerId;
  }
  public String getEmail()
  {
```

```
      return email;
   }
   public void setEmail(String email)
   {
      this.email = email;
   }
   public String getFirstName()
   {
      return firstName;
   }
   public void setFirstName(String firstName)
   {
      this.firstName = firstName;
   }
   public String getLastName()
   {
      return lastName;
   }
   public void setLastName(String lastName)
   {
      this.lastName = lastName;
   }
}
```

In the preceding code, the `@Entity` annotation lets GlassFish (or, for that matter, any other application server that is compliant with Java EE) know that this class is an entity.

The `@Table(name = "CUSTOMERS")` annotation lets the application server know what table to map the entity to. The value of the `name` element contains the name of the database table that the entity maps to. This annotation is optional; if the name of the class is the same as the name of the database table, then it isn't necessary to specify what table the entity maps to.

The `@Id` annotation indicates that the `customerId` field is the primary key (unique identifier) for our Entity.

The `@Column` annotation maps each field to a column in the table. If the name of the field matches the name of the database column, then this annotation is not needed. This is the reason why the `email` field is not annotated.

The `EntityManager` class (`EntityManager` is actually an interface; each Java EE compliant application server provides its own implementation) is used to persist Entities to a database. The following example illustrates its usage:

```
package net.ensode.glassfishbook.jpaintro.namedbean;

import javax.annotation.Resource;
```

```java
import javax.enterprise.context.RequestScoped;
import javax.inject.Named;
import javax.persistence.EntityManager;
import javax.persistence.PersistenceContext;
import javax.transaction.HeuristicMixedException;
import javax.transaction.HeuristicRollbackException;
import javax.transaction.NotSupportedException;
import javax.transaction.RollbackException;
import javax.transaction.SystemException;
import javax.transaction.UserTransaction;
import net.ensode.glassfishbook.jpaintro.entity.Customer;

@Named
@RequestScoped
public class JpaDemoBean {

    @PersistenceContext
    private EntityManager entityManager;

    @Resource
    private UserTransaction userTransaction;

    public String updateDatabase() {

        String retVal = "confirmation";

        Customer customer = new Customer();
        Customer customer2 = new Customer();
        Customer customer3;

        customer.setCustomerId(3L);
        customer.setFirstName("James");
        customer.setLastName("McKenzie");
        customer.setEmail("jamesm@notreal.com");

        customer2.setCustomerId(4L);
        customer2.setFirstName("Charles");
        customer2.setLastName("Jonson");
        customer2.setEmail("cjohnson@phony.org");

        try {
            userTransaction.begin();
            entityManager.persist(customer);
            entityManager.persist(customer2);
```

```
            customer3 = entityManager.find(Customer.class, 4L);
            customer3.setLastName("Johnson");
            entityManager.persist(customer3);
            entityManager.remove(customer);

            userTransaction.commit();
        } catch (HeuristicMixedException |
                HeuristicRollbackException |
                IllegalStateException |
                NotSupportedException |
                RollbackException |
                SecurityException |
                SystemException e) {
            retVal = "error";
            e.printStackTrace();
        }

        return retVal;
    }
}
```

The CDI named bean in the preceding code obtains an instance of a class implementing the `javax.persistence.EntityManager` interface via dependency injection. This is done by decorating the `EntityManager` variable with the `@PersistenceContext` annotation.

An instance of a class implementing the `javax.transaction.UserTransaction` interface is then injected via the `@Resource` annotation. This object is necessary since without it, invoking calls to persist Entities to the database would result in the code throwing a `javax.persistence.TransactionRequiredException`.

The `EntityManager` class performs many database-related tasks such as finding entities in the database, updating them, and deleting them.

Since JPA Entities are **Plain Old Java Objects (POJOs)**, they can be instantiated via the `new` operator.

>
> POJOs are Java objects that do not need to extend any specific parent class or implement any specific interface
>
> The call to the `setCustomerId()` method takes advantage of autoboxing, a feature added to the Java language in JDK 1.5. Note that the method takes an instance of `java.lang.Long` as its parameter, but we are using long primitives. The code compiles and executes properly thanks to this feature..

Calls to the `persist()` method on `EntityManager` must be in a transaction; therefore, it is necessary to start one by calling the `begin()` method on `UserTransaction`.

We then insert two new rows to the CUSTOMERS table by calling the `persist()` method on `entityManager` for the two instances of the `Customer` class we populated earlier in the code.

After persisting the data contained in the `customer` and `customer2` objects, we search the database for a row in the CUSTOMERS table with a primary key of 4. We do this by invoking the `find()` method on `entityManager`. This method takes the class of the Entity we are searching for as its first parameter and the primary key of the row corresponding to the object we want to obtain. This method is roughly equivalent to the `findByPrimaryKey()` method on an Entity Bean's home interface.

The primary key we set for the `customer2` object was 4; therefore, what we have now is a copy of this object. The last name for this customer was misspelled when we originally inserted his data into the database; we now correct Mr. Johnson's last name by invoking the `setLastName()` method on `customer3` and then update the information in the database by invoking `entityManager.persist()`.

We then delete the information for the `customer` object by invoking `entityManager.remove()` and passing the `customer` object as a parameter.

Finally, we commit the changes to the database by invoking the `commit()` method on `userTransaction`.

In order for our code to work as expected, an XML configuration file named `persistence.xml` must be deployed in the WAR file containing `JPADemoBean`. This file must be placed in the `WEB-INF/classes/META-INF/` directory inside the WAR file. The contents of this file corresponding to our code are shown next:

```xml
<?xml version="1.0" encoding="UTF-8"?>
<persistence version="2.1"
xmlns="http://java.sun.com/xml/ns/persistence"
xmlns:xsi="http://www.w3.org/2001/XMLSchema-instance"
xsi:schemaLocation="http://java.sun.com/xml/ns/persistence http://
java.sun.com/xml/ns/persistence/persistence_1_0.xsd">
   <persistence-unit name="customerPersistenceUnit">
     <jta-data-source>jdbc/__CustomerDBPool</jta-data-source>
   </persistence-unit>
</persistence>
```

The `persistence.xml` file must contain at least one `<persistence-unit>` element. Each `<persistence-unit>` element must provide a value for its `name` attribute and must contain a `<jta-data-source>` child element whose value is the JNDI name of the datasource to be used for the persistence unit.

More than one `<persistence-unit>` element is allowed because an application may access more than one database. A `<persistence-unit>` element is required for each database the application will access. If the application defines more than one `<persistence-unit>` element, then the `@PersistenceContext` annotation used to inject `EntityManager` must provide a value for its `unitName` element. The value for this element must match the `name` attribute of the corresponding `<persistence-unit>` element in `persistence.xml`.

>
> **Cannot persist the detached object exception**
>
> An application will frequently retrieve a JPA entity via the `EntityManager.find()` method and then pass this entity to a business or user interface layer, where it will potentially be modified. Later, the database data corresponding to the entity will be updated. In cases like this, invoking `EntityManager.persist()` will result in an exception. In order to update JPA entities this way, we need to invoke `EntityManager.merge()`. This method takes an instance of the JPA entity as its single argument and updates the corresponding row in the database with the data stored in it.

Entity relationships

In the previous section, we saw how to retrieve, insert, update, and delete single entities from the database. Entities are rarely isolated; in the vast majority of cases, they are related to other entities.

Entities can have one-to-one, one-to-many, many-to-one, and many-to-many relationships.

In the `CustomerDB` database, for example, there is a one-to-one relationship between the `LOGIN_INFO` table and the `CUSTOMERS` tables. This means that each customer has exactly one corresponding row in the `LOGIN_INFO` table. There is also a one-to-many relationship between the `CUSTOMERS` table and the `ORDERS` table. This is because a customer can place many orders, but each order belongs only to a single customer. Additionally, there is a many-to-many relationship between the `ORDERS` table and the `ITEMS` table. This is because an order can contain many items and an item can be in many orders.

In the next few sections, we discuss how to establish relationships between JPA entities.

One-to-one relationships

One-to-one relationships occur when an instance of an entity can have zero or one corresponding instance of another entity.

One-to-one entity relationships can be bidirectional (each entity is aware of the relationship) or unidirectional (only one of the entities is aware of the relationship). In the `CustomerDB` example database, the one-to-one mapping between the `LOGIN_INFO` and the `CUSTOMERS` tables is unidirectional. This is because the `LOGIN_INFO` table has a foreign key to the `CUSTOMERS` table, but not the other way around. As we will soon see, this fact does not stop us from creating a bidirectional one-to-one relationship between the `Customer` entity and the `LoginInfo` entity.

The source code for the `LoginInfo` entity, which maps to the `LOGIN_INFO` table, can be seen next:

```java
package net.ensode.glassfishbook.entityrelationship.entity;

import javax.persistence.Column;
import javax.persistence.Entity;
import javax.persistence.Id;
import javax.persistence.JoinColumn;
import javax.persistence.Table;

@Entity
@Table(name = "LOGIN_INFO")
public class LoginInfo
{
  @Id
  @Column(name = "LOGIN_INFO_ID")
  private Long loginInfoId;

  @Column(name = "LOGIN_NAME")
  private String loginName;

  private String password;

  @OneToOne
  @JoinColumn(name="CUSTOMER_ID")
  private Customer customer;

  public Long getLoginInfoId()
  {
    return loginInfoId;
  }
```

```java
    public void setLoginInfoId(Long loginInfoId)
    {
      this.loginInfoId = loginInfoId;
    }

    public String getPassword()
    {
      return password;
    }

    public void setPassword(String password)
    {
      this.password = password;
    }

    public String getLoginName()
    {
      return loginName;
    }

    public void setLoginName(String userName)
    {
      this.loginName = userName;
    }

    public Customer getCustomer()
    {
      return customer;
    }

    public void setCustomer(Customer customer)
    {
      this.customer = customer;
    }

}
```

The code for this entity is very similar to the code for the `Customer` entity; it defines fields that map to database columns. Each field whose name does not match the database column name is decorated with the `@Column` annotation; in addition to that, the primary key is decorated with the `@Id` annotation.

This code gets interesting in the declaration of the `customer` field. As can be seen in the code, the `customer` field is decorated with the `@OneToOne` annotation. This lets the application server (GlassFish) know that there is a one-to-one relationship between this entity and the `Customer` entity. The `customer` field is also decorated with the `@JoinColumn` annotation. This annotation lets the container know what column in the LOGIN_INFO table is the foreign key corresponding to the primary key on the CUSTOMER table. Since LOGIN_INFO, the table that the `LoginInfo` entity maps to, has a foreign key to the CUSTOMER table, the `LoginInfo` entity owns the relationship. If the relationship was unidirectional, we wouldn't have to make any changes to the `Customer` entity. However, since we would like to have a bidirectional relationship between these two entities, we need to add a `LoginInfo` field to the `Customer` entity, along with the corresponding getter and setter methods, as shown in the following code:

```java
package net.ensode.glassfishbook.entityrelationship.entity;

import java.io.Serializable;
import java.util.Set;

import javax.persistence.CascadeType;
import javax.persistence.Column;
import javax.persistence.Entity;
import javax.persistence.Id;
import javax.persistence.OneToMany;
import javax.persistence.OneToOne;
import javax.persistence.Table;

@Entity
@Table(name = "CUSTOMERS")
public class Customer implements Serializable
{
  @Id
  @Column(name = "CUSTOMER_ID")
  private Long customerId;

  @Column(name = "FIRST_NAME")
  private String firstName;

  @Column(name = "LAST_NAME")
  private String lastName;

  private String email;
```

```java
@OneToOne(mappedBy = "customer")
private LoginInfo loginInfo;

public Long getCustomerId()
{
    return customerId;
}

public void setCustomerId(Long customerId)
{
    this.customerId = customerId;
}

public String getEmail()
{
    return email;
}

public void setEmail(String email)
{
    this.email = email;
}

public String getFirstName()
{
    return firstName;
}

public void setFirstName(String firstName)
{
    this.firstName = firstName;
}

public String getLastName()
{
    return lastName;
}

public void setLastName(String lastName)
{
    this.lastName = lastName;
}
```

```java
public LoginInfo getLoginInfo()
{
  return loginInfo;
}

public void setLoginInfo(LoginInfo loginInfo)
{
  this.loginInfo = loginInfo;
}
```

The only change we need to make to the `Customer` entity to make the one-to-one relationship bidirectional is to add a `LoginInfo` field to it, along with the corresponding setter and getter methods. The `LoginInfo` field is decorated with the `@OneToOne` annotation. Since the `Customer` entity does not own the relationship (the table it maps to does not have a foreign key to the corresponding table), the `mappedBy` element of the `@OneToOne` annotation needs to be added. This element specifies what field in the corresponding entity has the other end of the relationship. In this particular case, the `customer` field in the `LoginInfo` entity corresponds to the other end of this one-to-one relationship.

The following Java class illustrates the use of the preceding entity:

```java
package net.ensode.glassfishbook.entityrelationship.namedbean;

import javax.annotation.Resource;
import javax.enterprise.context.RequestScoped;
import javax.inject.Named;
import javax.persistence.EntityManager;
import javax.persistence.PersistenceContext;
import javax.transaction.HeuristicMixedException;
import javax.transaction.HeuristicRollbackException;
import javax.transaction.NotSupportedException;
import javax.transaction.RollbackException;
import javax.transaction.SystemException;
import javax.transaction.UserTransaction;
import net.ensode.glassfishbook.entityrelationship.entity.Customer;
import net.ensode.glassfishbook.entityrelationship.entity.LoginInfo;

@Named
@RequestScoped
public class OneToOneRelationshipDemoBean {

    @PersistenceContext
    private EntityManager entityManager;
```

```java
    @Resource
    private UserTransaction userTransaction;

    public String updateDatabase() {
        String retVal = "confirmation";
        Customer customer;
        LoginInfo loginInfo = new LoginInfo();

        loginInfo.setLoginInfoId(1L);
        loginInfo.setLoginName("charlesj");
        loginInfo.setPassword("iwonttellyou");

        try {
            userTransaction.begin();

            customer = entityManager.find(Customer.class, 4L);
            loginInfo.setCustomer(customer);

            entityManager.persist(loginInfo);

            userTransaction.commit();

        } catch (NotSupportedException |
                SystemException |
                SecurityException |
                IllegalStateException |
                RollbackException |
                HeuristicMixedException |
                HeuristicRollbackException e) {
            retVal = "error";
            e.printStackTrace();
        }

        return retVal;
    }
}
```

In this example, we first create an instance of the `LoginInfo` entity and populate it with some data. We then obtain an instance of the `Customer` entity from the database by invoking the `find()` method of `EntityManager` (the data for this entity was inserted into the CUSTOMERS table in one of the previous examples). We then invoke the `setCustomer()` method on the `LoginInfo` entity, passing the customer object as a parameter. Finally, we invoke the `EntityManager.persist()` method to save the data in the database.

Behind the scenes, the CUSTOMER_ID column of the LOGIN_INFO table gets populated with the primary key of the corresponding row in the CUSTOMERS table. This can be easily verified by querying the CUSTOMERDB database.

>  Notice how the call to EntityManager.find() to obtain the customer entity is inside the same transaction where we call EntityManager.persist(). This must be the case; otherwise the database will not be updated successfully.

One-to-many relationships

JPA one-to-many entity relationships can be bidirectional (one entity contains a many-to-one relationship and the corresponding entity contains an inverse one-to-many relationship).

With SQL, one-to-many relationships are defined by foreign keys in one of the tables. The "many" part of the relationship is the one containing a foreign key to the "one" part of the relationship. One-to-many relationships defined in an RDBMS are typically unidirectional, since making them bidirectional usually results in denormalized data.

Just as when defining a unidirectional one-to-many relationship in an RDBMS, in JPA, the "many" part of the relationship is the one that has a reference to the "one" part of the relationship; therefore, the annotation used to decorate the appropriate setter method is @ManyToOne.

In the CUSTOMERDB database, there is a unidirectional one-to-many relationship between customers and orders. We define this relationship in the Order entity, as shown in the following code:

```
package net.ensode.glassfishbook.entityrelationship.entity;

import javax.persistence.Column;
import javax.persistence.Entity;
import javax.persistence.Id;
import javax.persistence.JoinColumn;
import javax.persistence.ManyToOne;
import javax.persistence.Table;

@Entity
@Table(name = "ORDERS")
public class Order
{
  @Id
```

```java
@Column(name = "ORDER_ID")
private Long orderId;

@Column(name = "ORDER_NUMBER")
private String orderNumber;

@Column(name = "ORDER_DESCRIPTION")
private String orderDescription;

@ManyToOne
@JoinColumn(name = "CUSTOMER_ID")
private Customer customer;

public Customer getCustomer()
{
  return customer;
}

public void setCustomer(Customer customer)
{
  this.customer = customer;
}

public String getOrderDescription()
{
  return orderDescription;
}

public void setOrderDescription(String orderDescription)
{
  this.orderDescription = orderDescription;
}

public Long getOrderId()
{
  return orderId;
}

public void setOrderId(Long orderId)
{
  this.orderId = orderId;
}
```

```java
  public String getOrderNumber()
  {
    return orderNumber;
  }

  public void setOrderNumber(String orderNumber)
  {
    this.orderNumber = orderNumber;
  }
}
```

If we were to define a unidirectional many-to-one relationship between the `Orders` entity and the `Customer` entity, we wouldn't need to make any changes to the `Customer` entity. To define a bidirectional one-to-many relationship between the two entities, a new field decorated with the `@OneToMany` annotation needs to be added to the `Customer` entity, as shown in the following code:

```java
package net.ensode.glassfishbook.entityrelationship.entity;

import java.io.Serializable;
import java.util.Set;

import javax.persistence.Column;
import javax.persistence.Entity;
import javax.persistence.Id;
import javax.persistence.OneToMany;
import javax.persistence.Table;

@Entity
@Table(name = "CUSTOMERS")
public class Customer implements Serializable
{
  @Id
  @Column(name = "CUSTOMER_ID")
  private Long customerId;

  @Column(name = "FIRST_NAME")
  private String firstName;

  @Column(name = "LAST_NAME")
  private String lastName;

  private String email;
```

```java
    @OneToOne(mappedBy = "customer")
    private LoginInfo loginInfo;

    @OneToMany(mappedBy="customer")
    private Set<Order> orders;

    public Long getCustomerId()
    {
      return customerId;
    }

    public void setCustomerId(Long customerId)
    {
      this.customerId = customerId;
    }

    public String getEmail()
    {
      return email;
    }

    public void setEmail(String email)
    {
      this.email = email;
    }

    public String getFirstName()
    {
      return firstName;
    }

    public void setFirstName(String firstName)
    {
      this.firstName = firstName;
    }

    public String getLastName()
    {
      return lastName;
    }

    public void setLastName(String lastName)
    {
      this.lastName = lastName;
```

```
  }

  public LoginInfo getLoginInfo()
  {
    return loginInfo;
  }

  public void setLoginInfo(LoginInfo loginInfo)
  {
    this.loginInfo = loginInfo;
  }

  public Set<Order> getOrders()
  {
    return orders;
  }

  public void setOrders(Set<Order> orders)
  {
    this.orders = orders;
  }
}
```

The only difference between this version of the Customer entity and the previous one is the addition of the orders field and related getter and setter methods. Of special interest is the @OneToMany annotation decorating this field. The mappedBy attribute must match the name of the corresponding field in the entity corresponding to the "many" part of the relationship. In simple terms, the value of the mappedBy attribute must match the name of the field decorated with the @ManyToOne annotation in the bean at the other side of the relationship.

The following example code illustrates how to persist one-to-many relationships to the database:

```
package net.ensode.glassfishbook.entityrelationship.namedbean;

import javax.annotation.Resource;
import javax.enterprise.context.RequestScoped;
import javax.inject.Named;
import javax.persistence.EntityManager;
import javax.persistence.PersistenceContext;
import javax.transaction.HeuristicMixedException;
import javax.transaction.HeuristicRollbackException;
import javax.transaction.NotSupportedException;
import javax.transaction.RollbackException;
```

```java
import javax.transaction.SystemException;
import javax.transaction.UserTransaction;
import net.ensode.glassfishbook.entityrelationship.entity.Customer;
import net.ensode.glassfishbook.entityrelationship.entity.Order;

@Named
@RequestScoped
public class OneToManyRelationshipDemoBean {

    @PersistenceContext
    private EntityManager entityManager;

    @Resource
    private UserTransaction userTransaction;

    public String updateDatabase() {
        String retVal = "confirmation";

        Customer customer;
        Order order1;
        Order order2;

        order1 = new Order();
        order1.setOrderId(1L);
        order1.setOrderNumber("SFX12345");
        order1.setOrderDescription("Dummy order.");

        order2 = new Order();
        order2.setOrderId(2L);
        order2.setOrderNumber("SFX23456");
        order2.setOrderDescription("Another dummy order.");

        try {
            userTransaction.begin();

            customer = entityManager.find(Customer.class, 4L);

            order1.setCustomer(customer);
            order2.setCustomer(customer);

            entityManager.persist(order1);
            entityManager.persist(order2);
```

```
                userTransaction.commit();

        } catch (NotSupportedException |
                SystemException |
                SecurityException |
                IllegalStateException |
                RollbackException |
                HeuristicMixedException |
                HeuristicRollbackException e) {
            retVal = "error";
            e.printStackTrace();
        }

        return retVal;
    }
}
```

The preceding code is pretty similar to the previous example. It instantiates two instances of the `Order` entity, populates them with some data; then, an instance of the `Customer` entity is located in a transaction and used as the parameter of the `setCustomer()` method of both instances of the `Order` entity. We then persist both `Order` entities by invoking `EntityManager.persist()` for each one of them.

Just as when dealing with one-to-one relationships, behind the scenes, the CUSTOMER_ID column of the ORDERS table in the CUSTOMERDB database is populated with the primary key corresponding to the related row in the CUSTOMERS table.

Since the relationship is bidirectional, we can obtain all orders related to a customer by invoking the `getOrders()` method on the `Customer` entity.

Many-to-many relationships

In the CUSTOMERDB database, there is a many-to-many relationship between the ORDERS table and the ITEMS table. We can map this relationship by adding a new `Collection<Item>` field to the `Order` entity and decorating it with the `@ManyToMany` annotation, as shown in the following code:

```
package net.ensode.glassfishbook.entityrelationship.entity;

import java.util.Collection;

import javax.persistence.Column;
import javax.persistence.Entity;
import javax.persistence.Id;
import javax.persistence.JoinColumn;
```

```java
import javax.persistence.JoinTable;
import javax.persistence.ManyToMany;
import javax.persistence.ManyToOne;
import javax.persistence.Table;

@Entity
@Table(name = "ORDERS")
public class Order
{
  @Id
  @Column(name = "ORDER_ID")
  private Long orderId;

  @Column(name = "ORDER_NUMBER")
  private String orderNumber;

  @Column(name = "ORDER_DESCRIPTION")
  private String orderDescription;

  @ManyToOne
  @JoinColumn(name = "CUSTOMER_ID")
  private Customer customer;

  @ManyToMany
  @JoinTable(name = "ORDER_ITEMS",
      joinColumns = @JoinColumn(name = "ORDER_ID",
          referencedColumnName = "ORDER_ID"),
          inverseJoinColumns = @JoinColumn(name = "ITEM_ID",
              referencedColumnName = "ITEM_ID"))
  private Collection<Item> items;

  public Customer getCustomer()
  {
    return customer;
  }

  public void setCustomer(Customer customer)
  {
    this.customer = customer;
  }

  public String getOrderDescription()
  {
```

```java
      return orderDescription;
   }

   public void setOrderDescription(String orderDescription)
   {
      this.orderDescription = orderDescription;
   }

   public Long getOrderId()
   {
      return orderId;
   }

   public void setOrderId(Long orderId)
   {
      this.orderId = orderId;
   }

   public String getOrderNumber()
   {
      return orderNumber;
   }

   public void setOrderNumber(String orderNumber)
   {
      this.orderNumber = orderNumber;
   }

   public Collection<Item> getItems()
   {
      return items;
   }

   public void setItems(Collection<Item> items)
   {
      this.items = items;
   }
}
```

Object Relational Mapping with JPA

As we can see in the preceding code, in addition to being decorated with the `@ManyToMany` annotation, the `items` field is also decorated with the `@JoinTable` annotation. As its name suggests, this annotation lets the application server know what table is used as a join table to create the many-to-many relationship between the two entities. This annotation has three relevant elements: the `name` element, which defines the name of the join table, and the `joinColumns` and `inverseJoinColumns` elements, which define the columns that serve as foreign keys in the join table pointing to the entities' primary keys. Values for the `joinColumns` and `inverseJoinColumns` elements are yet another annotation, the `@JoinColumn` annotation. This annotation has two relevant elements: the `name` element, which defines the name of the column in the join table, and the `referencedColumnName` element, which defines the name of the column in the entity table.

The `Item` entity is a simple entity mapping to the `ITEMS` table in the `CUSTOMERDB` database, as shown in the following code:

```java
package net.ensode.glassfishbook.entityrelationship.entity;

import java.util.Collection;

import javax.persistence.Column;
import javax.persistence.Entity;
import javax.persistence.Id;
import javax.persistence.ManyToMany;
import javax.persistence.Table;

@Entity
@Table(name = "ITEMS")
public class Item
{
  @Id
  @Column(name = "ITEM_ID")
  private Long itemId;

  @Column(name = "ITEM_NUMBER")
  private String itemNumber;

  @Column(name = "ITEM_SHORT_DESC")
  private String itemShortDesc;

  @Column(name = "ITEM_LONG_DESC")
  private String itemLongDesc;
```

```java
@ManyToMany(mappedBy="items")
private Collection<Order> orders;

public Long getItemId()
{
  return itemId;
}

public void setItemId(Long itemId)
{
  this.itemId = itemId;
}

public String getItemLongDesc()
{
  return itemLongDesc;
}

public void setItemLongDesc(String itemLongDesc)
{
  this.itemLongDesc = itemLongDesc;
}

public String getItemNumber()
{
  return itemNumber;
}

public void setItemNumber(String itemNumber)
{
  this.itemNumber = itemNumber;
}

public String getItemShortDesc()
{
  return itemShortDesc;
}

public void setItemShortDesc(String itemShortDesc)
{
  this.itemShortDesc = itemShortDesc;
}
```

```java
    public Collection<Order> getOrders()
    {
      return orders;
    }

    public void setOrders(Collection<Order> orders)
    {
      this.orders = orders;
    }

}
```

Just like one-to-one and one-to-many relationships, many-to-many relationships can be unidirectional or bidirectional. Since we would like the many-to-many relationship between the `Order` and `Item` entities to be bidirectional, we added a `Collection<Order>` field and decorated it with the `@ManyToMany` annotation. Since the corresponding field in the `Order` entity already has the join table defined, it is not necessary to do it again here. The entity containing the `@JoinTable` annotation is said to own the relationship. In a many-to-many relationship, either entity can own the relationship. In our example, the `Order` entity owns it, since its `Collection<Item>` field is decorated with the `@JoinTable` annotation.

Just as with the one-to-one and one-to-many relationships, the `@ManyToMany` annotation in the non-owning side of a bidirectional many-to-many relationship must contain a `mappedBy` element indicating what field in the owning entity defines the relationship.

Now that we have seen the changes necessary to establish a bidirectional many-to-many relationship between the `Order` and `Item` entities, we can see the relationship in action in the following example:

```java
package net.ensode.glassfishbook.entityrelationship.namedbean;

import java.util.ArrayList;
import java.util.Collection;
import javax.annotation.Resource;
import javax.enterprise.context.RequestScoped;
import javax.inject.Named;
import javax.persistence.EntityManager;
import javax.persistence.PersistenceContext;
import javax.transaction.HeuristicMixedException;
import javax.transaction.HeuristicRollbackException;
import javax.transaction.NotSupportedException;
import javax.transaction.RollbackException;
import javax.transaction.SystemException;
```

```java
import javax.transaction.UserTransaction;
import net.ensode.glassfishbook.entityrelationship.entity.Item;
import net.ensode.glassfishbook.entityrelationship.entity.Order;

@Named
@RequestScoped
public class ManyToManyRelationshipDemoBean {

    @PersistenceContext
    private EntityManager entityManager;

    @Resource
    private UserTransaction userTransaction;

    public String updateDatabase() {
        String retVal = "confirmation";

        Order order;
        Collection<Item> items = new ArrayList<Item>();
        Item item1 = new Item();
        Item item2 = new Item();

        item1.setItemId(1L);
        item1.setItemNumber("BCD1234");
        item1.setItemShortDesc("Notebook Computer");
        item1.setItemLongDesc("64 bit Quad core CPU, 4GB memory");

        item2.setItemId(2L);
        item2.setItemNumber("CDF2345");
        item2.setItemShortDesc("Cordless Mouse");
        item2.setItemLongDesc("Three button, infrared, "
                + "vertical and horizontal scrollwheels");

        items.add(item1);
        items.add(item2);

        try {
            userTransaction.begin();

            entityManager.persist(item1);
            entityManager.persist(item2);

            order = entityManager.find(Order.class, 1L);
            order.setItems(items);
```

```
            entityManager.persist(order);

        userTransaction.commit();

    } catch (NotSupportedException |
            SystemException |
            SecurityException |
            IllegalStateException |
            RollbackException |
            HeuristicMixedException |
            HeuristicRollbackException e) {
        retVal = "error";
        e.printStackTrace();
    }

    return retVal;
    }
}
```

The preceding code creates two instances of the `Item` entity and populates them with some data. It then adds these two instances to a collection. A transaction is then started. The two `Item` instances are persisted to the database. Then, an instance of the `Order` entity is retrieved from the database. The `setItems()` method of the `Order` entity instance is then invoked, passing the collection containing the two `Item` instances as a parameter. The `Customer` instance is then persisted into the database. At this point, two rows are created behind the scenes in the `ORDER_ITEMS` table, which is the join table between the `ORDERS` and `ITEMS` tables.

Composite primary keys

Most tables in the CUSTOMERDB database have a column that exists for the sole purpose of serving as a primary key (this type of primary key is sometimes referred to as a surrogate primary key or as an artificial primary key). However, some databases are not designed this way; instead, a column in the database that is known to be unique across rows is used as the primary key. If there is no column whose value is not guaranteed to be unique across rows, then a combination of two or more columns is used as the table's primary key. It is possible to map this kind of primary key to JPA entities using a primary key class.

There is one table in the CUSTOMERDB database that does not have a surrogate primary key; this table is the ORDER_ITEMS table. This table serves as a join table between the ORDERS table and the ITEMS table. In addition to having foreign keys for these two tables, the ORDER_ITEMS table has an additional column called ITEM_QTY that stores the quantity of each item in an order. Since this table does not have a surrogate primary key, the JPA entity mapping to it must have a custom primary key class. In this table, the combination of the ORDER_ID and ITEM_ID columns must be unique. Therefore, this is a good combination for a composite primary key, as shown in the following code example:

```java
package net.ensode.glassfishbook.compositeprimarykeys.entity;

import java.io.Serializable;

public class OrderItemPK implements Serializable
{
  public Long orderId;
  public Long itemId;

  public OrderItemPK()
  {

  }

  public OrderItemPK(Long orderId, Long itemId)
  {
    this.orderId = orderId;
    this.itemId = itemId;
  }

  @Override
  public boolean equals(Object obj)
  {
    boolean returnVal = false;

    if (obj == null)
    {
      returnVal = false;
    }
    else if (!obj.getClass().equals(this.getClass()))
    {
      returnVal = false;
    }
    else
    {
```

```java
        OrderItemPK other = (OrderItemPK) obj;

      if (this == other)
      {
        returnVal = true;
      }
      else if (orderId != null && other.orderId != null
           && this.orderId.equals(other.orderId))
      {
        if (itemId != null && other.itemId != null
            && itemId.equals(other.itemId))
        {
          returnVal = true;
        }
      }
      else
      {
        returnVal = false;
      }
    }

    return returnVal;
  }

  @Override
  public int hashCode()
  {
    if (orderId == null || itemId == null)
    {
      return 0;
    }
    else
    {
      return orderId.hashCode() ^ itemId.hashCode();
    }
  }
}
```

A custom primary key class must satisfy the following requirements:

- The class must be `public`
- It must implement `java.io.Serializable`
- It must have a `public` constructor that takes no arguments

- Its fields must be `public` or `protected`
- Its field names and types must match those of the entity
- It must override the default `hashCode()` and `equals()` methods defined in the `java.lang.Object` class

The `OrderItemPK` class in the preceding code meets all of these requirements. It also has a convenient constructor that takes two `Long` objects meant to initialize its `orderId` and `itemId` fields. This constructor was added for convenience and is not a requirement for the class to be used as a primary key class.

When an entity uses a custom primary key class, it must be decorated with the `@IdClass` annotation. Since the `OrderItem` class uses `OrderItemPK` as its custom primary key class, it must be decorated with the said annotation, as shown in the following code example:

```java
package net.ensode.glassfishbook.compositeprimarykeys.entity;

import javax.persistence.Column;
import javax.persistence.Entity;
import javax.persistence.Id;
import javax.persistence.IdClass;
import javax.persistence.Table;

@Entity
@Table(name = "ORDER_ITEMS")
@IdClass(value = OrderItemPK.class)
public class OrderItem
{
  @Id
  @Column(name = "ORDER_ID")
  private Long orderId;

  @Id
  @Column(name = "ITEM_ID")
  private Long itemId;

  @Column(name = "ITEM_QTY")
  private Long itemQty;

  public Long getItemId()
  {
    return itemId;
  }
```

```java
    public void setItemId(Long itemId)
    {
      this.itemId = itemId;
    }

    public Long getItemQty()
    {
      return itemQty;
    }

    public void setItemQty(Long itemQty)
    {
      this.itemQty = itemQty;
    }

    public Long getOrderId()
    {
      return orderId;
    }

    public void setOrderId(Long orderId)
    {
      this.orderId = orderId;
    }
}
```

There are two differences between this entity and entities we have seen previously. The first difference is that this entity is decorated with the `@IdClass` annotation, indicating the primary key class corresponding to it. The second difference is that this entity has more than one field decorated with the `@Id` annotation. Since this entity has a composite primary key, each field that is part of the primary key must be decorated with this annotation.

Obtaining a reference of an entity with a composite primary key is not very different from obtaining a reference to an entity with a primary key consisting of a single field. The following example demonstrates how to do this:

```java
package net.ensode.glassfishbook.compositeprimarykeys.namedbean;

import javax.enterprise.context.RequestScoped;
import javax.inject.Named;
import javax.persistence.EntityManager;
import javax.persistence.PersistenceContext;
import net.ensode.glassfishbook.compositeprimarykeys.entity.OrderItem;
```

```java
import net.ensode.glassfishbook.compositeprimarykeys.entity.
OrderItemPK;

@Named
@RequestScoped
public class CompositePrimaryKeyDemoBean {

    @PersistenceContext
    private EntityManager entityManager;

    private OrderItem orderItem;

    public String findOrderItem() {
        String retVal = "confirmation";

        try {
            orderItem = entityManager.find(OrderItem.class, new
OrderItemPK(1L, 2L));
        } catch (Exception e) {
            retVal = "error";
            e.printStackTrace();
        }

        return retVal;
    }

    public OrderItem getOrderItem() {
        return orderItem;
    }

    public void setOrderItem(OrderItem orderItem) {
        this.orderItem = orderItem;
    }

}
```

As can be seen in this example, the only difference between locating an entity with a composite primary key and an entity with a primary key consisting of a single field is that an instance of the custom primary key class must be passed as the second argument of the `EntityManager.find()` method; fields for this instance must be populated with the appropriate values for each field that is part of the primary key.

Introducing the Java Persistence Query Language

All of our examples that obtain entities from the database so far have conveniently assumed that the primary key for the entity is known ahead of time. We all know that, frequently, this is not the case. Whenever we need to search for an entity by a field other than the entity's primary key, we must use the **Java Persistence Query Language (JPQL)**.

JPQL is a SQL-like language used for retrieving, updating, and deleting entities in a database. The following example illustrates how to use JPQL to retrieve a subset of states from the US_STATES table in the CUSTOMERDB database:

```java
package net.ensode.glassfishbook.jpql.namedbean;

import java.util.List;
import javax.enterprise.context.RequestScoped;
import javax.inject.Named;
import javax.persistence.EntityManager;
import javax.persistence.PersistenceContext;
import javax.persistence.Query;
import net.ensode.glassfishbook.jpql.entity.UsState;

@Named
@RequestScoped
public class SelectQueryDemoBean {

    @PersistenceContext
    private EntityManager entityManager;

    private List<UsState> matchingStatesList;

    public String findStates() {
        String retVal = "confirmation";

        try {
            Query query = entityManager
                    .createQuery(
                    "SELECT s FROM UsState s WHERE s.usStateNm "
                    + "LIKE :name");
            query.setParameter("name", "New%");
            matchingStatesList = query.getResultList();
        } catch (Exception e) {
            retVal = "error";
```

```java
            e.printStackTrace();
        }
        return retVal;
    }

    public List<UsState> getMatchingStatesList() {
        return matchingStatesList;
    }

    public void setMatchingStatesList(List<UsState>
  matchingStatesList) {
        this.matchingStatesList = matchingStatesList;
    }

}
```

The preceding code invokes the `EntityManager.createQuery()` method, passing a string containing a JPQL query as a parameter. This method returns an instance of `javax.persistence.Query`. The query retrieves all `UsState` entities whose names start with the string `"New"`.

As can be seen in the preceding code, JPQL is similar to SQL. However there are some differences that may confuse readers with SQL knowledge. The equivalent SQL code for the query in the code will be:

```
SELECT * from US_STATES s where s.US_STATE_NM like 'New%'
```

The first difference between JPQL and SQL is that in JPQL, we always use entity names, whereas in SQL table names are used. The `s` after the entity name in the JPQL query is an alias for the entity. Table aliases are optional in SQL, but entity aliases are required in JPQL. Keeping these differences in mind, the JPQL query should now be a lot less confusing.

The `:name` parameter in the query is a named parameter; named parameters are meant to be substituted with actual values. This is done by invoking the `setParameter()` method in the instance of `javax.persistence.Query` returned by the call to `EntityManager.createQuery()`. A JPQL query can have multiple named parameters.

To actually run the query and retrieve the entities from the database, the `getResultList()` method must be invoked in the instance of `javax.persistence.Query` obtained from `EntityManager.createQuery()`. This method returns an instance of a class implementing the `java.util.List` interface. This list contains the entities matching the query criteria. If no entities match the criteria, then an empty list is returned.

If we are certain that the query will return exactly one entity, then the `getSingleResult()` method may be alternatively called on `Query`; this method returns an object that must be cast to the appropriate entity.

Our example uses the `LIKE` operator to find entities whose names start with the string `"New"`. This is accomplished by substituting the query's named parameter with the value `"New%"`. The percent sign at the end of the parameter value means that any number of characters after the word `"New"` will match the expression. The percent sign can be used anywhere in the parameter value; for example, a value of `"%Dakota"` would match any entities whose name end in `"Dakota"` and a value of `"A%a"` would match any states whose name start with an uppercase `"A"` and end with a lowercase `"a"`. There can be more than one percent sign in a parameter value. The underscore sign (_) can be used to match a single character; all the rules for the percent sign apply to the underscore as well.

In addition to the `LIKE` operator, there are other operators that can be used to retrieve entities from the database, as follows:

- The `=` operator will retrieve entities whose field to the left of the operator exactly match the value to the right of the operator
- The `>` operator will retrieve entities whose field to the left of the operator is greater than the value to the right of the operator
- The `<` operator will retrieve entities whose field to the left of the operator is less than the value to the right of the operator
- The `>=` operator will retrieve entities whose field to the left of the operator is greater than, or equal to, the value to the right of the operator
- The `<=` operator will retrieve entities whose field to the left of the operator is less than, or equal to, the value to the right of the operator

All of the preceding operators work the same way as the equivalent operators in SQL. Just as in SQL, the preceding operators can be combined with the `AND` and `OR` operators. Conditions combined with the `AND` operator match if both conditions are true, and conditions combined with the `OR` operator match if at least one of the conditions are true.

If we intend to use a query many times, it can be stored in a named query. Named queries can be defined by decorating the relevant entity class with the `@NamedQuery` annotation. This annotation has two elements, a name element used to set the name of the query and a query element that defines the query itself. To execute a named query, the `createNamedQuery()` method must be invoked in an instance of `EntityManager`. This method takes a string of type `String` containing the query name as its sole parameter and returns an instance of `javax.persistence.Query`.

In addition to retrieving entities, JPQL can be used to modify or delete entities. However, entity modification and deletion can be done programmatically via the `EntityManager` interface too; doing so results in code that tends to be more readable than when using JPQL. Because of this, we will not cover entity modification and deletion via JPQL. Readers interested in writing JPQL queries to modify and delete entities, as well as readers wishing to know more about JPQL are encouraged to review the Java Persistence 2.1 specification. This specification can be downloaded from `http://jcp.org/en/jsr/detail?id=338`.

Introducing the Criteria API

One of the main additions to JPA in Version 2.0 was the introduction of the Criteria API. The Criteria API is meant as a complement to the JPQL.

Although JPQL is very flexible, it has some problems that make working with it more difficult than necessary. For starters, JPQL queries are stored as strings, and the compiler has no way of validating JPQL syntax. Additionally, JPQL is not type safe; we could write a JPQL query in which our where clause could have a string value for a numeric property and our code would compile and deploy just fine.

To get around the JPQL limitations described in the previous paragraph, the Criteria API was introduced in JPA in Version 2.0 of the specification. The Criteria API allows us to write JPA queries programmatically, without having to rely on JPQL.

The following code example illustrates how to use the Criteria API in our Java EE applications:

```
package net.ensode.glassfishbook.criteriaapi.namedbean;

import java.util.List;
import javax.enterprise.context.RequestScoped;
import javax.inject.Named;
import javax.persistence.EntityManager;
import javax.persistence.PersistenceContext;
import javax.persistence.TypedQuery;
import javax.persistence.criteria.CriteriaBuilder;
import javax.persistence.criteria.CriteriaQuery;
import javax.persistence.criteria.Path;
import javax.persistence.criteria.Predicate;
import javax.persistence.criteria.Root;
import javax.persistence.metamodel.EntityType;
import javax.persistence.metamodel.Metamodel;
import javax.persistence.metamodel.SingularAttribute;
import net.ensode.glassfishbook.criteriaapi.entity.UsState;
```

Object Relational Mapping with JPA

```java
@Named
@RequestScoped
public class CriteriaApiDemoBean {

    @PersistenceContext
    private EntityManager entityManager;

    private List<UsState> matchingStatesList;

    public String findStates() {
        String retVal = "confirmation";
        try {
            CriteriaBuilder criteriaBuilder =
              entityManager.getCriteriaBuilder();
            CriteriaQuery<UsState> criteriaQuery =
              criteriaBuilder.
                    createQuery(UsState.class);
            Root<UsState> root =
             criteriaQuery.from(UsState.class);

            Metamodel metamodel = entityManager.getMetamodel();
            EntityType<UsState> usStateEntityType =
              metamodel.entity(
                    UsState.class);
            SingularAttribute<UsState, String> usStateAttribute
                    =
                    usStateEntityType.getDeclaredSingularAttribute(
                      "usStateNm",
                      String.class);
            Path<String> path = root.get(usStateAttribute);
            Predicate predicate = criteriaBuilder.like(
                    path, "New%");
            criteriaQuery = criteriaQuery.where(predicate);

            TypedQuery typedQuery = entityManager.createQuery(
                    criteriaQuery);

            matchingStatesList = typedQuery.getResultList();

        } catch (Exception e) {
            retVal = "error";
            e.printStackTrace();
        }
```

```
        return retVal;
    }

    public List<UsState> getMatchingStatesList() {
        return matchingStatesList;
    }

    public void setMatchingStatesList(List<UsState>
      matchingStatesList) {
        this.matchingStatesList = matchingStatesList;
    }

}
```

This example is equivalent to the JPQL example we saw earlier in this chapter. This example, however, takes advantage of the Criteria API instead of relying on JPQL.

When writing code using the Criteria API, the first thing we need to do is obtain an instance of a class implementing the `javax.persistence.criteria.CriteriaBuilder` interface. As we can see in our example, we need to obtain the said instance by invoking the `getCriteriaBuilder()` method on our `EntityManager` instance.

From our `CriteriaBuilder` implementation, we need to obtain an instance of a class implementing the `javax.persistence.criteria.CriteriaQuery` interface. We do this by invoking the `createQuery()` method in our `CriteriaBuilder` implementation. Note that `CriteriaQuery` is generically typed. The generic type argument dictates the type of result that our `CriteriaQuery` implementation will return upon execution. By taking advantage of generics in this way, the Criteria API allows us to write type-safe code.

Once we have obtained a `CriteriaQuery` implementation, from it we can obtain an instance of a class implementing the `javax.persistence.criteria.Root` interface. The `Root` implementation dictates what JPA Entity we will be querying from. It is analogous to the FROM query in JPQL (and SQL).

The next two lines in our example take advantage of another new addition to the JPA specification, the **Metamodel API**. In order to take advantage of the Metamodel API, we need to obtain an implementation of the `javax.persistence.metamodel.Metamodel` interface by invoking the `getMetamodel()` method on our `EntityManager` instance.

Object Relational Mapping with JPA

From our `Metamodel` implementation, we can obtain a generically typed instance of the `javax.persistence.metamodel.EntityType` interface. The generic type argument indicates the JPA entity our `EntityType` implementation corresponds to. The `EntityType` interface implementation allows us to browse the persistent attributes of our JPA entities at runtime, which is exactly what we do in the next line in our example. In our case, we are getting an instance of `SingularAttribute`, which maps to a simple, singular attribute in our JPA entity. The `EntityType` interface implementation has methods to obtain attributes that map to collections, sets, lists, and maps. Obtaining these types of attributes is very similar to obtaining `SingularAttribute`; therefore, we won't be covering those in depth. Please refer to the Java EE 7 API documentation at `http://docs.oracle.com/javaee/7/api/` for more information.

As we can see in our example, `SingularAttribute` contains two generic type arguments. The first argument dictates the JPA entity we are working with, and the second one indicates the type of the attribute. We obtain our `SingularAttribute` implementation by invoking the `getDeclaredSingularAttribute()` method on our `EntityType` interface implementation and passing the attribute name (as declared in our JPA entity) as a string.

Once we have obtained our `SingularAttribute` implementation, we need to obtain a `javax.persistence.criteria.Path` implementation by invoking the `get()` method in our `Root` instance and passing `SingularAttribute` as a parameter.

In our example, we will get a list of all the states in the United States whose names start with the string `"New"`. This, of course, is a job for the `like` condition. We can do this with the criteria API by invoking the `like()` method on our `CriteriaBuilder` implementation. The `like()` method takes our `Path` implementation as its first parameter and the value to search for as its second parameter.

The `CriteriaBuilder` interface implementation has a number of methods that are analogous to SQL and JPQL clauses such as `equals()`, `greaterThan()`, `lessThan()`, `and()`, `or()`, and so on and so forth (for the complete list, refer to the Java EE 7 documentation at `http://docs.oracle.com/javaee/7/api/`). These methods can be combined to create complex queries via the Criteria API.

The `like()` method in `CriteriaBuilder` returns an implementation of the `javax.persistence.criteria.Predicate` interface, which we need to pass to the `where()` method in our `CriteriaQuery` implementation. This method returns a new instance of `CriteriaBuilder`, which we assign to our `CriteriaBuilder` variable.

At this point, we are ready to build our query. When working with the Criteria API, we deal with the `javax.persistence.TypedQuery` interface, which can be thought of as a type-safe version of the `Query` interface we use with JPQL. We obtain an instance of `TypedQuery` by invoking the `createQuery()` method in `EntityManager` and passing our `CriteriaQuery` implementation as a parameter.

To obtain our query results as a list, we simply invoke `getResultList()` on our `TypedQuery` implementation. It is worth reiterating that the Criteria API is type safe; therefore, attempting to assign the results of `getResultList()` to a list of the wrong type would result in a compilation error.

Updating data with the Criteria API

When the JPA Criteria API was initially added to JPA 2.0, it only supported selecting data from the database. Modifying existing data was not supported.

JPA 2.1, introduced in Java EE 7, adds support for updating database data via the `CriteriaUpdate` interface; the following example illustrates how to use it:

```java
package net.ensode.glassfishbook.criteriaupdate.namedbean;

//imports omitted for brevity

@Named
@RequestScoped
public class CriteriaUpdateDemoBean {

    @PersistenceContext
    private EntityManager entityManager;

    @Resource
    private UserTransaction userTransaction;

    private int updatedRows;

    public String updateData() {
        String retVal = "confirmation";

        try {

            userTransaction.begin();
            insertTempData();

            CriteriaBuilder criteriaBuilder =
                entityManager.getCriteriaBuilder();
```

```
            CriteriaUpdate<Address> criteriaUpdate =
              criteriaBuilder.createCriteriaUpdate(Address.class);
            Root<Address> root =
              criteriaUpdate.from(Address.class);
            criteriaUpdate.set("city", "New York");
            criteriaUpdate.where(criteriaBuilder.equal(
              root.get("city"), "New Yorc"));

            Query query =
              entityManager.createQuery(criteriaUpdate);

            updatedRows = query.executeUpdate();
            userTransaction.commit();
        } catch (Exception e) {
            retVal = "error";
            e.printStackTrace();
        }
        return retVal;
    }

    public int getUpdatedRows() {
        return updatedRows;
    }

    public void setUpdatedRows(int updatedRows) {
        this.updatedRows = updatedRows;
    }

    private void insertTempData() throws NotSupportedException,
            SystemException, RollbackException,
HeuristicMixedException,
            HeuristicRollbackException {
      //body omitted since it is not relevant to the discussion at hand
      //full source code available as part of this book's code download
    }
```

What this example is actually doing is finding all of the database rows with a city `"New Yorc"` (a typo) and replacing the value with the correct spelling, `"New York"`.

Just as in the previous example, we obtain an instance of a class implementing the `CriteriaBuilder` interface by invoking the `getCriteriaBuilder()` method on our `EntityManager` instance.

We then obtain an instance of a class implementing `CriteriaUpdate` by invoking `createCriteriaUpdate()` on our `CriteriaBuilder` instance.

The next step is to obtain an instance of a class implementing `Root` by invoking the `from()` method on our `CriteriaUpdate` instance.

We then invoke the `set()` method on `CriteriaUpdate` to specify the new values our rows will have after they have been updated. The first parameter of the `set()` method must be a string matching the property name in the `Entity` class, and the second parameter must be the new value.

At this point, we build the `where` clause by invoking the `where()` method on `CriteriaUpdate` and passing the `Predicate` returned by the `equal()` method invoked in `CriteriaBuilder`.

Then, we get a `Query` implementation by invoking `createQuery()` on `EntityManager` and passing our `CriteriaUpdate` instance as a parameter.

Finally, we execute our query, as usual, by invoking `executeUpdate()` on our `Query` implementation.

Deleting data with the Criteria API

In addition to adding support for data update via the Criteria API, JPA 2.1 added the ability to bulk-delete database rows with the new `CriteriaDelete` interface. The following code snippet illustrates its usage:

```java
package net.ensode.glassfishbook.criteriadelete.namedbean;

//imports omitted

@Named
@RequestScoped
public class CriteriaDeleteDemoBean {

    @PersistenceContext
    private EntityManager entityManager;

    @Resource
    private UserTransaction userTransaction;

    private int deletedRows;

    public String deleteData() {
        String retVal = "confirmation";
```

Object Relational Mapping with JPA

```java
        try {
            userTransaction.begin();

            CriteriaBuilder criteriaBuilder =
              entityManager.getCriteriaBuilder();
            CriteriaDelete<Address> criteriaDelete =
              criteriaBuilder.createCriteriaDelete(Address.class);
            Root<Address> root =
              criteriaDelete.from(Address.class);
            criteriaDelete.where(criteriaBuilder.or(criteriaBuilder.
                    equal(
                    root.get("city"), "New York"),
                    criteriaBuilder.equal(root.get("city"), "New
                      York")));

            Query query = entityManager.createQuery(criteriaDelete);

            deletedRows = query.executeUpdate();
            userTransaction.commit();
        } catch (Exception e) {
            retVal = "error";
            e.printStackTrace();
        }
        return retVal;
    }

    public int getDeletedRows() {
        return deletedRows;
    }

    public void setDeletedRows(int updatedRows) {
        this.deletedRows = updatedRows;
    }
}
```

To use `CriteriaDelete`, we first obtain an instance of `CriteriaBuilder` as usual, and then invoke the `createCriteriaDelete()` method on our `CriteriaBuilder` instance to obtain an implementation of `CriteriaDelete`.

Once we have an instance of `CriteriaDelete`, we build the `where` clause as it is usually done with the Criteria API.

Once we have built our `where` clause, we obtain an implementation of the `Query` interface and invoke `executeUpdate()` on it as usual.

Bean Validation support

Another feature introduced in JPA 2.0 is support for JSR 303, Bean Validation. Bean Validation support allows us to annotate our JPA entities with Bean Validation annotations. These annotations allow us to easily validate user input and perform data sanitation.

Taking advantage of Bean Validation is very simple. All we need to do is annotate our JPA Entity fields or getter methods with any of the validation annotations defined in the `javax.validation.constraints` package. Once our fields are annotated as needed, the `EntityManager` will prevent non-validated data from being persisted.

The following code example is a modified version of the `Customer` JPA entity we saw earlier in this chapter. It has been modified to take advantage of Bean Validation in some of its fields.

```
net.ensode.glassfishbook.beanvalidation.entity;

import java.io.Serializable;

import javax.persistence.Column;
import javax.persistence.Entity;
import javax.persistence.Id;
import javax.persistence.Table;
import javax.validation.constraints.NotNull;
import javax.validation.constraints.Size;

@Entity
@Table(name = "CUSTOMERS")
public class Customer implements Serializable
{
  @Id
  @Column(name = "CUSTOMER_ID")
  private Long customerId;

  @Column(name = "FIRST_NAME")
  @NotNull
  @Size(min=2, max=20)
  private String firstName;

  @Column(name = "LAST_NAME")
  @NotNull
  @Size(min=2, max=20)
  private String lastName;
```

```java
    private String email;

    public Long getCustomerId()
    {
      return customerId;
    }

    public void setCustomerId(Long customerId)
    {
      this.customerId = customerId;
    }

    public String getEmail()
    {
      return email;
    }

    public void setEmail(String email)
    {
      this.email = email;
    }

    public String getFirstName()
    {
      return firstName;
    }

    public void setFirstName(String firstName)
    {
      this.firstName = firstName;
    }

    public String getLastName()
    {
      return lastName;
    }

    public void setLastName(String lastName)
    {
      this.lastName = lastName;
    }
}
```

In this example, we used the `@NotNull` annotation to prevent `firstName` and `lastName` of our entity from being persisted with `null` values. We also used the `@Size` annotation to restrict the minimum and maximum length of these fields.

That is all we need to do to take advantage of Bean Validation in JPA. If our code attempts to persist or update an instance of our entity that does not pass the declared validation, an exception of type `javax.validation.ConstraintViolationException` will be thrown, and the entity will not be persisted.

As we can see, Bean Validation pretty much automates data validation, freeing us from having to manually write validation code.

In addition to the two annotations discussed in the previous example, the `javax.validation.constraints` package contains several additional annotations we can use to automate validation on our JPA entities. Please refer to the Java EE 7 API documentation at `http://docs.oracle.com/javaee/7/api/` for the complete list.

Final notes

In the examples of this chapter, we showed how a database is accessed directly from CDI named beans serving as controllers. We did this to get the point across without bogging ourselves down with details. In general, accessing the database directly from controllers is not a good practice. Database access code should be encapsulated in **Data Access Objects (DAOs)**.

> For more information on the DAO design pattern, see `http://www.oracle.com/technetwork/java/dao-138818.html`.

Named beans typically assume the role of controllers and/or models when using the Model-View-Controller (MVC) design pattern: a practice so common that it has become the de facto standard for Java EE applications.

> For more information about the MVC design pattern, see `http://www.oracle.com/technetwork/java/mvc-140477.html`.

Additionally, we chose not to show any user interface code in our examples since it is irrelevant to the topic at hand; however, the code downloads for this chapter includes JSF pages that invoke the named beans in this chapter and display a confirmation page once the named bean invocation finishes.

Summary

This chapter covered how to access data in a database via JPA.

We covered how to mark a Java class as a JPA entity by decorating it with the `@Entity` annotation. Additionally, we covered how to map an entity to a database table via the `@Table` annotation. We also covered how to map entity fields to database columns via the `@Column` annotation, as well as how to declare an entity's primary key via the `@Id` annotation.

Using the `javax.persistence.EntityManager` interface to find, persist, and update JPA entities was also covered.

Defining both unidirectional and bidirectional one-to-one, one-to-many, and many-to-many relationships between JPA entities was covered as well.

Additionally, we covered how to use JPA composite primary keys by developing custom primary key classes.

We then went on to cover how to retrieve entities from a database by using the JPQL.

We discussed additional JPA features, such as the Criteria API, which allows us to build JPA queries programmatically; the Metamodel API, which allows us to take advantage of Java's type safety when working with JPA; and Bean Validation, which allows us to easily validate input by simply annotating our JPA entity fields.

In the next chapter, we will cover **Enterprise JavaBeans (EJBs)**.

4
Enterprise JavaBeans

Enterprise JavaBeans are server side components that encapsulate business logic of an application. Enterprise JavaBeans simplify application development by automatically managing transaction management and security. There are two types of Enterprise JavaBeans: Session beans, which execute business logic, and message-driven beans, which act as a message listener.

Readers familiar with J2EE may notice that Entity Beans haven't been mentioned in the previous paragraph. In Java EE 5, Entity Beans were deprecated in favor of the **Java Persistence API (JPA)**. Entity Beans are still supported for backwards compatibility, however, the preferred way of performing Object-relational mapping is through JPA.

The following topics will be covered in this chapter:

- Session beans
    - A simple session bean
    - A more realistic example
    - Using a session bean to implement the DAO design pattern
    - Singleton session beans
- Message-driven beans
- Transactions in Enterprise JavaBeans
    - Container-managed transactions
    - Bean-managed transactions
- Enterprise JavaBeans life cycles
    - A stateful session bean life cycle
    - A stateless session bean life cycle

- Message-driven bean life cycle
- The EJB Timer Service
- EJB Security

Introduction to session beans

As we've previously mentioned, session beans typically encapsulate business logic. In Java EE, only one or two artifacts need to be created in order to create a session bean, namely, the bean itself and an optional business interface. These artifacts need to be decorated with the proper annotations to let the EJB container know they are session beans.

J2EE required application developers to create several artifacts in order to create a session bean. These artifacts included the bean itself, a local or remote interface (or both), a local home or a remote home interface (or both), and an XML deployment descriptor. As we shall see in this chapter, EJB development was greatly simplified in Java EE.

Developing a simple session bean

The following example illustrates a very simple session bean:

```
package net.ensode.glassfishbook;

import javax.ejb.Stateless;

@Stateless
public class SimpleSessionBean implements SimpleSession
{
  private String message =
      "If you don't see this, it didn't work!";

  public String getMessage()
  {
    return message;
  }
}
```

The `@Stateless` annotation lets the EJB container know that this class is a stateless session bean. There are three types of session beans: stateless, stateful, and singleton. Before we explain the difference between these types of session beans, we need to clarify how an instance of an EJB is provided to an EJB client application.

When a stateless or stateful session bean is deployed, the EJB container creates a series of instances of each session bean. This is what is typically referred to as an EJB pool. When an EJB client application obtains an instance of EJB, the application server (GlassFish, in our case) provides one of the instances in the pool to the client application.

The difference between stateful and stateless session beans is that stateful session beans maintain a conversational state with the client, whereas stateless session beans do not. In simple terms, what this means is that when an EJB client application obtains an instance of a stateful session bean, we are guaranteed that the values of any instance variables in the bean will be consistent across method calls. It is safe to modify any instance variables on a stateful session bean, since they will retain their values for the next method call. The EJB container saves the conversational state by passivating stateful session beans, and retrieves that state when the bean is activated. Conversational state is the reason why the life cycle of stateful session beans is a bit more complex than that of stateless session beans and message driven beans (EJB life cycle is discussed later in this chapter).

The EJB container may provide any instance of EJB from the pool when an EJB client application requests an instance of a stateless session bean. Since we are not guaranteed the same instance for every method call, values set to any instance variables in a stateless session bean may be "lost" (they are not really lost; the modification is in another instance of the EJB in the pool).

Other than being decorated with the `@Stateless` annotation, there is nothing special about the previous class. Notice that it implements an interface called `SimpleSession`. This interface is the bean's business interface. The `SimpleSession` interface is shown in the following code:

```
package net.ensode.glassfishbook;

import javax.ejb.Remote;

@Remote
public interface SimpleSession
{
  public String getMessage();
}
```

Enterprise JavaBeans

The only peculiar thing about this interface is that it is decorated with the `@Remote` annotation. This annotation indicates that this is a remote business interface. What this means is that the interface may be in a different JVM than the client application invoking it. Remote business interfaces may even be invoked across the network.

Business interfaces may also be decorated with the `@Local` interface. This annotation indicates that the business interface is a local business interface. Local business interface implementations must be in the same JVM as the client application invoking its methods.

Since remote business interfaces can be invoked either from the same JVM or a different one than the client application, at first glance, we might be tempted to make all of our business interfaces remote. Before doing so, we must remind ourselves of the fact that the flexibility provided by remote business interfaces comes with a performance penalty, since method invocations are made under the assumption that they will be made across the network. As a matter of fact, most typical Java EE applications consist of web applications acting as client applications for EJBs; in such cases, the client application and the EJB are running on the same JVM, therefore local interfaces are used a lot more frequently than remote business interfaces.

Once we have compiled the session bean and its corresponding business interface, we need to place them in a JAR file and deploy them. Just like with WAR files, the easiest way to deploy an EJB JAR file is by copying it to `[glassfish installation directory]/glassfish/domains/domain1/autodeploy`.

Now that we have seen the session bean and its corresponding business interface, let's take a look at a client sample application:

```
package net.ensode.glassfishbook;

import javax.ejb.EJB;

public class SessionBeanClient
{
  @EJB
  private static SimpleSession simpleSession;

  private void invokeSessionBeanMethods()
  {
    System.out.println(simpleSession.getMessage());

    System.out.println("\nSimpleSession is of type: "
        + simpleSession.getClass().getName());
  }
```

```
    public static void main(String[] args)
    {
      new SessionBeanClient().invokeSessionBeanMethods();
    }

}
```

The previous code simply declares an instance variable of the type net.ensode.SimpleSession, which is the business interface for our session bean. The instance variable is decorated with the @EJB annotation. The @EJB annotation lets the EJB container know that this variable is a business interface for a session bean. The EJB container then injects an implementation of the business interface for the client code to use.

Since our client is a standalone application (as opposed to being a Java EE artifact, such as a WAR file or another EJB JAR file), in order for it to be able to access the code deployed in the server, it must be placed in a JAR file and executed through the appclient utility. The appclient utility is a GlassFish-specific tool that allows standalone Java applications to access resources deployed to the application server. This utility can be found at [glassfish installation directory]/glassfish/bin/. Assuming that this directory is in the PATH environment variable and that we've placed our client code in a JAR file called simplesessionbeanclient.jar, we will execute the previous client code by typing the following command in the command line:

appclient -client simplesessionbeanclient.jar

Executing the previous command results in the following console output:

If you don't see this, it didn't work!

SimpleSession is of type: net.ensode.glassfishbook._SimpleSession_Wrapper

That is the output of the SessionBeanClient class.

> We are using Maven to build our code. For this example, we used the Maven Assembly plugin (http://maven.apache.org/plugins/maven-assembly-plugin/) to build a client JAR file that includes all dependencies; this frees us from having to specify all the dependent JAR files in the -classpath command-line option of the appclient utility. To build this JAR file, simply invoke mvn assembly:assembly from the command line.

The first line of the output is simply the return value of the `getMessage()` method we implemented in the session bean. The second line of output displays the fully qualified class name of the class implementing the business interface. Notice that the class name is not the fully qualified name of the session bean we wrote; instead, what is actually provided is an implementation of the business interface created behind the scenes by the EJB container.

A more realistic example

In the previous section, we saw a very simple, "Hello world" type of example. In this section, we will show a more realistic example. Session beans are frequently used as **Data Access Objects (DAOs)**. Sometimes, they are used as wrappers for JDBC calls and other times, they are used to wrap calls to obtain or modify JPA entities. In this section, we will take the latter approach.

The following example illustrates how to implement the DAO design pattern in a session bean. Before looking at the bean implementation, let's look at the business interface it corresponds to:

```java
package net.ensode.glassfishbook;

import javax.ejb.Remote;

@Remote
public interface CustomerDao
{
  public void saveCustomer(Customer customer);

  public Customer getCustomer(Long customerId);

  public void deleteCustomer(Customer customer);
}
```

As we can see, the previous code is a remote interface implementing three methods: the `saveCustomer()` method saves customer data to the database, the `getCustomer()` method obtains data for a customer from the database, and the `deleteCustomer()` method deletes customer data from the database. Two of these methods take an instance of the `Customer` entity we developed in *Chapter 3, Object Relational Mapping with JPA*, as their parameters. The third method, `getCustomer()`, takes a `Long` value representing the ID of the `Customer` object we wish to retrieve from the database.

Let's now take a look at the session bean implementing the previous business interface. As we are about to see in the following code, there are some differences between the way the JPA code is implemented in a session bean and the way it is implemented in a plain old Java object:

```java
package net.ensode.glassfishbook;

import javax.ejb.Stateful;
import javax.persistence.EntityManager;
import javax.persistence.PersistenceContext;

@Stateful
public class CustomerDaoBean implements CustomerDao {

    @PersistenceContext
    private EntityManager entityManager;

    public void saveCustomer(Customer customer) {
        if (customer.getCustomerId() == null) {
            saveNewCustomer(customer);
        } else {
            updateCustomer(customer);
        }
    }

    private void saveNewCustomer(Customer customer) {
        entityManager.persist(customer);
    }

    private void updateCustomer(Customer customer) {
        entityManager.merge(customer);
    }

    public Customer getCustomer(Long customerId) {
        Customer customer;

        customer = entityManager.find(Customer.class, customerId);

        return customer;
    }

    public void deleteCustomer(Customer customer) {
        entityManager.remove(customer);
    }
}
```

The main difference between our session bean and previous JPA examples is that JPA calls were wrapped between calls to `UserTransaction.begin()` and `UserTransaction.commit()`. The reason we had to do this is because JPA calls are required to be wrapped in a transaction; if they are not wrapped in a transaction, most JPA calls will throw `TransactionRequiredException`. In this case we don't have to explicitly wrap JPA calls in a transaction as in previous examples, since session bean methods are implicitly transactional; there is nothing we need to do to make them that way. This default behavior is what is known as **Container-Managed Transactions**. Container-managed transactions are discussed in detail later in this chapter.

> As mentioned in *Chapter 3, Object Relational Mapping with JPA*, when a JPA entity is retrieved from one transaction and updated to a different transaction, the `EntityManager.merge()` method needs to be invoked to update the data in the database. Invoking `EntityManager.persist()` in this case will result in a `Cannot persist detached object` exception.

Invoking session beans from web applications

Frequently, Java EE applications consist of web applications acting as clients for EJBs. Before Java EE 6, the most common way of deploying a Java EE application that consists of both a web application and one or more session beans was by packaging both the WAR file for the web application and the EJB JAR files into an EAR (Enterprise Archive) file.

Java EE 6 simplified the packaging and deployment of applications consisting of both EJB's and web components.

In this section, we will develop a JSF application with a CDI named bean acting as a client to the DAO session bean we just discussed in the previous section.

In order to make this application act as an EJB client, we will develop a `CustomerController` named bean so that it delegates the logic to save a new customer to the database to the `CustomerDaoBean` session bean we developed in the previous section. We will develop a `CustomerController` named bean, as shown in the following code:

```
package net.ensode.glassfishbook.jsfjpa;

//imports omitted for brevity
```

```java
@Named
@RequestScoped
public class CustomerController implements Serializable {

    @EJB
    private CustomerDaoBean customerDaoBean;

    private Customer customer;

    private String firstName;
    private String lastName;
    private String email;

    public CustomerController() {
        customer = new Customer();
    }

    public String saveCustomer() {
        String returnValue = "customer_saved";

        try {
            populateCustomer();
            customerDaoBean.saveCustomer(customer);
        } catch (Exception e) {
            e.printStackTrace();
            returnValue = "error_saving_customer";
        }

        return returnValue;
    }

    private void populateCustomer() {
        if (customer == null) {
            customer = new Customer();
        }
        customer.setFirstName(getFirstName());
        customer.setLastName(getLastName());
        customer.setEmail(getEmail());
    }

    //setters and getters omitted for brevity

}
```

Enterprise JavaBeans

As we can see, all we had to do was declare an instance of the `CustomerDaoBean` session bean and decorate it with the `@EJB` annotation so that an instance of the corresponding EJB is injected, and then invoke the EJB `saveCustomer()` method.

Notice that we injected an instance of the session bean directly into our client code. The reason we can do this is because of a feature introduced in Java EE 6. When using Java EE 6 or newer, we can do away with local interfaces and use session bean instances directly in our client code.

Now that we have modified our web application to be a client for our session bean, we need to package it in a WAR (web archive) file and deploy it in order to use it.

Introduction to singleton session beans

A new type of session bean that was introduced in Java EE 6 is the singleton session bean. A single instance of each singleton session bean exists per application.

Singleton session beans are useful to cache database data. Caching frequently used data in a singleton session bean increases performance, since it greatly minimizes trips to the database. The common pattern is to have a method in our bean decorated with the `@PostConstruct` annotation; in this method, we retrieve the data we want to cache. Then we provide a setter method for the bean's clients to call. The following example illustrates this technique:

```java
package net.ensode.glassfishbook.singletonsession;

import java.util.List;
import javax.annotation.PostConstruct;
import javax.ejb.Singleton;
import javax.persistence.EntityManager;
import javax.persistence.PersistenceContext;
import javax.persistence.Query;
import net.ensode.glassfishbook.entity.UsStates;

@Singleton
public class SingletonSessionBean implements
    SingletonSessionBeanRemote {

  @PersistenceContext
  private EntityManager entityManager;
  private List<UsStates> stateList;

  @PostConstruct
  public void init() {
```

```
    Query query = entityManager.createQuery(
        "Select us from UsStates us");
    stateList = query.getResultList();
  }

  @Override
  public List<UsStates> getStateList() {
    return stateList;
  }
}
```

Since our bean is a singleton, all of its clients would access the same instance, avoiding multiple queries to the database. Additionally, since it is a singleton, it is safe to specify an instance variable, as all clients access the same instance of the bean.

Asynchronous method calls

Sometimes it is useful to do some processing asynchronously, that is, invoke a method call and return control to the client immediately, without making the client wait for the method to finish.

In earlier versions of Java EE, the only way to invoke EJB methods asynchronously was using message-driven beans (which is discussed in the next section). Although message-driven beans are fairly easy to write, they do require some configuration before they can be used, such as setting up JMS message queues or topics.

EJB 3.1 introduced the `@Asynchronous` annotation, which can be used to mark a method in a session bean as asynchronous. When an EJB client invokes an asynchronous method, control immediately goes back to the client, without waiting for the method to finish.

Asynchronous methods can only return void or an implementation of the `java.util.concurrent.Future` interface. The `Future` interface was introduced in Java 5 and represents the result of an asynchronous computation. The following example illustrates both scenarios:

```
package net.ensode.glassfishbook.asynchronousmethods;

import java.util.concurrent.Future;
import java.util.logging.Level;
import java.util.logging.Logger;
import javax.ejb.AsyncResult;
import javax.ejb.Asynchronous;
import javax.ejb.Stateless;
```

```java
@Stateless
public class AsynchronousSessionBean implements
    AsynchronousSessionBeanRemote {

  private static Logger logger = Logger.getLogger(
      AsynchronousSessionBean.class.getName());

  @Asynchronous
  @Override
  public void slowMethod() {
    long startTime = System.currentTimeMillis();
    logger.info("entering " + this.getClass().getCanonicalName()
        + ".slowMethod()");
    try {
      Thread.sleep(10000); //simulate processing for 10 seconds
    } catch (InterruptedException ex) {
      Logger.getLogger(AsynchronousSessionBean.class.getName()).
          log(Level.SEVERE, null, ex);
    }
    logger.info("leaving " + this.getClass().getCanonicalName()
        + ".slowMethod()");
    long endTime = System.currentTimeMillis();
    logger.info("execution took " + (endTime - startTime)
        + " milliseconds");
  }

  @Asynchronous
  @Override
  public Future<Long> slowMethodWithReturnValue() {
    try {
      Thread.sleep(15000); //simulate processing for 15 seconds
    } catch (InterruptedException ex) {
      Logger.getLogger(AsynchronousSessionBean.class.getName()).
          log(Level.SEVERE, null, ex);
    }

    return new AsyncResult<Long>(42L);
  }
}
```

When our asynchronous method returns void, the only thing we need to do is decorate the method with the @Asynchronous annotation, then call it as usual from the client code.

If we need a return value, this value needs to be wrapped in an implementation of the `jav.util.concurrent.Future` interface. The Java EE API provides a convenience implementation in the form of the `javax.ejb.AsyncResult` class. Both the `Future` interface and the `AsyncResult` class use generics, so we need to specify our return type as the type parameter of these artifacts.

The `Future` interface has several methods we can use to cancel the execution of an asynchronous method, check to see whether or not the method is finished, get the return value of the method, and check to see whether or not the method is canceled. The following table lists these methods:

Method	Description
`cancel(boolean mayInterruptIfRunning)`	This method cancels method execution. If the boolean parameter is `true`, this method will attempt to cancel the method execution even if it is already running.
`get()`	This method will return the "unwrapped" return value of the method; it will be of the type parameter of the `Future` interface implementation returned by the method.
`get(long timeout, TimeUnit unit)`	This method will attempt to get the unwrapped return value of the method; the return value will be of the type parameter of the `Future` interface implementation returned by the method. This method will block for the amount of time specified by the first parameter. The unit of time to wait is determined by the second parameter, the `TimeUnit` enum has constants for NANOSECONDS, MILLISECONDS, SECONDS, MINUTES, and so on. Refer to its Javadoc documentation for the complete list.
`isCancelled()`	This method returns `true` if the method has been cancelled; otherwise, it returns `false`.
`isDone()`	This method returns `true` if the method has finished executing; otherwise, it returns `false`.

As we can see, the `@Asynchronous` annotation makes it very easy to make asynchronous calls without suffering the overhead of having to set up message queues or topics. It is certainly a welcome addition to the EJB specification.

Message-driven beans

The **Java Message Service (JMS)** is a Java EE API used for asynchronous communication between different applications. JMS messages are stored in either message queues or message topics.

The purpose of a message-driven bean is to consume messages from a JMS queue or a JMS topic, depending on the messaging domain used (refer to *Chapter 8, The Java Message Service*). A message-driven bean must be decorated with the `@MessageDriven` annotation. The `mappedName` attribute of this annotation must contain the JNDI name of the JMS message queue or JMS message topic that the bean will be consuming messages from. The following example illustrates a simple message driven bean:

```java
package net.ensode.glassfishbook;

import javax.ejb.MessageDriven;
import javax.jms.JMSException;
import javax.jms.Message;
import javax.jms.MessageListener;
import javax.jms.TextMessage;

@MessageDriven(mappedName = "jms/GlassFishBookQueue")
public class ExampleMessageDrivenBean implements MessageListener
{
  public void onMessage(Message message)
  {
    TextMessage textMessage = (TextMessage) message;
    try
    {
      System.out.print("Received the following message: ");
      System.out.println(textMessage.getText());
      System.out.println();
    }
    catch (JMSException e)
    {
      e.printStackTrace();
    }
  }
}
```

It is recommended, but not required, for message-driven beans to implement the `javax.jms.MessageListener` interface. However, message-driven beans must have a method called `onMessage()` whose signature is identical to that in the previous example.

Client applications never invoke a message-driven bean's methods directly. Instead, they put messages in a message queue or topic, then the bean consumes those messages and acts appropriately. The previous example simply prints the message to standard output, since message-driven beans execute within an EJB container; standard output gets redirected to a log. To see the messages in the GlassFish's server log, open the `[GlassFish installation directory]/glassfish/domains/domain1/logs/server.log` file.

Transactions in Enterprise JavaBeans

As we mentioned earlier in this chapter, by default, all EJB methods are automatically wrapped in a transaction. This default behavior is known as **Container-managed transactions**, since transactions are managed by the EJB container. Application developers may also choose to manage transactions themselves; this can be accomplished using bean-managed transactions. Both of these approaches are discussed in the following sections.

Container-managed transactions

Because EJB methods are transactional by default, we run into an interesting dilemma when an EJB method is invoked from client code that is already in a transaction. How should the EJB container behave? Should it suspend the client transaction, execute its method in a new transaction, then resume the client transaction? Should it not create a new transaction and execute its method as part of the client transaction? Should it throw an exception?

By default, if an EJB method is invoked by a client code that is already in a transaction, the EJB container will simply execute the session bean method as part of the client transaction. If this is not the behavior we need, we can change it by decorating the method with the `@TransactionAttribute` annotation. This annotation has a `value` attribute that determines how the EJB container will behave when the session bean method is invoked within an existing transaction and also when it is invoked outside any transactions. The value of the `value` attribute is typically a constant defined in the `javax.ejb.TransactionAttributeType` enum.

Enterprise JavaBeans

The following table lists the possible values for the `@TransactionAttribute` annotation:

@TransactionAttribute value	Description
`TransactionAttributeType.MANDATORY`	Forces the method to be invoked as part of a client transaction. If this method is called outside any transactions, it will throw a `TransactionRequiredException` exceptiom
`TransactionAttributeType.NEVER`	The method is never executed in a transaction. If it is invoked as part of a client transaction, it will throw a `RemoteException` exception No transaction is created if the method is not invoked within a client transaction.
`TransactionAttributeType.NOT_SUPPORTED`	The method is invoked as part of a client transaction, the client transaction is suspended and the method is executed outside any transaction. After the method is executed, the client transaction is resumed. No transaction is created if the method is not invoked within the client transaction.
`TransactionAttributeType.REQUIRED`	The method is invoked as part of a client transaction, it is executed as part of that transaction. If the method is invoked outside a transaction, a new transaction is created for the method. This is the default behavior.
`TransactionAttributeType.REQUIRES_NEW`	The method is invoked as part of a client transaction, that transaction is suspended, and a new transaction is created for the method. Once the method executes, the client transaction is resumed. If the method is called outside a transaction, a new transaction is created for the method.
`TransactionAttributeType.SUPPORTS`	The method is invoked as part of a client transaction, it is executed as part of that transaction. If the method is invoked outside a transaction, no new transaction is created for the method.

Although the default transaction attribute is reasonable in most cases, it is good to be able to override this default if necessary. For example, transactions have a performance impact. Therefore, being able to turn off transactions for a method that does not need them is beneficial. For a case like this, we would decorate our method, as illustrated in the following code snippet:

```
@TransactionAttribute(value=TransactionAttributeType.NEVER)
public void doitAsFastAsPossible()
{
   //performance critical code goes here.
}
```

Other transaction attribute types can be declared by annotating the methods with the corresponding constant in the `TransactionAttributeType` enum.

If we wish to override the default transaction attribute consistently across all methods in a session bean, we can decorate the session bean class with the `@TransactionAttribute` annotation; the value of its `value` attribute will be applied to every method in the session bean.

Container-managed transactions are automatically rolled back whenever an exception is thrown within an EJB method. Additionally, we can programmatically roll back a container-managed transaction by invoking the `setRollbackOnly()` method on an instance of `javax.ejb.EJBContext` corresponding to the session bean in question. The following example is a new version of the session bean we saw earlier in this chapter, modified to roll back transactions if necessary:

```
package net.ensode.glassfishbook;

//imports omitted

@Stateless
public class CustomerDaoRollbackBean implements
  CustomerDaoRollback
{
  @Resource
  private EJBContext ejbContext;

  @PersistenceContext
  private EntityManager entityManager;

  @Resource(name = "jdbc/__CustomerDBPool")
  private DataSource dataSource;

  public void saveNewCustomer(Customer customer)
  {
    if (customer == null || customer.getCustomerId() != null)
    {
      ejbContext.setRollbackOnly();
    }
    else
    {
      customer.setCustomerId(getNewCustomerId());
      entityManager.persist(customer);
    }
  }
```

```
      public void updateCustomer(Customer customer)
      {
        if (customer == null || customer.getCustomerId() == null)
        {
          ejbContext.setRollbackOnly();
        }
        else
        {
          entityManager.merge(customer);
        }
      }
    //Additional methods omitted for brevity.

    }
```

In this version of the DAO session bean, we deleted the `saveCustomer()` method and made the `saveNewCustomer()` and `updateCustomer()` methods public. Each of these methods now checks to see whether or not the `customerId` field is set correctly for the operation we are trying to perform (`null` for inserts and not `null` for updates). It also checks to make sure the object to be persisted is not `null`. If any of the checks result in invalid data, the method simply rolls back the transaction by invoking the `setRollBackOnly()` method on the injected instance of `EJBContext` and does not update the database.

Bean-managed transactions

As we have seen, container-managed transactions make it ridiculously easy to write code that is wrapped in a transaction. After all, there is nothing special that we need to do to make them that way; as a matter of fact, some developers are sometimes not even aware that they are writing code that will be transactional in nature when they develop session beans. Container-managed transactions cover most of the typical cases that we will encounter. However, they do have a limitation: each method can be wrapped in at most a single transaction. With container-managed transactions, it is not possible to implement a method that generates more than one transaction, this can be accomplished using bean-managed transactions, as shown in the following code:

```
    package net.ensode.glassfishbook;

    import java.sql.Connection;
    import java.sql.PreparedStatement;
    import java.sql.ResultSet;
    import java.sql.SQLException;
    import java.util.List;
```

```java
import javax.annotation.Resource;
import javax.ejb.Stateless;
import javax.ejb.TransactionManagement;
import javax.ejb.TransactionManagementType;
import javax.persistence.EntityManager;

//imports omitted

@Stateless
@TransactionManagement(value = TransactionManagementType.BEAN)
public class CustomerDaoBmtBean implements CustomerDaoBmt
{
  @Resource
  private UserTransaction userTransaction;

  @PersistenceContext
  private EntityManager entityManager;

  @Resource(name = "jdbc/__CustomerDBPool")
  private DataSource dataSource;

  public void saveMultipleNewCustomers(
      List<Customer> customerList)
  {
    for (Customer customer : customerList)
    {
      try
      {
        userTransaction.begin();
        customer.setCustomerId(getNewCustomerId());
        entityManager.persist(customer);
        userTransaction.commit();
      }
      catch (Exception e)
      {
        e.printStackTrace();
      }
    }
  }

  private Long getNewCustomerId()
  {
    Connection connection;
    Long newCustomerId = null;
```

```java
        try
        {
          connection = dataSource.getConnection();
          PreparedStatement preparedStatement =
              connection.prepareStatement("select " +
              "max(customer_id)+1 as new_customer_id " +
              "from customers");

          ResultSet resultSet = preparedStatement.executeQuery();

          if (resultSet != null && resultSet.next())
          {
            newCustomerId = resultSet.getLong("new_customer_id");
          }

          connection.close();
        }
        catch (SQLException e)
        {
          e.printStackTrace();
        }

        return newCustomerId;
    }
}
```

In this example, we implemented a method named `saveMultipleNewCustomers()`. This method takes a `List` of customers as its sole parameter. The intention of this method is to save as many elements in `ArrayList` as possible. An exception saving one of the entities should not stop the method from attempting to save the remaining elements. This behavior is not possible using container-managed transactions, since if an exception is thrown when saving one of the entities it would roll back the whole transaction. The only way to achieve this behavior is through bean-managed transactions.

As shown in the previous example, we declare that the session bean uses bean-managed transactions by decorating the class with the `@TransactionManagement` annotation, and using `TransactionManagementType.BEAN` as the value for its `value` attribute (the only other valid value for this attribute is `TransactionManagementType.CONTAINER`, but since this is the default value, it is not necessary to specify it).

To be able to programmatically control transactions, we inject an instance of `javax.transaction.UserTransaction`, which is then used in the `for` loop within the `saveMultipleNewCustomers()` method to begin and commit transactions in each iteration of the loop.

If we need to roll back a bean-managed transaction, we can do so by simply calling the `rollback()` method on the appropriate instance of `javax.transaction.UserTransaction`.

Before moving on, it is worth noting that even though all the examples in this section were implemented as session beans, the concepts apply to message-driven beans as well.

Enterprise JavaBean life cycles

Enterprise JavaBeans go through different states in their life cycle. Each type of EJB has different states. States specific to each type of EJB are discussed in the next sections.

The stateful session bean life cycle

Readers with experience in previous versions of J2EE may remember that in previous versions of the specification, session beans were required to implement the `javax.ejb.SessionBean` interface. This interface provided methods to be executed at certain points in the session bean's life cycle. Methods provided by the `SessionBean` interface include:

- `ejbActivate()`
- `ejbPassivate()`
- `ejbRemove()`
- `setSessionContext(SessionContext ctx)`

The first three methods were meant to be executed at certain points in the bean's life cycle. In most cases, there was nothing to do in the implementation of these methods. This fact resulted in the vast majority of session beans implementing empty versions of these methods. Thankfully, starting with Java EE 5, it is no longer necessary to implement the `SessionBean` interface, however, if necessary, we can still write methods that will get executed at certain points in the bean's life cycle. We can achieve this by decorating methods with specific annotations.

Before explaining the annotations available to implement life cycle methods, a brief explanation of the session bean life cycle is in order. The life cycle of a stateful session bean is different from that of a stateless session bean.

A stateful session bean's life cycle contains three states: **Does Not Exist**, **Ready**, and **Passive**, as shown in the following diagram:

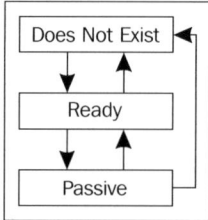

Before a stateful session bean is deployed, it is in the Does Not Exist state. Upon successful deployment, the EJB container does any required dependency injections for the bean and the bean goes into the Ready state. At this point, the bean is ready to have its methods called by a client application.

When a stateful session bean is in Ready state, the EJB container may decide to passivate it, that is, to move it from main memory to secondary storage. When this happens, the bean goes into **Passive** state. If an instance of a stateful session bean hasn't been accessed for a period of time, the EJB container will set the bean to the Does Not Exist state. By default, GlassFish will send a stateful session bean to the Does Not Exist state after 90 minutes of inactivity. This default can be changed by going through the following steps:

1. Log in to the GlassFish administration console.
2. Expand the **Configuration** node in the tree to the left-hand side.
3. Expand the **server-config** node.
4. Click on the **EJB Container** node.
5. Scroll down towards the bottom of the page and modify the value of the **Removal Timeout** text field.

6. Click on the **Save** button, as shown in the following screenshot:

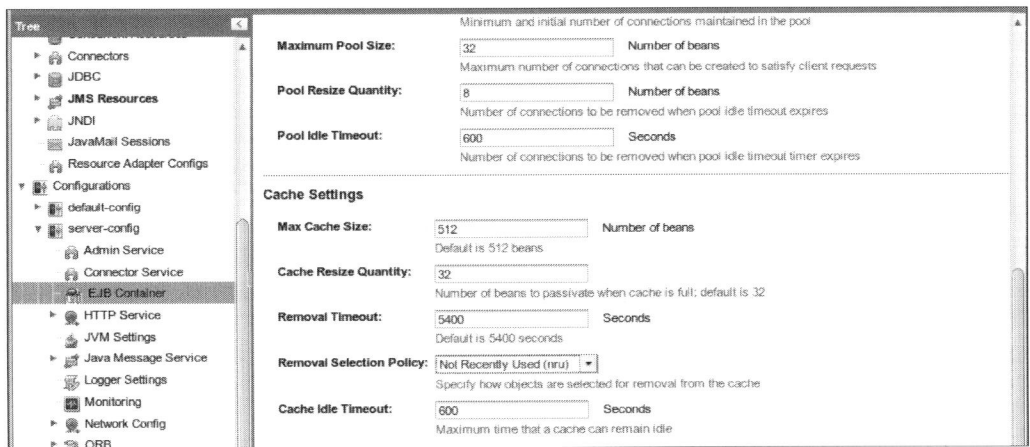

This technique sets the timeout value for all stateful session beans. If we need to modify the timeout value for a specific session bean, we need to include a `glassfish-ejb-jar.xml` deployment descriptor in the JAR file containing the session bean. In this deployment descriptor, we can set the timeout value as the value of the `<removal-timeout-in-seconds>` element, as shown in the following code:

```xml
<?xml version="1.0" encoding="UTF-8"?>
<!DOCTYPE glassfish-ejb-jar PUBLIC "-//GlassFish.org//DTD
  GlassFish Application Server 3.1 EJB 3.1//EN"
    "http://glassfish.org/dtds/glassfish-ejb-jar_3_1-1.dtd">
<glassfish-ejb-jar>
  <enterprise-beans>
    <ejb>
      <ejb-name>MyStatefulSessionBean</ejb-name>
      <bean-cache>
          <removal-timeout-in-seconds>
              600
          </removal-timeout-in-seconds>
      </bean-cache>
    </ejb>
  </enterprise-beans>
</glassfish-ejb-jar>
```

Even though we are not required to create an `ejb-jar.xml` file for our session beans anymore (which used to be the case in previous versions of the J2EE specification), we can still write one if we wish to. The `<ejb-name>` element in the `glassfish-ejb-jar.xml` deployment descriptor must match the value of the element of the same name in `ejb-jar.xml`. If we choose not to create an `ejb-jar.xml` file, this value must match the name of the EJB class. The timeout value for the stateful session bean must be the value of the `<removal-timeout-in-seconds>` element; as the name of the element suggests, the unit of time to use is seconds. In the previous example, we set the timeout value to 600 seconds, or 10 minutes.

Any methods in a stateful session bean decorated with the `@PostActivate` annotation will be invoked just after the stateful session bean has been activated. This is equivalent to implementing the `ejbActivate()` method in previous versions of J2EE. Similarly, any method decorated with the `@PrePassivate` annotation will be invoked just before the stateful session bean is passivated; this is equivalent to implementing the `ejbPassivate()` method in previous versions of J2EE.

When a stateful session bean in the Ready state times out and is sent to the Does not Exist state, any method decorated with the `@PreDestroy` annotation is executed. If the session bean times out in the Passive state, methods decorated with the `@PreDestroy` annotation are not executed. Additionally, if a client of the stateful session bean executes a method decorated with the `@Remove` annotation, all methods decorated with the `@PreDestroy` annotation are executed and the bean is marked for garbage collection. Decorating a method with the `@Remove` annotation is equivalent to implementing the `ejbRemove()` method in previous versions of the J2EE specification.

The `@PostActivate`, `@PrePassivate`, and `@Remove` annotations are valid only for stateful session beans, whereas the `@PreDestroy` and `@PostConstruct` annotations are valid for stateful session beans, stateless session beans, and message-driven beans.

The stateless session bean life cycle

A stateless session bean life cycle contains only the **Does Not Exist** and **Ready** states, as shown in the following diagram:

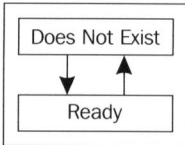

Stateless session beans are never passivated. A stateless session bean's methods can be decorated with the `@PostConstruct` and `@PreDestroy` annotations. Just like with stateful session beans, any methods decorated with the `@PostConstruct` annotation will be executed when the stateless session bean goes from the Does Not Exist to the Ready State, and any methods decorated with the `@PreDestroy` annotation will be executed when a stateless session bean goes from the Ready state to the Does Not Exist state. Stateless session beans are never passivated, any `@PrePassivate` and `@PostActivate` annotations in a stateless session bean are simply ignored by the EJB container.

Just like with stateful session beans, we can control how GlassFish manages the life cycle of stateless session beans (and message-driven beans) via the administration web console, as shown in the following screenshot:

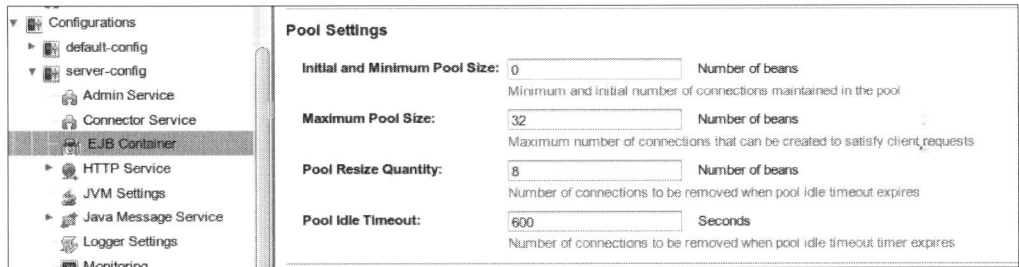

- **Initial and Minimum Pool Size** refers to the minimum number of beans in the pool
- **Maximum Pool Size** refers to the maximum number of beans in the pool
- **Pool Resize Quantity** refers to how many beans will be removed from the pool when the **Pool Idle Timeout** value expires
- **Pool Idle Timeout** refers to the number of seconds of inactivity to let pass before removing beans from the pool

The previous settings affect all `poolable` EJBs, such as stateless session beans and message-driven beans. Just as with stateful session beans, these settings can be overridden on a case-by-case basis by adding a GlassFish specific `glassfish-ejb-jar.xml` deployment descriptor, as shown in the following code:

```
<?xml version="1.0" encoding="UTF-8"?>
<!DOCTYPE glassfish-ejb-jar PUBLIC "-//GlassFish.org//DTD
  GlassFish Application Server 3.1 EJB 3.1//EN"
    "http://glassfish.org/dtds/glassfish-ejb-jar_3_1-1.dtd">
<glassfish-ejb-jar>
```

```xml
<enterprise-beans>
    <ejb>
        <ejb-name>MyStatelessSessionBean</ejb-name>
        <bean-pool>
            <steady-pool-size>10</steady-pool-size>
            <max-pool-size>60</max-pool-size>
            <resize-quantity>5</resize-quantity>
            <pool-idle-timeout-in-seconds>
                900
            </pool-idle-timeout-in-seconds>
        </bean-pool>
    </ejb>
</enterprise-beans>
</glassfish-ejb-jar>
```

- The `<steady-pool-size>` line corresponds to **Initial and Minimum Pool Size** in the GlassFish web console
- The `<max-pool-size>` line corresponds to **Maximum Pool Size** in the GlassFish web console
- The `<resize-quantity>` line corresponds to **Pool Resize Quantity** in the GlassFish web console
- The `<pool-idle-timeout-in-seconds>` line corresponds to **Pool Idle Timeout** in the GlassFish web console

Message-driven bean life cycle

Just like stateless session beans, message-driven beans exist only in the Does Not Exist and Ready states, as shown in the following diagram:

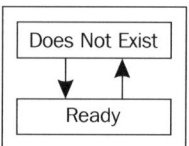

The above image is exactly the same as the previous one. Message-driven beans have the same life cycle as stateless session beans. Therefore, the image to illustrate the life cycle was re-used.

A message-driven bean can have methods decorated with the `@PostConstruct` and `@PreDestroy` methods. Methods decorated with the `@PostConstruct` method are executed just before the bean goes into the Ready state. Methods decorated with the `@PreDestroy` annotation are executed just before the bean goes to the Does Not Exist state.

Introduction to the EJB Timer Service

Stateless session beans and message-driven beans can have a method that is executed periodically at regular intervals of time. This can be accomplished using the **EJB Timer Service**. The following example illustrates how to take advantage of this feature:

```java
package net.ensode.glassfishbook;

//imports omitted

@Stateless
public class EjbTimerExampleBean implements EjbTimerExample
{
  private static Logger logger = Logger.getLogger(EjbTimerExampleBean.class
      .getName());
  @Resource
  TimerService timerService;

  public void startTimer(Serializable info)
  {
    Timer timer = timerService.createTimer
      (new Date(), 5000, info);
  }

  public void stopTimer(Serializable info)
  {
    Timer timer;
    Collection timers = timerService.getTimers();

    for (Object object : timers)
    {
      timer = ((Timer) object);

      if (timer.getInfo().equals(info))
      {
        timer.cancel();
```

```
            break;
        }
    }
}

@Timeout
public void logMessage(Timer timer)
{
    logger.info("This message was triggered by :" +
        timer.getInfo() + " at "
        + System.currentTimeMillis());
}
}
```

In our example, we injected an implementation of the `javax.ejb.TimerService` interface by decorating an instance variable of this type with the `@Resource` annotation. We then created a timer by invoking the `createTimer()` method of the `TimerService` instance.

There are several overloaded versions of the `createTimer()` method. The one we chose to use takes an instance of `java.util.Date` as its first parameter; this parameter is used to indicate the first time the timer should expire (go off). In the example, we chose to use a brand new instance of the `Date` class, which, in effect, makes the timer expire immediately. The second parameter of the `createTimer()` method is the amount of time to wait, in milliseconds, before the timer expires again. In our example, the timer is set to expire every five seconds. The third parameter of the `createTimer()` method can be an instance of any class implementing the `java.io.Serializable` interface. Since a single EJB can have several timers executing concurrently, this third parameter is used to uniquely identify each of the timers. If we don't need to identify the timers, `null` can be passed as a value for this parameter.

[The EJB method invoking `TimerService.createTimer()` must be called from an EJB client. Placing this call in an EJB method decorated with the `@PostConstruct` annotation to start the timer automatically when the bean is placed in the Ready state will result in an `IllegalStateException` exception to be thrown.]

We can stop a timer by invoking its `cancel()` method. There is no way to directly obtain a single timer associated with an EJB. What we need to do is invoke the `getTimers()` method on the instance of `TimerService` that is linked to the EJB; this method will return a Collection containing all the timers associated with the EJB. We can then iterate through the collection and cancel the correct one by invoking its `getInfo()` method. This method will return the `Serializable` object we passed as a parameter to the `createTimer()` method.

Finally, any EJB method decorated with the `@Timeout` annotation will be executed when a timer expires. Methods decorated with this annotation must return void and take a single parameter of type `javax.ejb.Timer`. In our example, the method simply writes a message to the server log.

The following class is a standalone client for the previous EJB:

```java
package net.ensode.glassfishbook;

import javax.ejb.EJB;

public class Client
{
  @EJB
  private static EjbTimerExample ejbTimerExample;

  public static void main(String[] args)
  {
    try
    {
      System.out.println("Starting timer 1...");
      ejbTimerExample.startTimer("Timer 1");
      System.out.println("Sleeping for 2 seconds...");
      Thread.sleep(2000);
      System.out.println("Starting timer 2...");
      ejbTimerExample.startTimer("Timer 2");
      System.out.println("Sleeping for 30 seconds...");
      Thread.sleep(30000);
      System.out.println("Stopping timer 1...");
      ejbTimerExample.stopTimer("Timer 1");
      System.out.println("Stopping timer 2...");
      ejbTimerExample.stopTimer("Timer 2");
      System.out.println("Done.");
    }
    catch (InterruptedException e)
    {
      e.printStackTrace();
    }
  }
}
```

The previous example simply starts a timer, waits for a couple of seconds, and then starts a second timer. It then sleeps for 30 seconds and then stops both timers. After deploying the EJB and executing the client, we should see some entries like the following in the server log:

```
[2013-08-26T20:44:55.180-0400] [glassfish 4.0] [INFO] []
   [net.ensode.glassfishbook.EjbTimerExampleBean] [tid:
    _ThreadID=147 _ThreadName=__ejb-thread-pool1] [timeMillis:
      1377564295180] [levelValue: 800] [[

This message was triggered by :Timer 1 at 1377564295180]]

[2013-08-26T20:44:57.203-0400] [glassfish 4.0] [INFO] []
   [net.ensode.glassfishbook.EjbTimerExampleBean] [tid:
    _ThreadID=148 _ThreadName=__ejb-thread-pool2] [timeMillis:
      1377564297203] [levelValue: 800] [[

This message was triggered by :Timer 2 at 1377564297203]]

[2013-08-26T20:44:58.888-0400] [glassfish 4.0] [INFO] []
   [net.ensode.glassfishbook.EjbTimerExampleBean] [tid:
    _ThreadID=149 _ThreadName=__ejb-thread-pool3] [timeMillis:
      1377564298888] [levelValue: 800] [[

This message was triggered by :Timer 1 at 1377564298888]]

[2013-08-26T20:45:01.156-0400] [glassfish 4.0] [INFO] []
   [net.ensode.glassfishbook.EjbTimerExampleBean] [tid:
    _ThreadID=150 _ThreadName=__ejb-thread-pool4] [timeMillis:
      1377564301156] [levelValue: 800] [[

This message was triggered by :Timer 2 at 1377564301156]]
```

These entries are created each time one of the timers expires.

Calendar-based EJB timer expressions

The example in the previous section has one disadvantage: the `startTimer()` method in the session bean must be invoked from a client in order to start the timer. This restriction makes it difficult to have the timer start as soon as the bean is deployed.

Java EE 6 introduced calendar-based EJB timer expressions. Calendar-based expressions allow one or more methods in our session beans to be executed at a certain date and time. For example, we could configure one of our methods to be executed every night at 8:10 p.m., which is exactly what the following example does:

```
package com.ensode.glassfishbook.calendarbasedtimer;

import java.util.logging.Logger;
```

```java
import javax.ejb.Stateless;
import javax.ejb.LocalBean;
import javax.ejb.Schedule;

@Stateless
@LocalBean
public class CalendarBasedTimerEjbExampleBean {

  private static Logger logger = Logger.getLogger(
      CalendarBasedTimerEjbExampleBean.class.getName());

  @Schedule(hour = "20", minute = "10")
  public void logMessage() {
    logger.info("This message was triggered at:"
        + System.currentTimeMillis());
  }
}
```

As you can see in this example, we set up the time when the method will be executed via the `javax.ejb.Schedule` annotation. In this particular example, we set up our method to be executed at 8:10 p.m. by setting the `hour` attribute of the `@Schedule` annotation to `"20"`, and its minute attribute to `"10"`. The value of the `hour` attribute is 24 hour based; hour 20 is equivalent to 8:00 p.m.

The `@Schedule` annotation has several other attributes that allows a lot of flexibility in specifying when the method should be executed; we could, for instance, have a method being executed on the third Friday of every month, or the last day of the month, and so on and so forth.

The following table lists all the attributes in the `@Schedule` annotation that allow us to control when the annotated method will be executed:

Attribute	Description	Example values	Default value
dayOfMonth	The day of the month.	`"3"`: the third day of the month `"Last"`: the last day of the month `"-2"`: two days before the end of the month `"1st Tue"`: the first Tuesday of the month	`"*"`
dayOfWeek	The day of the week	`"3"`: every Wednesday `"Thu"`: every Thursday	`"*"`

[153]

Attribute	Description	Example values	Default value
hour	The hour of the day (24 hour based)	`"14"`: 2:00 p.m.	`"0"`
minute	The minute of the hour	`"10"`: ten minutes after the hour	`"0"`
month	The month of the year	`"2"`: February `"March"`: March	`"*"`
second	The second of the minute	`"5"`: five seconds after the minute	`"0"`
timezone	The timezone ID	`"America/New York"`	`""`
year	The four-digit year	`"2010"`	`"*"`

In addition to single values, most attributes accept the asterisk (`"*"`) as a wildcard, meaning that the annotated method will be executed regularly (every day, hour, and so on).

Additionally, we can specify more than one value by separating the values with commas, for example, if we need a method to be executed every Tuesday and Thursday, we could annotate the method as `@Schedule(dayOfWeek="Tue, Thu")`.

We can also specify a range of values; the first and last values are separated by a hyphen (-). To execute a method from Monday through Friday, we could use `@Schedule(dayOfWeek="Mon-Fri")`.

Additionally, we could specify that we need the method to be executed every n units of time (for example, every day, every 2 hours, every 10 minutes, and so on). To do something like this, we could use `@Schedule(hour="*/12")`, which would execute the method every 12 hours.

As we can see, the `@Schedule` annotation provides a lot of flexibility in terms of how to specify when we need our methods executed. In addition, it provides us the advantage of not needing a client call to activate the scheduling. It also has the advantage of using cron-like syntax; therefore, developers familiar with this Unix tool will feel right at home using this annotation.

EJB Security

Enterprise JavaBeans allow us to declaratively decide which users can access their methods. For example, some methods might only be available to users in certain roles. A typical scenario is that only users with the role of administrator can add, delete, or modify other users in the system.

The following example is a slightly modified version of the DAO session bean we saw earlier in this chapter. In this version, some methods that were previously private are made public. Additionally, the session bean was modified to allow only users in certain roles to access its methods.

```java
package net.ensode.glassfishbook;

// imports omitted

@Stateless
@RolesAllowed("appadmin")
public class CustomerDaoBean implements CustomerDao
{
  @PersistenceContext
  private EntityManager entityManager;

  @Resource(name = "jdbc/__CustomerDBPool")
  private DataSource dataSource;

  public void saveCustomer(Customer customer)
  {
    if (customer.getCustomerId() == null)
    {
      saveNewCustomer(customer);
    }
    else
    {
      updateCustomer(customer);
    }
  }

  public Long saveNewCustomer(Customer customer)
  {
    entityManager.persist(customer);

    return customer.getCustomerId();
  }
```

```java
    public void updateCustomer(Customer customer)
    {
      entityManager.merge(customer);
    }

    @RolesAllowed(
    { "appuser", "appadmin" })
    public Customer getCustomer(Long customerId)
    {
      Customer customer;

      customer = entityManager.find(Customer.class, customerId);

      return customer;
    }

    public void deleteCustomer(Customer customer)
    {
      entityManager.remove(customer);
    }
}
```

As we can see, we declare what roles have access to the methods using the `@RolesAllowed` annotation. This annotation can take either a single string or an array of strings as its parameter. When a single string is used as a parameter for this annotation, only users with the role specified by the parameter can access the method. If an array of Strings is used as the parameter, users with any of the roles specified by the array's elements can access the method.

The `@RolesAllowed` annotation can be used to decorate an EJB class, in which case, its values apply to either all the methods in the EJB, or to one or more methods. In the second case, its values apply only to the method the annotation is decorating. If, like in our previous example, both the EJB class and one or more of its methods are decorated with the `@RolesAllowed` annotation, the method level annotation takes precedence.

Application roles need to be mapped to a security realm's group name (refer to *Chapter 9, Securing Java EE Applications*, for details). This mapping, along with what realm to use, is set in the `glassfish-ejb-jar.xml` deployment descriptor, as shown in the following code:

```xml
<?xml version="1.0" encoding="UTF-8"?>
<!DOCTYPE glassfish-ejb-jar PUBLIC "-//GlassFish.org//DTD
  GlassFish Application Server 3.1 EJB 3.1//EN"
    "http://glassfish.org/dtds/glassfish-ejb-jar_3_1-1.dtd">
<glassfish-ejb-jar>
```

```xml
<security-role-mapping>
    <role-name>appuser</role-name>
    <group-name>appuser</group-name>
</security-role-mapping>
<security-role-mapping>
    <role-name>appadmin</role-name>
    <group-name>appadmin</group-name>
</security-role-mapping>
<enterprise-beans>
    <ejb>
        <ejb-name>CustomerDaoBean</ejb-name>
        <ior-security-config>
            <as-context>
                <auth-method>username_password</auth-method>
                <realm>file</realm>
                <required>true</required>
            </as-context>
        </ior-security-config>
    </ejb>
</enterprise-beans>
</glassfish-ejb-jar>
```

The `<security-role-mapping>` element of `glassfish-ejb-jar.xml` performs the mapping between application roles and the security realm's group. The value of the `<role-name>` subelement must contain the application role; this value must match the value used in the `@RolesAllowed` annotation. The value of the `<group-name>` subelement must contain the name of the security group in the security realm used by the EJB. In our example, we map two application roles to their corresponding groups in the security realm. Although in this particular example the name of the application role and the security group match, this does not need to be the case.

Automatically matching roles to security groups

It is possible to automatically match any application roles to identically named security groups in the security realm. This can be accomplished by logging in to the GlassFish web console, clicking on the **Configuration** node, clicking on **Security**, then clicking on the checkbox labeled **Default Principal To Role Mapping**, and saving this configuration change.

As shown in our example, the security realm to use for authentication is defined in the `<realm>` subelement of the `<as-context>` element. The value of this subelement must match the name of a valid security realm in the application server. Other sub elements of the `<as-context>` element include `<auth-method>`, the only valid value for this element is `username_password`, and `<required>`, the only valid values of which are `true` and `false`.

Client authentication

If the client code accessing a secured EJB is part of a web application the user of which has already been authenticated (the user logged in through the web interface), then the user's credentials will be used to determine whether or not the user should be allowed to access the method they are trying to execute.

Standalone clients must be executed through the `appclient` utility. The following code illustrates a typical client for the previous, secured session bean:

```java
package net.ensode.glassfishbook;

import javax.ejb.EJB;

public class Client
{
  @EJB
  private static CustomerDao customerDao;

  public static void main(String[] args)
  {
    Long newCustomerId;

    Customer customer = new Customer();
    customer.setFirstName("Mark");
    customer.setLastName("Butcher");
    customer.setEmail("butcher@phony.org");

    System.out.println("Saving New Customer...");
    newCustomerId = customerDao.saveNewCustomer(customer);

    System.out.println("Retrieving customer...");
    customer = customerDao.getCustomer(newCustomerId);
    System.out.println(customer);
  }
}
```

As we can see, there is nothing the code is doing in order to authenticate the user. The session bean is simply injected into the code via the `@EJB` annotation and used as usual. The reason this works is because the `appclient` utility takes care of authenticating the user after invoking the client code via the `appclient` utility as follows:

```
appclient -client ejbsecurityclient.jar
```

The `appclient` utility will present the user with a log in window when it attempts to invoke a secure method on EJB, as shown in the following screenshot:

Assuming that the credentials are correct and the user has the appropriate permissions, the EJB code will execute, and we should see the expected output from the `Client` class:

```
Saving New Customer...
Retrieving customer...
customerId = 29
firstName = Mark
lastName = Butcher
email = butcher@phony.org
```

Summary

In this chapter, we covered how to implement business logic via stateless and stateful session beans. Additionally, we covered how to implement message-driven beans to consume JMS messages.

We also explained how to take advantage of the transactional nature of EJBs to simplify implementing the Data Access Object (DAO) pattern.

Additionally, we explained the concept of container-managed transactions and how to control them using the appropriate annotations. We also explained how to implement Bean Managed Transactions for cases in which container-managed transactions are not enough to satisfy our requirements.

Life cycles for the different types of Enterprise JavaBeans were covered, including an explanation on how to have EJB methods automatically invoked by the EJB container at certain points in the life cycle.

We also covered how to have EJB methods invoked periodically by the EJB container by taking advantage of the EJB timer service.

Finally, we explained how to make sure EJB methods are only invoked by authorized users by annotating the EJB classes and/or methods and by adding the appropriate entries to the `glassfish-ejb-jar.xml` deployment descriptor.

In the next chapter, we will cover Contexts and Dependency Injection.

Contexts and Dependency Injection

Contexts and Dependency Injection (**CDI**) was added to the Java EE specification in Java EE 6. It provides several advantages that were previously unavailable to Java EE developers, such as allowing any JavaBean to be used as a **JavaServer Faces** (**JSF**) managed bean, including stateless and stateful session beans. As the name implies, CDI simplifies dependency injection in Java EE applications.

In this chapter, we will cover the following topics:

- Named beans
- Dependency injection
- Scopes
- Qualifiers

Named beans

CDI provides us with the ability to name our beans via the @Named annotation. Named beans allow us to easily inject our beans into other classes that depend on them (see the *Dependency injection* section), and to easily refer to them from JSF pages via the unified expression language.

The following example shows us the @Named annotation in action:

```
package net.ensode.cdidependencyinjection.beans;

import javax.enterprise.context.RequestScoped;
import javax.inject.Named;
```

```
@Named
@RequestScoped
public class Customer {

  private String firstName;
  private String lastName;

  public String getFirstName() {
    return firstName;
  }

  public void setFirstName(String firstName) {
    this.firstName = firstName;
  }

  public String getLastName() {
    return lastName;
  }

  public void setLastName(String lastName) {
    this.lastName = lastName;
  }
}
```

As we can see, all we need to do to name our class is to decorate it with the `@Named` annotation. By default, the name of the bean will be the class name with its first letter switched to lowercase; in our example, the name of the bean would be `customer`. If we wish to use a different name, we can do so by setting the `value` attribute of the `@Named` annotation. For example, if we wanted to use the name `customerBean` for our bean in the previous example, we could have done so by modifying the `@Named` annotation as follows:

```
@Named(value="customerBean")
```

Or, we could have simply used the following code:

```
@Named("customerBean")
```

Since the `value` attribute's name does not need to be specified, if we don't use an attribute name, then `value` is implied.

The CDI name can be used to access our bean from JSF pages using the unified expression language, as shown in the following code:

```
<?xml version='1.0' encoding='UTF-8' ?>
<!DOCTYPE html PUBLIC "-//W3C//DTD XHTML 1.0 Transitional//EN"
  "http://www.w3.org/TR/xhtml1/DTD/xhtml1-transitional.dtd">
<html xmlns="http://www.w3.org/1999/xhtml"
```

```
        xmlns:h="http://java.sun.com/jsf/html">
    <h:head>
      <title>Enter Customer Information</title>
    </h:head>
    <h:body>
      <h:form>
        <h:panelGrid columns="2">
          <h:outputLabel for="firstName" value="First Name"/>
          <h:inputText id="firstName"
                                value="#{customer.firstName}"/>
          <h:outputLabel for="lastName" value="Last Name"/>
          <h:inputText id="lastName"
                                value="#{customer.lastName}"/>
          <h:panelGroup/>
        </h:panelGrid>
      </h:form>
    </h:body>
</html>
```

As we can see, named beans are accessed from JSF pages exactly like standard JSF managed beans. This allows JSF to access any named bean, decoupling the Java code from the JSF API.

When deployed and executed, our simple application looks like the following screenshot (shown after the user has entered some data):

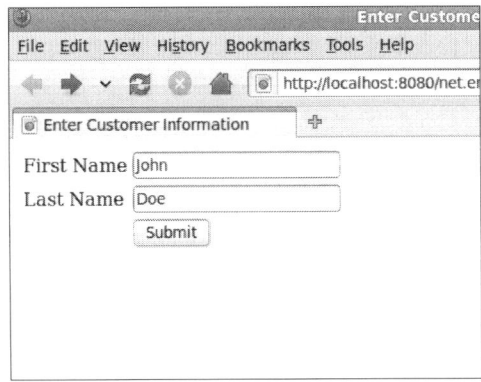

Dependency injection

Dependency injection is a technique that is used to supply external dependencies to a Java class. Java EE 5 introduced dependency injection via the `@Resource` annotation; however, this annotation is limited to injecting resources such as database connections, JMS resources, and so on. CDI includes the `@Inject` annotation, which can be used to inject instances of Java classes into any dependent objects.

JSF applications typically follow the **Model-View-Controller (MVC)** design pattern. As such, some JSF-managed beans frequently take on the role of controllers in the pattern, while others take on the role of the model. This approach typically requires the controller-managed bean to have access to one or more of the model-managed beans.

Because of the pattern described in the previous paragraph, one of the most frequently asked JSF questions is how to access one managed bean from another. There is more than one way to do this; however, before CDI, none of the ways were straightforward. Before CDI, the easiest way was to declare a managed property in the controller-managed bean, which required modifying the application's `faces-config.xml` file; another approach was to use code like the following one:

```
ELContext elc = FacesContext.getCurrentInstance().getELContext();
SomeBean someBean
    = (SomeBean) FacesContext.getCurrentInstance().getApplication()
        .getELResolver().getValue(elc, null, "someBean");
```

In this example, `someBean` is the name of the bean as specified in the application's `faces-config.xml`. As we can see, neither approach is simple or easy to remember. Fortunately, code like this is not needed anymore thanks to CDI's dependency injection capabilities, as shown in the following code:

```
package net.ensode.cdidependencyinjection.ejb;

import java.util.logging.Logger;
import javax.inject.Inject;
import javax.inject.Named;

@Named
@RequestScoped
public class CustomerController {

    private static final Logger logger = Logger.getLogger(
        CustomerController.class.getName());
    @Inject
```

```
    private Customer customer;

    public String saveCustomer() {

      logger.info("Saving the following information \n" + customer.
          toString());

      //If this was a real application, we would have code to save
      //customer data to the database here.

      return "confirmation";
    }
  }
```

Notice that all we had to do to initialize our customer instance was to decorate it with the `@Inject` annotation. When the bean is constructed by the application server, an instance of the `Customer` bean is automatically injected into this field. Notice that the injected bean is used in the `saveCustomer()` method. As we can see, CDI makes accessing one bean from another a snap, a far cry from the code we had to use in previous versions of the Java EE specification.

Working with CDI Qualifiers

In some instances, the type of the bean we wish to inject into our code may be an interface or a Java superclass, but we may be interested in injecting a subclass or a class implementing the interface. For cases like this, CDI provides qualifiers that we can use to indicate the specific type we wish to inject into our code.

A CDI qualifier is an annotation that must be decorated with the `@Qualifier` annotation. This annotation can then be used to decorate the specific subclass or interface implementation that we wish to qualify. Additionally, the injected field in the client code needs to be decorated with the qualifier as well.

Suppose our application could have a special kind of customer; for example, frequent customers could be given the status of premium customers. To handle these premium customers, we could extend our `Customer` named bean and decorate it with the following qualifier:

```
package net.ensode.cdidependencyinjection.qualifiers;

import static java.lang.annotation.ElementType.TYPE;
import static java.lang.annotation.ElementType.FIELD;
import static java.lang.annotation.ElementType.PARAMETER;
import static java.lang.annotation.ElementType.METHOD;
import static java.lang.annotation.RetentionPolicy.RUNTIME;
import java.lang.annotation.Retention;
```

```
import java.lang.annotation.Target;
import javax.inject.Qualifier;

@Qualifier
@Retention(RUNTIME)
@Target({METHOD, FIELD, PARAMETER, TYPE})
public @interface Premium {
}
```

Like we mentioned previously, qualifiers are standard annotations; they typically have retention of runtime and can target methods, fields, parameters, or types, as illustrated in the previous example by the value of the `@Retention` annotation. The only difference between a qualifier and a standard annotation is that qualifiers are decorated with the `@Qualifier` annotation.

Once we have our qualifier in place, we need to use it to decorate the specific subclass or interface implementation:

```
package net.ensode.cdidependencyinjection.beans;

import javax.enterprise.context.RequestScoped;
import javax.inject.Named;
import net.ensode.cdidependencyinjection.qualifiers.Premium;

@Named
@RequestScoped
@Premium
public class PremiumCustomer extends Customer {

  private Integer discountCode;

  public Integer getDiscountCode() {
    return discountCode;
  }

  public void setDiscountCode(Integer discountCode) {
    this.discountCode = discountCode;
  }
}
```

Once we have decorated the specific instance that we need to qualify, we can use our qualifiers in the client code to specify the exact type of dependency we need:

```
package net.ensode.cdidependencyinjection.beans;

import java.util.Random;
import java.util.logging.Logger;
```

```java
import javax.enterprise.context.RequestScoped;
import javax.inject.Inject;
import javax.inject.Named;
import net.ensode.cdidependencyinjection.qualifiers.Premium;

@Named
@RequestScoped
public class CustomerController {

  private static final Logger logger = Logger.getLogger(
      CustomerController.class.getName());
  @Inject
  @Premium
  private Customer customer;

  public String saveCustomer() {

    PremiumCustomer premiumCustomer = (PremiumCustomer) customer;

    premiumCustomer.setDiscountCode(generateDiscountCode());

    logger.info("Saving the following information \n"
        + premiumCustomer.getFirstName() + " "
        + premiumCustomer.getLastName()
        + ", discount code = "
        + premiumCustomer.getDiscountCode());

    //If this was a real application, we would have code to save
    //customer data to the database here.

    return "confirmation";
  }

  public Integer generateDiscountCode() {
    return new Random().nextInt(100000);
  }
}
```

As we used our `@Premium` qualifier to decorate the customer field, an instance of `PremiumCustomer` is injected into that field, since this class is also decorated with the `@Premium` qualifier.

Contexts and Dependency Injection

As far as our JSF pages go, we simply access our named bean as usual, using its name:

```xml
<?xml version='1.0' encoding='UTF-8' ?>
<!DOCTYPE html PUBLIC "-//W3C//DTD XHTML 1.0 Transitional//EN"
  "http://www.w3.org/TR/xhtml1/DTD/xhtml1-transitional.dtd">
<html xmlns="http://www.w3.org/1999/xhtml"
      xmlns:h="http://java.sun.com/jsf/html">
    <h:head>
        <title>Enter Customer Information</title>
    </h:head>
    <h:body>
        <h:form>
            <h:panelGrid columns="2">
                <h:outputLabel for="firstName" value="First
                  Name"/>
                <h:inputText id="firstName"
                  value="#{premiumCustomer.firstName}"/>
                <h:outputLabel for="lastName" value="Last Name"/>
                <h:inputText id="lastName"
                   value="#{premiumCustomer.lastName}"/>
                <h:outputLabel for="discountCode" value="Discount
                  Code"/>
                <h:inputText id="discountCode"
                   value="#{premiumCustomer.discountCode}"/>
                <h:panelGroup/>
                <h:commandButton value="Submit"
                   action="#{customerController.saveCustomer}"/>
            </h:panelGrid>
        </h:form>
    </h:body>
</html>
```

In this example, we are using the default name for our bean, which is the class name with the first letter switched to lowercase.

Our simple application renders and acts just like a plain (that is, not using CDI) JSF application as far as the user is concerned. Take a look at the following screenshot:

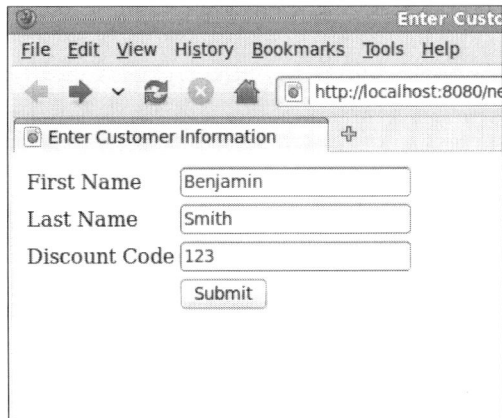

Named bean scopes

Just like JSF-managed beans, CDI named beans are scoped. This means that CDI beans are contextual objects. When a named bean is needed, either because of injection or because it is referred from a JSF page, CDI looks for an instance of the bean in the scope it belongs to and injects it to the dependent code. If no instance is found, one is created and stored in the appropriate scope for future use. The different scopes are the context in which the bean exists.

The following table lists the different valid CDI scopes:

Scope	Annotation	Description
Request	`@RequestScoped`	Request scoped beans are shared through the duration of a single request. A single request could refer to an HTTP request, an invocation to a method in an EJB, a web service invocation, or sending a JMS message to a message-driven bean.
Conversation	`@ConversationScoped`	The conversation scope can span multiple requests, but it is typically shorter than the session scope.
Session	`@SessionScoped`	Session scoped beans are shared across all requests in an HTTP session. Each user of an application gets its own instance of a session scoped bean.

Scope	Annotation	Description
Application	`@ApplicationScoped`	Application scoped beans live through the whole application lifetime. Beans in this scope are shared across user sessions.
Dependent	`@Dependent`	Dependent scoped beans are not shared; any time a dependent scoped bean is injected, a new instance is created.

As we can see, CDI includes all scopes supported by JSF; it also adds a couple of its own. CDI's request scope differs from JSF's request scope in which a request does not necessarily refer to an HTTP request; it could simply be an invocation on an EJB method, a web service invocation, or sending a JMS message to a message driven bean.

The conversation scope does not exist in JSF. This scope is longer than the request scope but shorter than the session scope, and it typically spans three or more pages. Classes wishing to access a conversation scoped bean must have an instance of `javax.enterprise.context.Conversation` injected. At the point where we want to start the conversation, the `begin()` method must be invoked on this object. At the point where we want to end the conversation, the `end()` method must be invoked on it.

CDI's session scope behaves just like its JSF counterpart. The lifecycle of session scoped beans is tied to the life of an HTTP session.

CDI's application scope also behaves just like the equivalent scope in JSF. Application scoped beans are tied to the life of an application. A single instance of each application scoped beans exists per application, which means that the same instance is accessible to all HTTP sessions.

Just like the conversation scope, CDI's dependent scope does not exist in JSF. A new dependent scoped bean is instantiated every time it is needed, usually, when it is injected into a class that depends on it.

Suppose we wanted to have a user enter some data that would be stored in a single named bean; however, this bean has several fields and therefore, we would like to split the data entry into several pages. This is a fairly common situation and one that was not easy to handle using previous versions of JSF (JSF 2.2 added Faces Flows to solve this problem; refer to *Chapter 2, JavaServer Faces*) or the servlet API, for that matter. The reason this situation is not trivial to manage using these technologies is that we can only put a class in the request scope, in which case, the class is destroyed after every single request, losing its data in the process; or in session scope, in which the class sticks around in the memory long after it is needed.

Chapter 5

For cases like this, CDI's conversation scope is a good solution, as shown in the following code:

```
package net.ensode.conversationscope.model;

import java.io.Serializable;
import javax.enterprise.context.ConversationScoped;
import javax.inject.Named;
import org.apache.commons.lang.builder.ReflectionToStringBuilder;

@Named
@ConversationScoped
public class Customer implements Serializable {

    private String firstName;
    private String middleName;
    private String lastName;
    private String addrLine1;
    private String addrLine2;
    private String addrCity;
    private String state;
    private String zip;
    private String phoneHome;
    private String phoneWork;
    private String phoneMobile;

    //getters and setters omitted for brevity

    @Override
    public String toString() {
        return ReflectionToStringBuilder.reflectionToString(this);
    }
}
```

We declare that our bean is conversation scoped by decorating it with the `@ConversationScoped` annotation. Conversation scoped beans also need to implement `java.io.Serializable`. Other than these two requirements, there is nothing special about our code. It is a simple JavaBean code with private properties and corresponding getter and setter methods.

> We are using the Apache `commons-lang` library in our code to easily implement a `toString()` method for our bean. The `commons-lang` library has several utility methods like this that implement frequently needed, tedious to code functionality. commons-lang is available in the central Maven repositories at http://commons.apache.org/lang.

[171]

Contexts and Dependency Injection

In addition to having our conversation scoped bean injected, our client code must also have an instance of `javax.enterprise.context.Conversation` injected, as illustrated in the following example:

```java
package net.ensode.conversationscope.controller;

import java.io.Serializable;
import javax.enterprise.context.Conversation;
import javax.enterprise.context.RequestScoped;
import javax.inject.Inject;
import javax.inject.Named;
import net.ensode.conversationscope.model.Customer;

@Named
@RequestScoped
public class CustomerInfoController implements Serializable {

    @Inject
    private Conversation conversation;
    @Inject
    private Customer customer;

    public String customerInfoEntry() {
        conversation.begin();
        System.out.println(customer);
        return "page1";
    }

    public String navigateToPage1() {
        System.out.println(customer);
        return "page1";
    }

    public String navigateToPage2() {
        System.out.println(customer);
        return "page2";
    }

    public String navigateToPage3() {
        System.out.println(customer);
        return "page3";
    }

    public String navigateToConfirmationPage() {
        System.out.println(customer);
        conversation.end();
```

```
            return "confirmation";
        }
    }
```

Conversations can be either long running or transient. Transient conversations finish at the end of a request. Long running conversations span multiple requests. In most cases, we will use long running conversations to hold a reference to a conversation scoped bean across multiple HTTP requests in a web application.

A long running conversation starts when the `begin()` method is invoked in the injected conversation instance, and it ends when we invoke the `end()` method on this same object.

JSF pages simply access our CDI beans as usual:

```
<?xml version='1.0' encoding='UTF-8' ?>
<!DOCTYPE html PUBLIC "-//W3C//DTD XHTML 1.0 Transitional//EN"
   "http://www.w3.org/TR/xhtml1/DTD/xhtml1-transitional.dtd">
<html xmlns="http://www.w3.org/1999/xhtml"
      xmlns:h="http://java.sun.com/jsf/html">
    <h:head>
        <title>Customer Information</title>
    </h:head>
    <h:body>
        <h3>Enter Customer Information (Page 1 of 3)</h3>
        <h:form>
            <h:panelGrid columns="2">
                <h:outputLabel for="firstName" value="First Name"/>
                <h:inputText id="firstName"
                                    value="#{customer.firstName}"/>
                <h:outputLabel for="middleName" value="Middle Name"/>
                <h:inputText id="middleName"
                                    value="#{customer.middleName}"/>
                <h:outputLabel for="lastName" value="Last Name"/>
                <h:inputText id="lastName"
                                    value="#{customer.lastName}"/>
                <h:panelGroup/>
                <h:commandButton value="Next"
                    action="#{customerInfoController.navigateToPage2}"/>
            </h:panelGrid>
        </h:form>
    </h:body>
</html>
```

As we navigate from one page to the next, we keep the same instance of our conversation scoped bean. Therefore, all user-entered data remains. When the `end()` method is called on our conversation bean, the conversation ends and our conversation scoped bean is destroyed.

Keeping our bean in the conversation scope simplifies the task of implementing wizard-style user interfaces, where data can be entered across several pages, as shown in the following screenshot:

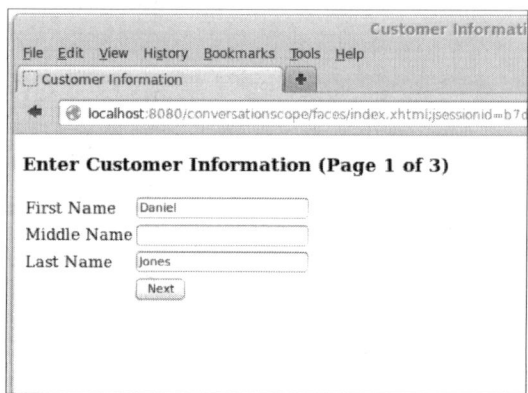

In our example, after clicking on the **Next** button on the first page, we can see our partially populated bean in the GlassFish log:

```
INFO:    HYPERLINK "mailto:net.ensode.conversationscope.model.
Customer@6e1c51b4"net.ensode.conversationscope.model.Customer@6e1c
51b4[firstName=Daniel,middleName=,lastName=Jones,addrLine1=,addrLi
ne2=,addrCity=,state=AL,zip=<null>,phoneHome=<null>,phoneWork=<nul
l>,phoneMobile=<null>]
```

At this point, the second page in our simple wizard is displayed as follows:

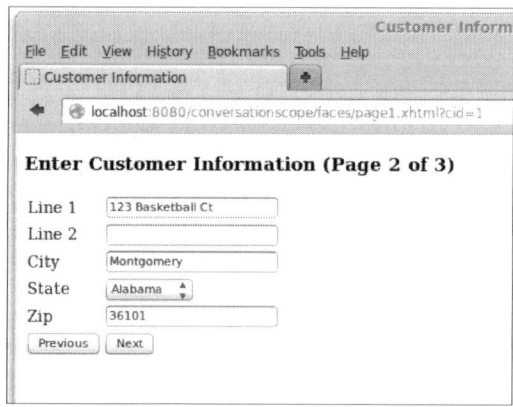

By clicking on **Next**, we can see that additional fields are populated in our conversation scoped bean.

```
INFO: net.ensode.conversationscope.model.Customer@6e1c51b4[firstName=Dani
el,middleName=,lastName=Jones,addrLine1=123 Basketball Ct,addrLine2=,addr
City=Montgomery,state=AL,zip=36101,phoneHome=<null>,phoneWork=<null>,phon
eMobile=<null>]
```

When we submit the third page in our wizard, additional bean properties corresponding to the fields on that page are populated, as shown in the following screenshot:

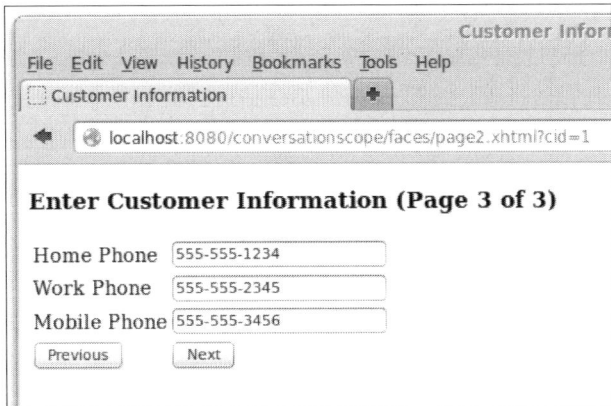

When we are at the point where we don't need to keep the customer information in mind anymore, we need to call the `end()` method on the conversation bean that was injected into our code. This is exactly what we do in our code before displaying the confirmation page:

```
public String navigateToConfirmationPage() {
    System.out.println(customer);
    conversation.end();
    return "confirmation";
}
```

After the request to show the confirmation page is completed, our conversation scoped bean is destroyed, as we invoked the `end()` method in our injected `Conversation` class.

Summary

In this chapter, we provided an introduction to Contexts and Dependency Injection. We covered how JSF pages can access CDI named beans as if they were JSF managed beans. We also covered how CDI makes it easy to inject dependencies into our code via the `@Inject` annotation. Additionally, we explained how we can use qualifiers to determine the specific implementation of a dependency to be injected into our code. Finally, we covered all the scopes that a CDI bean can be placed into, which include the equivalents to all the JSF scopes, plus an additional two scopes not included in JSF, namely, the conversation scope and the dependent scope.

In the next chapter, we will cover processing JavaScript Object Notation (JSON) formatted data using the new JSON-P API.

6
JSON Processing with JSON-P

JSON, or the **JavaScript Object Notation**, is a human-readable data interchange format. As its name implies, JSON is derived from JavaScript. Java EE 7 introduced JSON-P, the Java API for JSON Processing as **Java Specification Request (JSR)** 353.

Traditionally, XML has been the format of choice for data interchange between disparate systems. While XML is undoubtedly very popular, JSON has been gaining ground in recent years as an arguably simpler format for data exchange. Several Java libraries exist for parsing and generating JSON data from Java code. Java EE standardized this functionality via the Java API for JSON Processing.

JSON-P includes two APIs for processing JSON—the Model API and the Streaming API; both of these APIs will be covered in this chapter.

In this chapter, we will cover the following topics:

- The JSON-P Model API
    - Generating JSON data with the Model API
    - Parsing JSON data with the Model API
- The JSON-P Streaming API
    - Generating JSON data with the Streaming API
    - Parsing JSON data with the Streaming API

The JSON-P Model API

The JSON-P Model API allows us to generate a preloaded, fully traversable, in-memory representation of a JSON object. This API is more flexible than the Streaming API discussed in the *The JSON-P Streaming API* section. However, the JSON-P Model API is slower and requires more memory, which can be a concern when handling large volumes of data.

Generating JSON data with the Model API

At the heart of the JSON-P Model API is the `JsonObjectBuilder` class. This class has several overloaded `add()` methods that can be used to add properties and their corresponding values to the generated JSON data.

The following code sample illustrates how to generate JSON data using the Model API:

```
packagepackagenet.ensode.glassfishbook.jsonpobject;

//other imports omitted for brevity.
importimportjavax.inject.Named;
importimportjavax.json.Json;
importimportjavax.json.JsonObject;
importimportjavax.json.JsonReader;
importimportjavax.json.JsonWriter;

@Named
@SessionScoped
public class JsonpBean implements Serializable{

    private String jsonStr;

    @Inject
    private Customer customer;

    public String buildJson() {
JsonObjectBuilderjsonObjectBuilder =
Json.createObjectBuilder();
JsonObjectjsonObject = jsonObjectBuilder.
                add("firstName", "Scott").
                add("lastName", "Gosling").
                add("email", "sgosling@example.com").
                build();
```

```
    StringWriterstringWriter = new StringWriter();
        try (JsonWriter jsonWriter = Json.createWriter(stringWriter))
        {
            jsonWriter.writeObject(jsonObject);
        }

        setJsonStr(stringWriter.toString());

        return "display_json";

    }
    //getters and setters omitted for brevity
}
```

> Our example is a CDI named bean that corresponds to a larger JSF application; the other parts of the application are not shown since they are not relevant to the discussion. The complete sample application is included as part of this book's example code download.

As can be seen in the previous example, we generate an instance of JsonObject by invoking the add() method on JsonObjectBuilder. In our example, we see how we can add String values to our JsonObject by invoking the add() method on JsonObjectBuilder. The first parameter of the add() method is the property name of the generated JSON object, and the second parameter corresponds to the value of the said property. The return value of the add() method is another instance of JsonObjectBuilder; therefore, invocations to the add() method can be chained as shown in the example.

Once we have added all the desired properties, we need to invoke the build() method of JsonObjectBuilder, which returns an instance of a class implementing the JsonObject interface.

In many cases, we may want to generate a String representation of the JSON object we created so that it can be processed by another process or service. We can do this by creating an instance of a class implementing the JsonWriter interface; invoking the static createWriter() method of the Json class, and passing an instance of StringWriter as its sole parameter. Once we have an instance of the JsonWriter implementation, we need to invoke its writeObject() method, passing our JsonObject instance as its sole parameter.

At this point, our StringWriter instance will have the String representation of our JSON object as its value. So, invoking its toString() method will return a String value containing our JSON object.

JSON Processing with JSON-P

Our specific example will generate a JSON string that looks as follows:

```
{"firstName":"Scott","lastName":"Gosling","email":
    "sgosling@example.com"}
```

Although we added only `String` objects to our JSON object in our example, we are not limited to this type of value. `JsonObjectBuilder` has several overloaded versions of its `add()` method, allowing us to add several different types of values to our JSON objects.

The following table summarizes all of the available versions of the `add()` method:

JsonObjectBuilder methods	Description
`add(String name, BigDecimal value)`	This method adds a `BigDecimal` value to our JSON object.
`add(String name, BigInteger value)`	This method adds a `BigInteger` value to our JSON object.
`add(String name, JsonArrayBuilder value)`	This method adds an array to our JSON object. A `JsonArrayBuilder` implementation allows us to create JSON arrays.
`add(String name, JsonObjectBuilder value)`	This method adds another JSON object to our original JSON object (the property values for JSON objects can be other JSON objects). The added `JsonObject` implementation is built from the provided `JsonObjectBuilder` parameter.
`add(String name, JsonValue value)`	This method adds another JSON object to our original JSON object (the property values for JSON objects can be other JSON objects).
`add(String name, String value)`	This method adds a `String` value to our JSON object.
`add(String name, boolean value)`	This method adds a `boolean` value to our JSON object.
`add(String name, double value)`	This method adds a `double` value to our JSON object.
`add(String name, int value)`	This method adds an `int` value to our JSON object.
`add(String name, long value)`	This method adds a `long` value to our JSON object.

In all cases, the first parameter of the `add()` method corresponds to the name of the property in our JSON object and the second parameter corresponds to the value of the property.

Parsing JSON data with the Model API

In the last section, we saw how to generate JSON data from our Java code with the Model API. In this section, we will see how we can read and parse the existing JSON data. The following code sample illustrates how to do this:

```java
packagepackagenet.ensode.glassfishbook.jsonpobject;

//other imports omitted
importimportjavax.json.Json;
importimportjavax.json.JsonObject;
importimportjavax.json.JsonReader;
importimportjavax.json.JsonWriter;

@Named
@SessionScoped
public class JsonpBean implements Serializable{

    private String jsonStr;

    @Inject
    private Customer customer;

    public String parseJson() {
JsonObjectjsonObject;

try (JsonReaderjsonReader = Json.createReader(
        new StringReader(jsonStr))) {
        jsonObject = jsonReader.readObject();
    }

    customer.setFirstName(
      jsonObject.getString("firstName"));
    customer.setLastName(
      jsonObject.getString("lastName"));
    customer.setEmail(jsonObject.getString("email"));

    return "display_parsed_json";
    }
    //getters and setters omitted
}
```

JSON Processing with JSON-P

To parse an existing JSON string, we need to create a `StringReader` object, passing a `String` object containing the JSON data to be parsed as a parameter. We then pass the resulting `StringReader` instance to the static `createReader()` method of the `Json` class. This method invocation will return an instance of `JsonReader`. We can then obtain an instance of `JsonObject` by invoking the `readObject()` method.

In our example, we used the `getString()` method to obtain the values for all the properties in our JSON object; the first and only argument for this method is the name of the property we wish to retrieve. Unsurprisingly, the return value is the value of the property.

In addition to the `getString()` method, there are several other similar methods to obtain the values of other types. The following table summarizes these methods:

JsonObject methods	Description
`get(Object key)`	This method returns an instance of a class implementing the `JsonValue` interface.
`getBoolean(String name)`	This method returns a `boolean` value corresponding to the given key.
`getInt(String name)`	This method returns an `int` value corresponding to the given key.
`getJsonArray(String name)`	This method returns the instance of a class implementing the `JsonArray` interface that corresponds to the given key.
`getJsonNumber(String name)`	This method returns the instance of a class implementing the `JsonNumber` interface that corresponds to the given key.
`getJsonObject(String name)`	This method returns the instance of a class implementing the `JsonObject` interface that corresponds to the given key.
`getJsonString(String name)`	This method returns the instance of a class implementing the `JsonString` interface that corresponds to the given key.
`getString(String Name)`	This method returns a `String` corresponding to the given key.

In all cases, the `String` parameter of the method corresponds to the key name and the return value is the JSON property value that we wish to retrieve.

The JSON-P Streaming API

The JSON-P Streaming API allows the sequential reading of a JSON object from a stream (a subclass of `java.io.OutputStream`, or a subclass of `java.io.Writer`). It is faster and more memory efficient than the Model API. However, the tradeoff is that it is more limited, since the JSON data needs to be read sequentially and we cannot access specific JSON properties directly, the way the Model API allows.

Generating JSON data with the Streaming API

The JSON Streaming API has a `JsonGenerator` class that we can use to generate JSON data and write it to a stream. This class has several overloaded `write()` methods which can be used to add properties and their corresponding values to the generated JSON data.

The following code sample illustrates how to generate JSON data using the Streaming API:

```
packagepackagenet.ensode.glassfishbook.jsonpstreaming;

//other imports omitted
import javax.json.Json;
import javax.json.stream.JsonGenerator;
import javax.json.stream.JsonParser;
import javax.json.stream.JsonParser.Event;

@Named
@SessionScoped
public class JsonpBean implements Serializable {

    private String jsonStr;

    @Inject
    private Customer customer;

    public String buildJson() {

StringWriterstringWriter = new StringWriter();
try (JsonGeneratorjsonGenerator =
Json.createGenerator(stringWriter)) {
        jsonGenerator.writeStartObject().
                write("firstName", "Larry").
                write("lastName", "Gates").
                write("email", "lgates@example.com").
                writeEnd();
    }
```

```
            setJsonStr(stringWriter.toString());

            return "display_json";
        }

        //getters and setters omitted
    }
```

We create an instance of `JsonGenerator` by invoking the `createGenerator()` static method of the `Json` class. The JSON-P Streaming API provides two overloaded versions of the `createGenerator()` method; one takes an instance of a class that extends `java.io.Writer` (such as `StringWriter`, which we used in our example), and the other takes an instance of a class that extends `java.io.OutputStream`.

Before we can start adding properties to the generated JSON stream, we need to invoke the `writeStartObject()` method on `JsonGenerator`. This method writes the JSON start object character (represented by an opening curly brace ({) in JSON strings) and returns another instance of `JsonGenerator`, allowing us to chain the `write()` invocations to add properties to our JSON stream.

The `write()` method in `JsonGenerator` allows us to add properties to the JSON stream that we generate. Its first parameter is a `String` corresponding to the name of the property we add, and the second parameter is the value of the property.

In our example, we are adding only the `String` values to the JSON stream that we create; however, we are not limited to `Strings`. The JSON-P Streaming API provides several overloaded `write()` methods that allow us to add several different types of data to our JSON stream. The following table summarizes all of the available versions of the `write()` method:

JsonGenerator write() methods	Description
`write(String name, BigDecimal value)`	This method writes a `BigDecimal` value to our JSON stream.
`write(String name, BigInteger value)`	This method writes a `BigInteger` value to our JSON stream.
`write(String name, JsonValue value)`	This method writes a JSON object to our JSON stream (the property values for JSON streams can be other JSON objects).
`write(String name, String value)`	This method writes a `String` value to our JSON stream.
`write(String name, boolean value)`	This method writes a `boolean` value to our JSON stream.

JsonGenerator write() methods	Description
`write(String name, double value)`	This method writes a `double` value to our JSON stream.
`write(String name, int value)`	This method writes an `int` value to our JSON stream.
`write(String name, long value)`	This method writes a `long` value to our JSON stream.

In all cases, the first parameter of the `write()` method corresponds to the name of the property we are adding to our JSON stream, and the second parameter corresponds to the value of the property.

Once we are done adding properties to our JSON stream, we need to invoke the `writeEnd()` method on `JsonGenerator`; this method adds the JSON end object character (represented by a closing curly brace (}) in JSON strings).

At this point, our stream or reader is populated with the JSON data we generated; what we do with it depends on our application logic. In our example, we simply invoked the `toString()` method of our `StringReader` class to obtain the `String` representation of the JSON data we created.

Parsing JSON data with the Streaming API

In the last section, we saw how to generate JSON data from our Java code with the Streaming API. In this section, we will see how we can read and parse the existing JSON data we receive from a stream. The following code sample illustrates how to do this:

```
package net.ensode.glassfishbook.jsonpstreaming;

//other imports omitted
import javax.json.Json;
import javax.json.stream.JsonGenerator;
import javax.json.stream.JsonParser;
import javax.json.stream.JsonParser.Event;

@Named
@SessionScoped
public class JsonpBean implements Serializable {

    private String jsonStr;
```

JSON Processing with JSON-P

```java
        @Inject
        private Customer customer;

        public String parseJson() {
    StringReaderstringReader = new StringReader(jsonStr);
    JsonParserjsonParser = Json.createParser(stringReader);
            Map<String, String> keyValueMap = new HashMap<>();
            String key = null;
            String value = null;

            while (jsonParser.hasNext()) {
                JsonParser.Event event = jsonParser.next();

                if (event.equals(Event.KEY_NAME)) {
                    key = jsonParser.getString();
                } else if (event.equals(Event.VALUE_STRING)) {
                    value = jsonParser.getString();
                }

                keyValueMap.put(key, value);
            }

            customer.setFirstName(keyValueMap.get("firstName"));
            customer.setLastName(keyValueMap.get("lastName"));
            customer.setEmail(keyValueMap.get("email"));

            return "display_parsed_json";
        }

        //getters and setters omitted

    }
```

The first thing we need to do in order to read JSON data using the Streaming API is to create an instance of `JsonParser` by invoking the static `createJsonParser()` method on the `Json` class. There are two overloaded versions of the `createJsonParser()` method; one takes an instance of a class that extends `java.io.InputStream`, and the other takes an instance of a class that extends `java.io.Reader`. In our example, we use the latter by passing an instance of `java.io.StringReader`, which is a subclass of `java.io.Reader`.

The next step is to loop through the JSON data to obtain the data to be parsed. We can achieve this by invoking the `hasNext()` method on `JsonParser`, which returns `true` if there is more data to be read and returns `false` otherwise.

We then need to read the next piece of data in our stream. The `JsonParser.next()` method returns an instance of `JsonParser.Event` that indicates the type of data we just read. In our example, we check only for key names (that is, `"firstName"`, `"lastName"`, and `"email"`) and the corresponding string values. We can check for the type of data we just read by comparing the event returned by `JsonParser.next()` against several values defined in the `Event` enum defined in `JsonParser`.

The following table summarizes all of the possible constants that can be returned by `JsonParser.next()`:

JsonParser Event constants	Description
`Event.START_OBJECT`	This constant indicates the start of a JSON object.
`Event.END_OBJECT`	This constant indicates the end of a JSON object.
`Event.START_ARRAY`	This constant indicates the start of an array
`Event.END_ARRAY`	This constant indicates the end of an array.
`Event.KEY_NAME`	This constant indicates the name of a JSON property that was read. We can obtain the key name by invoking `getString()` on `JsonParser`.
`Event.VALUE_TRUE`	This constant indicates that a `boolean` value of `true` was read.
`Event.VALUE_FALSE`	This constant indicates that a `boolean` value of `false` was read.
`Event.VALUE_NULL`	This constant indicates that a `null` value was read.
`Event.VALUE_NUMBER`	This constant indicates that a numeric value was read.
`Event.VALUE_STRING`	This constant indicates that a string value was read.

As shown in the example, the `String` values can be retrieved by invoking `getString()` on `JsonParser`. Numeric values can be retrieved in several different formats; the following table summarizes the methods in `JsonParser` that can be used to retrieve numeric values:

JsonParser methods	Description
`getInt()`	This method retrieves the numeric value as `int`.
`getLong()`	This method retrieves the numeric value as `long`.
`getBigDecimal()`	This method retrieves the numeric value as an instance of `java.math.BigDecimal`.

`JsonParser` also provides a convenience `isIntegralNumber()` method that returns `true` if the numeric value can be safely cast to an `int` or a `long` type.

What we do with the values we obtain from the stream depends on our application logic. In our example, we place them in Map and then use the said Map to populate a Java class.

Summary

In this chapter, we covered the Java API for JSON Processing (JSON-P). We covered both major JSON-P's APIs: the Model API and the Streaming API.

We illustrated how to generate JSON data via JSON-P's Model API, specifically the JsonBuilder class. We also covered how to parse JSON data via JSON-P's Model API via the JsonReader class.

Additionally, we explained how to generate JSON data via JSON-P's Streaming API by employing the JsonGenerator class.

Lastly, we covered how to parse JSON data via JSON-P's Streaming API, specifically via the JsonParser class.

In the next chapter, we will cover the Java API for WebSocket.

7
WebSockets

Traditionally, web applications have been developed using the request/response model followed by the HTTP protocol. In this model, the request is always initiated by the client and then the server returns a response back to the client.

There has never been any way for the server to send data to the client independently (without having to wait for a request from the browser) until now. The WebSocket protocol allows full-duplex, two-way communication between the client (browser) and the server.

Java EE 7 introduces the Java API for WebSocket, which allows us to develop WebSocket endpoints in Java. The Java API for WebSocket is a brand-new technology in the Java EE Standard.

> A socket is a two-way pipe that stays alive longer than a single request. Applied to an HTML5-compliant browser, this would allow for continuous communication to or from a web server without the need to load a new page (similar to AJAX).

In this chapter, we will cover the following topics:

- Developing WebSocket server endpoints
- Developing WebSocket clients in JavaScript
- Developing WebSocket clients in Java

Developing a WebSocket server endpoint

A WebSocket server endpoint is a Java class deployed to the application server that handles WebSocket requests.

WebSockets

There are two ways in which we can implement a WebSocket server endpoint via the Java API for WebSocket: either by developing an endpoint programmatically, in which case we need to extend the `javax.websocket.Endpoint` class, or by decorating **Plain Old Java Objects** (**POJOs**) with WebSocket-specific annotations. The two approaches are very similar; therefore, we will be discussing only the annotation approach in detail and briefly explaining the second approach, that is, developing WebSocket server endpoints programmatically, later in this section.

In this chapter, we will develop a simple web-based chat application, taking full advantage of the Java API for WebSocket.

Developing an annotated WebSocket server endpoint

The following Java class code illustrates how to develop a WebSocket server endpoint by annotating a Java class:

```java
package net.ensode.glassfishbook.websocketchat.serverendpoint;

import java.io.IOException;
import java.util.logging.Level;
import java.util.logging.Logger;
import javax.websocket.OnClose;
import javax.websocket.OnMessage;
import javax.websocket.OnOpen;
import javax.websocket.Session;
import javax.websocket.server.ServerEndpoint;

@ServerEndpoint("/websocketchat")
public class WebSocketChatEndpoint {

  private static final Logger LOG =
    Logger.getLogger(WebSocketChatEndpoint.class.getName());

  @OnOpen
  public void connectionOpened() {
    LOG.log(Level.INFO, "connection opened");
  }

  @OnMessage
  public synchronized void processMessage(Session session, String
    message) {
    LOG.log(Level.INFO, "received message: {0}", message);
```

```
      try {
        for (Session sess : session.getOpenSessions()) {
          if (sess.isOpen()) {
            sess.getBasicRemote().sendText(message);
          }
        }
      } catch (IOException ioe) {
        LOG.log(Level.SEVERE, ioe.getMessage());
      }
    }

    @OnClose
    public void connectionClosed() {
      LOG.log(Level.INFO, "connection closed");
    }

}
```

The class-level `@ServerEndpoint` annotation indicates that the class is a WebSocket server endpoint. The **URI (Uniform Resource Identifier)** of the server endpoint is the value specified within the parentheses following the annotation (which is "/websocketchat" in this example)—WebSocket clients will use this URI to communicate with our endpoint.

The `@OnOpen` annotation is used to decorate a method that needs to be executed whenever a WebSocket connection is opened by any of the clients. In our example, we are simply sending some output to the server log, but of course, any valid server-side Java code can be placed here.

Any method annotated with the `@OnMessage` annotation will be invoked whenever our server endpoint receives a message from a client. Since we are developing a chat application, our code simply broadcasts the message it receives to all connected clients.

In our example, the `processMessage()` method is annotated with `@OnMessage`, and takes two parameters: an instance of a class implementing the `javax.websocket.Session` interface and a `String` parameter containing the message that was received. Since we are developing a chat application, our WebSocket server endpoint simply broadcasts the received message to all connected clients.

The `getOpenSessions()` method of the `Session` interface returns a set of session objects representing all open sessions. We iterate through this set to broadcast the received message to all connected clients by invoking the `getBasicRemote()` method on each session instance and then invoking the `sendText()` method on the resulting `RemoteEndpoint.Basic` implementation returned by calling the previous method.

The `getOpenSessions()` method on the `Session` interface returns all the open sessions at the time it was invoked. It is possible for one or more of the sessions to have closed after the method was invoked; therefore, it is recommended to invoke the `isOpen()` method on a `Session` implementation before attempting to return data back to the client. An exception may be thrown if we attempt to access a closed session.

Finally, we need to decorate a method with the `@OnClose` annotation in case we need to handle the event when a client disconnects from the server endpoint. In our example, we simply log a message into the server log.

There is one additional annotation that we didn't use in our example—the `@OnError` annotation; it is used to decorate a method that needs to be invoked in case there's an error while sending or receiving data to or from the client.

As we can see, developing an annotated WebSocket server endpoint is straightforward. We simply need to add a few annotations, and the application server will invoke our annotated methods as necessary.

If we wish to develop a WebSocket server endpoint programmatically, we need to write a Java class that extends `javax.websocket.Endpoint`. This class has the `onOpen()`, `onClose()`, and `onError()` methods that are called at appropriate times during the endpoint's life cycle. There is no method equivalent to the `@OnMessage` annotation to handle incoming messages from clients. The `addMessageHandler()` method needs to be invoked in the session, passing an instance of a class implementing the `javax.websocket.MessageHandler` interface (or one of its subinterfaces) as its sole parameter.

> In general, it is easier and more straightforward to develop annotated WebSocket endpoints compared to their programmatic counterparts. Therefore, we recommend that you use the annotated approach whenever possible.

Developing WebSocket clients

Most WebSocket clients are implemented as HTML5 web pages, taking advantage of the JavaScript WebSocket API. As such, they must be accessed using an HTML5-compliant web browser (most modern web browsers are HTML5 compliant).

The Java API for WebSocket provides a client API that allows us to develop WebSocket clients as standalone Java applications. We will cover how to do this in a later section, *Developing WebSocket clients in Java*.

Developing JavaScript client-side WebSocket code

In this section, we will cover how to develop client-side JavaScript code to interact with the WebSocket endpoint we developed in the previous section.

The client page for our WebSocket example is implemented as a JSF page using HTML5-friendly markup (as explained in *Chapter 2, JavaServer Faces*).

Our client page consists of a text area where we can see what the users of our application are saying (it is, after all, a chat application) and an input text we can use to send a message to the other users, as shown in the following screenshot:

WebSockets

The markup for our client page looks like the following:

```xml
<?xml version="1.0" encoding="UTF-8"?>
<!DOCTYPE html>
<html xmlns="http://www.w3.org/1999/xhtml"xmlns:jsf="http://xmlns.jcp.or
  g/jsf">
  <head>
    <title>WebSocket Chat</title>
    <meta name="viewport" content="width=device-width"/>
    <script type="text/javascript">
      var websocket;
      function init() {
        websocket = new WebSocket('ws://localhost:8080/
          websocketchat/websocketchat');

        websocket.onopen = function(event) {
          websocketOpen(event)
        };
        websocket.onmessage = function(event) {
          websocketMessage(event)
        };
        websocket.onerror = function(event) {
          websocketError(event)
        };
      }

      function websocketOpen(event) {
        console.log("webSocketOpen invoked");
      }

      function websocketMessage(event) {
        console.log("websocketMessage invoked");
        document.getElementById('chatwindow').value += '\r' +
          event.data;
      }

      function websocketError(event) {
        console.log("websocketError invoked");
      }

      function sendMessage() {
        var userName =
        document.getElementById('userName').value;
        var msg =
```

```
          document.getElementById('chatinput').value;

          websocket.send(userName + ": " + msg);
        }
        function closeConnection(){
          websocket.close();
        }

        window.addEventListener("load", init);
    </script>
  </head>
  <body>
    <form jsf:prependId="false">
      <input type="hidden" id="userName" value="#
        {user.userName}"/>
      <table border="0">
      <tbody>
        <tr>
          <td>
            <label for="chatwindow">
              Chat Window
            </label>
          </td>
          <td>
            <textArea id="chatwindow" rows="10"/>
          </td>
        </tr>
        <tr>
          <td>
            <label for="chatinput">
              Type Something Here
            </label>
          </td>
          <td>
            <input type="text" id="chatinput"/>
            <input id="sendBtn" type="button" value="Send"
              onclick="sendMessage()"/>
          </td>
        </tr>
        <tr>
          <td></td>
          <td>
            <input type="button" id="exitBtn" value="Exit"
              onclick="closeConnection()"/>
```

```
                </td>
              </tr>
          </tbody>
        </table>
      </form>
    </body>
</html>
```

The last line of our JavaScript code (`window.addEventListener("load", init);`) sets our JavaScript `init()` function to be executed as soon as the page loads.

Within the `init()` method, we initialize a new JavaScript `websocket` object, passing the URI of our server endpoint as a parameter. This tells our JavaScript code the location of our server endpoint.

The JavaScript `websocket` object has a number of function types used to handle different events, such as opening the connection, receiving a message, and handling errors. We need to set these types to our own JavaScript functions so that we can handle these events, which is what we do in our `init()` method right after invoking the constructor for the JavaScript `websocket` object. In our example, the functions we assigned to the `websocket` object simply delegate their functionality to standalone JavaScript functions.

Our `websocketOpen()` function is called every time the WebSocket connection is opened. In our example, we simply send a message to the browser's JavaScript console.

The `webSocketMessage()` function is invoked every time the browser receives a WebSocket message from our WebSocket endpoint. In our example, we updated the contents of the text area whose `id` is `chatWindow` and the contents of the message.

The `websocketError()` function is called every time there is a WebSocket-related error. In our example, we simply send a message to the browser's JavaScript console.

The JavaScript `sendMessage()` function sends a message to the WebSocket server endpoint, containing both the username and the contents of the text input whose `id` is `chatinput`. This function is called when the user clicks on the button whose `id` is `sendBtn`.

The `closeConnection()` JavaScript function closes the connection to our WebSocket server endpoint. This function is called when the user clicks on the button whose `id` is `exitBtn`.

As we can see from this example, writing client-side JavaScript code to interact with WebSocket endpoints is fairly straightforward.

Developing WebSocket clients in Java

Although developing web-based WebSocket clients is currently the most common way of developing WebSocket clients, the Java API for WebSocket provides a client API that we can use to develop WebSocket clients in Java.

In this section, we will be developing a simple WebSocket client using the client API of the Java API for WebSocket. The final product looks as shown in the following screenshot:

However, we won't be covering the GUI code in this section (developed using the Swing framework), since it is not relevant to this discussion. The complete code for the example, including the GUI code, can be downloaded from the Packt Publishing website at www.packtpub.com.

Just as with WebSocket server endpoints, Java WebSocket clients can be developed either programmatically or using annotations. Once again, we will cover only the annotation approach: developing a programmatic client is very similar to the way programmatic server endpoints are developed, that is, programmatic clients must extend javax.websocket.Endpoint and override the appropriate methods.

Without further ado, the following is the code for our Java WebSocket client:

```
package net.ensode.websocketjavaclient;

import java.io.IOException;
import java.net.URI;
import java.net.URISyntaxException;
import javax.websocket.ClientEndpoint;
import javax.websocket.CloseReason;
import javax.websocket.ContainerProvider;
import javax.websocket.DeploymentException;
import javax.websocket.OnClose;
```

```java
import javax.websocket.OnError;
import javax.websocket.OnMessage;
import javax.websocket.OnOpen;
import javax.websocket.Session;
import javax.websocket.WebSocketContainer;

@ClientEndpoint
public class WebSocketClient {

  private String userName;
  private Session session;
  private final WebSocketJavaClientFrame webSocketJavaClientFrame;

  public WebSocketClient(WebSocketJavaClientFrame
    webSocketJavaClientFrame) {
    this.webSocketJavaClientFrame = webSocketJavaClientFrame;

    try {
      WebSocketContainer webSocketContainer =
        ContainerProvider.getWebSocketContainer();
      webSocketContainer.connectToServer(this, new URI(
        "ws://localhost:8080/websocketchat/websocketchat"));
    }
    catch (DeploymentException | IOException | URISyntaxException
      ex) {
      ex.printStackTrace();
    }

  }

  @OnOpen
  public void onOpen(Session session) {
    System.out.println("onOpen() invoked");
    this.session = session;
  }

  @OnClose
  public void onClose(CloseReason closeReason) {
    System.out.println("Connection closed, reason: "+
      closeReason.getReasonPhrase());
  }

  @OnError
  public void onError(Throwable throwable) {
    System.out.println("onError() invoked");
```

```
      throwable.printStackTrace();
    }

    @OnMessage
    public void onMessage(String message, Session session) {
      System.out.println("onMessage() invoked");
      webSocketJavaClientFrame.getChatWindowTextArea().
        setText(webSocketJavaClientFrame.getChatWindowTextArea()
        .getText() + "\n" + message);
    }

    public void sendMessage(String message) {
      try {
        System.out.println("sendMessage() invoked, message = " +
          message);
        session.getBasicRemote().sendText(userName + ": " +
          message);
      }
      catch (IOException ex) {
        ex.printStackTrace();
      }
    }

    public String getUserName() {
      return userName;
    }

    public void setUserName(String userName) {
      this.userName = userName;
    }

}
```

The class-level @ClientEndPoint annotation denotes that our class is a WebSocket client—all Java WebSocket clients must be annotated with this annotation.

The code to establish a connection to the WebSocket server endpoint is in our class constructor. First, we need to invoke ContainerProvider.getWebSocketContainer() to obtain an instance of javax.websocket.WebSocketContainer. We then establish a connection by invoking the connectToServer() method on our WebSocketContainer instance; then we pass a class annotated with @ClientEndpoint as the first parameter (we use this in our example since the connection code is within our WebSocket Java client code); and then we pass a URI object containing the WebSocket server endpoint URI as the second parameter.

After the connection is established, we are ready to respond to WebSocket events. Alert readers may have noticed that the exact same annotations we used to develop our server endpoint are used again in our client code.

Any method annotated with the `@OnOpen` annotation will be invoked automatically when the connection to the WebSocket server endpoint is established. The method must return void and can have an optional parameter of the type `javax.websocket.Session`. In our example, we send some output to the console and initialize a class variable with the `Session` instance, which we received as a parameter.

Methods annotated with the `@OnClose` annotation are invoked whenever the WebSocket session is closed. The annotated method can have optional parameters of the types `javax.websocket.Session` and `CloseReason`. In our example, we chose to use only the `CloseReason` optional parameter since its class has a handy `getReasonPhrase()` method that provides a short explanation of why the session was closed.

The `@OnError` annotation is used to decorate any methods that are called when an error occurs. Methods annotated with `@OnError` must have a parameter of type `java.lang.Throwable` (the parent class of `java.lang.Exception`), and can have an optional parameter of type `Session`. In our example, we simply send the stack trace of the `Throwable` parameter to `stderr`.

Methods annotated with `@OnMessage` are invoked every time an incoming WebSocket message is received. The `@OnMessage` methods can have different parameters depending on the type of message received and how we wish to handle it. In our example, we used the most common case: receiving a text message. In this particular case, we need a `String` parameter that will hold the contents of the message, and an optional `Session` parameter.

Refer to the JavaDoc documentation for `@OnMessage`, available at http://docs.oracle.com/javaee/7/api/javax/websocket/OnMessage.html for information on how to handle other types of messages.

In our example, we simply update the **Chat Window** text area, appending the received message to its contents.

To send a WebSocket message, we invoke the `getBasicRemote()` method on our `Session` instance, then invoke the `sendText()` method on the resulting `RemoteEndpoint.Basic` implementation returned by this call (if this looks familiar, it is because we did the exact same thing in the WebSocket server endpoint code). In our example, we do this in the `sendMessage()` method.

Additional information about the Java API for WebSocket

In this chapter, we covered the bulk of the functionality provided by the Java API for WebSocket. For additional information, refer to the user guide for Tyrus, the Java API for WebSocket reference implementation, at `https://tyrus.java.net/documentation/1.3.1/user-guide.html`.

Summary

In this chapter, we covered the Java API for WebSocket, which is a new Java EE API to develop WebSocket server endpoints and clients.

We first saw how to develop WebSocket server endpoints by taking advantage of the Java API for WebSockets. We focused on developing annotation-based WebSocket endpoints.

Then, we covered how to develop web-based WebSocket clients using JavaScript and the JavaScript built-in WebSocket API.

Finally, we explained how to develop WebSocket client applications in Java via the `@ClientEndpoint` annotation.

In the next chapter, we will cover the **Java Message Service (JMS)**.

The Java Message Service

The **Java Message Service** (**JMS**) **API** provides a mechanism for Java EE applications to send messages to each other. Java EE 7 introduces JMS 2.0, a new version of JMS that greatly simplifies the development of applications involving messaging functionality.

JMS applications do not communicate directly; instead, message producers send messages to a destination, and message consumers receive that message from the destination.

The message destination is a message queue when the **Point-to-Point** (**PTP**) messaging domain is used, and a message topic when the Publish/Subscribe (pub/sub) messaging domain is used.

In this chapter, we will cover the following topics:

- Setting up GlassFish for JMS
- Working with message queues
- Working with message topics

Setting up GlassFish for JMS

Before we can start writing code to take advantage of the JMS API, we need to configure some GlassFish resources. Specifically, we need to set up a JMS Connection Factory, a message queue, and a message topic.

The Java Message Service

 Java EE 7 requires all compliant application servers to provide a default JMS connection factory. GlassFish, which is a fully compliant Java EE 7 application server (and the Java EE 7 reference implementation), complies with this requirement; so strictly speaking, we don't really need to set up a connection factory, however, in many cases we may need to set one up. Therefore, in the following section we illustrate how set up can be done.

Setting up a JMS connection factory

The easiest way to set up a JMS connection factory is via GlassFish's web console. Recall from *Chapter 1, Getting Started with GlassFish*, that the web console can be accessed by starting our domain by entering the following command in the command line:

```
asadmin start-domain domain1
```

Then, go to `http://localhost:4848` and log in.

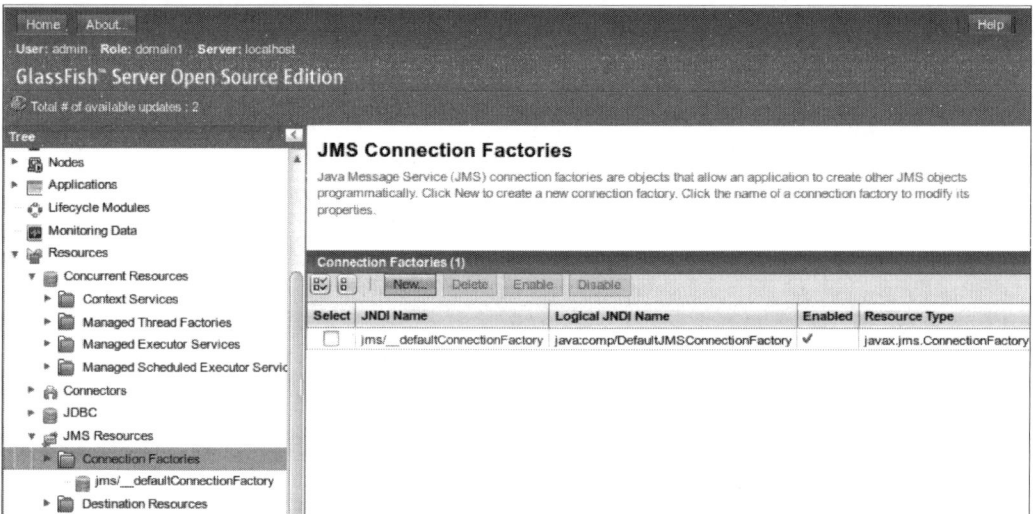

Chapter 8

A connection factory can be added by expanding the **Resources** node in the tree to the left-hand side of the web console; to do this, expand the **JMS Resources** node, click on the **Connection Factories** node, and then click on the **New...** button in the main area of the web console.

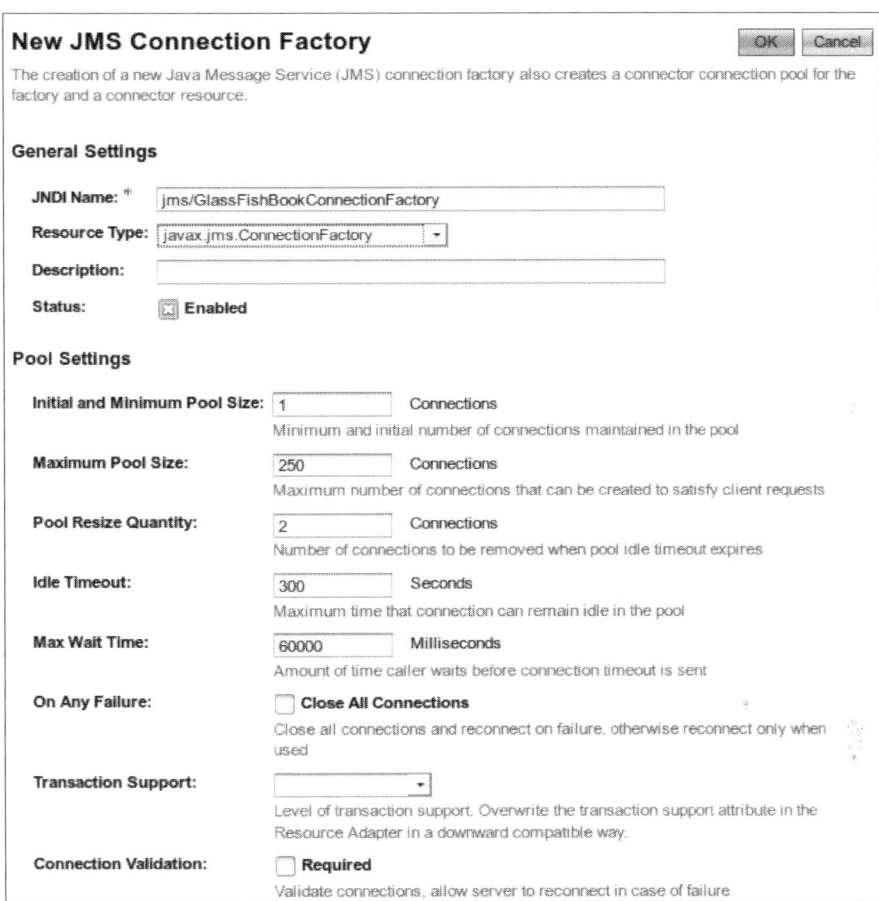

For our purposes, we can maintain most of the defaults; the only thing we need to do is enter a pool name in the **JNDI Name** field and pick a resource type for our connection factory.

It is always a good idea to use a pool name starting with `"jms/"` when naming JMS resources. This way, JMS resources can be easily identified when browsing a JNDI tree.

In the field labeled **JNDI Name**, enter `jms/GlassFishBookConnectionFactory`. Our code examples later in this chapter will use this JNDI name to obtain a reference to this connection factory.

The **Resource Type** dropdown has the following three options:

- **javax.jms.TopicConnectionFactory**: This option is used to create a connection factory that creates JMS topics for JMS clients using the pub/sub messaging domain
- **javax.jms.QueueConnectionFactory**: This option is used to create a connection factory that creates JMS queues for JMS clients using the PTP messaging domain
- **javax.jms.ConnectionFactory**: This option is used to create a connection factory that creates either JMS topics or JMS queues

For our example, we will select **javax.jms.ConnectionFactory**; this way, we can use the same connection factory for all of our examples, those using the PTP messaging domain and the pub/sub messaging domain.

After entering the pool name in the **JNDI Name** field for our connection factory, selecting a connection factory type, and optionally entering a description for our connection factory, we need to click on the **OK** button for the changes to take effect.

We should then see our newly created connection factory (**jms/GlassFishBookConnectionFactory**) listed in the main area of the GlassFish web console, as shown in the following screenshot:

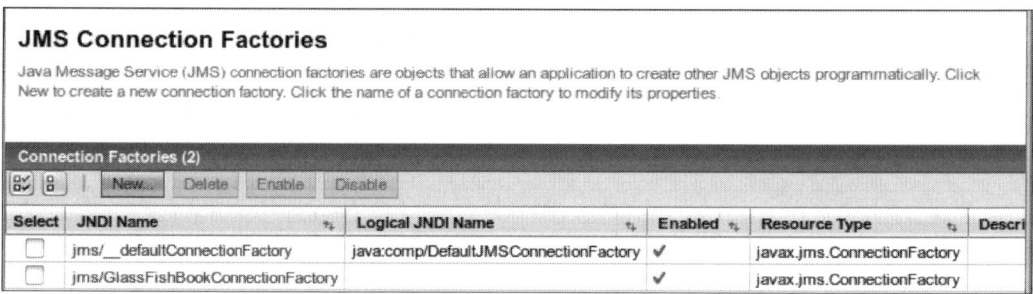

Setting up a JMS queue

A JMS queue can be added by going through the following steps:

1. Expand the **Resources** node in the tree at the left-hand side of the web console.
2. Enter a value in the **JNDI Name** field.
3. Enter a value in the **Physical Destination Name** field.
4. Select **javax.jms.Queue** in the **Resource Type** field.
5. Click on the **OK** button.

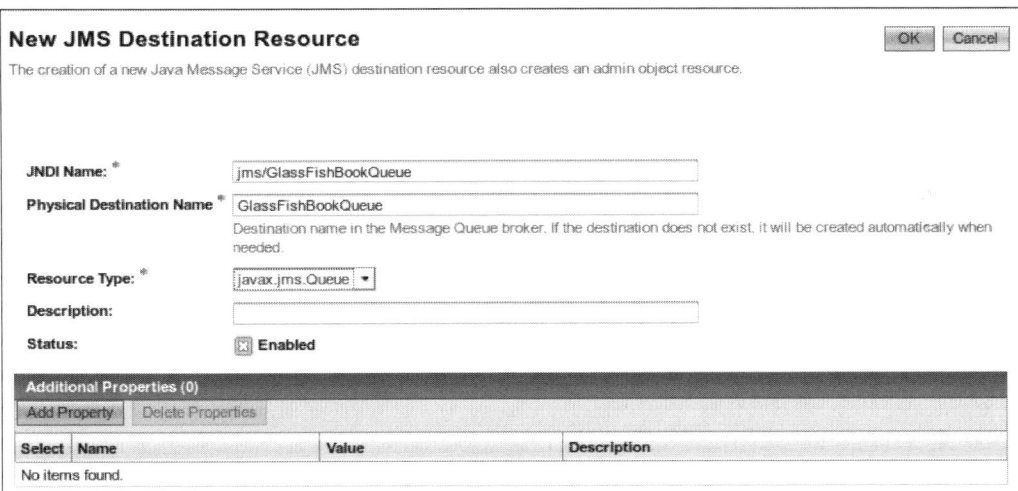

In our example, the JNDI name of the message queue is `jms/GlassFishBookQueue`. The resource type for message queues must be `javax.jms.Queue`. Additionally, a value must be entered in the **Physical Destination Name** field. In our example, we use `GlassFishBookQueue` as the value for this field.

After clicking on the **OK** button, we should see the newly created queue, as shown in the following screenshot:

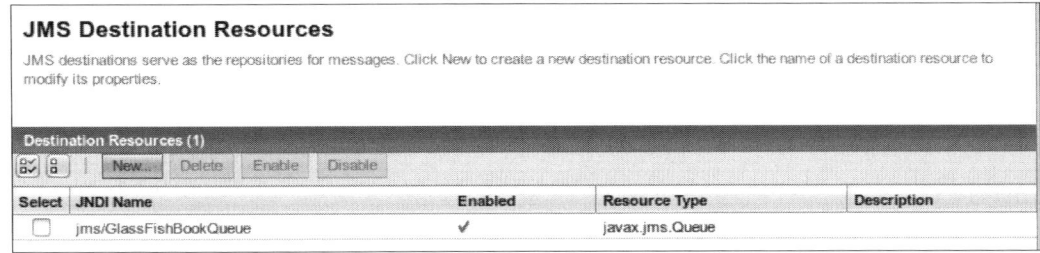

Setting up a JMS topic

Setting up a JMS topic in GlassFish is very similar to setting up a message queue. Perform the following steps:

1. Expand the JMS **Resources** node.
2. Click on the **Destination** node.
3. Click on the **New...** button in the main area of the web console.
4. Enter a name for our topic in the **JNDI Name** field.
5. Enter a physical destination name for our topic in the **Physical Destination Name** field.
6. Select **javax.jms.Topic** from the **Resource Type** dropdown.
7. Click on the **OK** button, shown in the following screenshot:

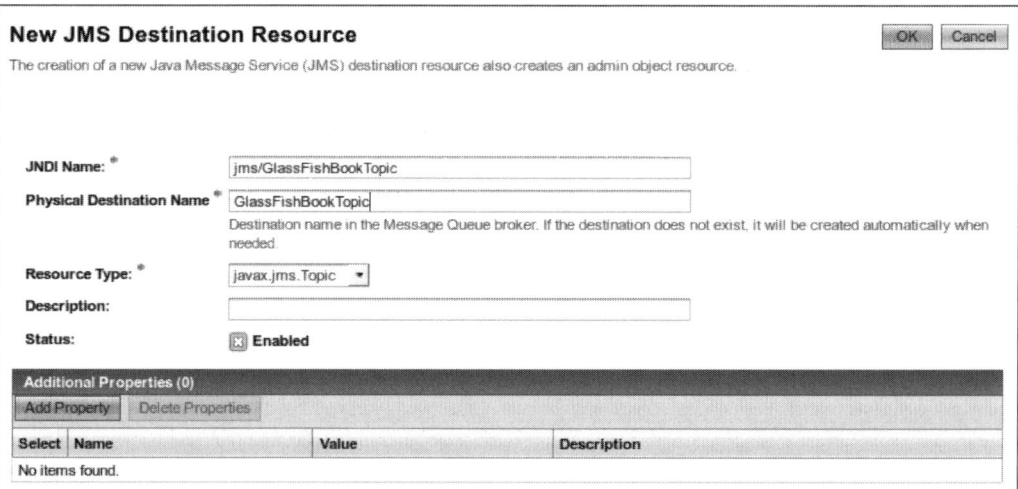

Our examples will use `jms/GlassFishBookTopic` in the **JNDI Name** field. Since this is a message topic, **Resource Type** must be set to `javax.jms.Topic`. The **Description** field is optional. The **Physical Destination Name** property is required; for our example, we will use `GlassFishBookTopic` as the value for this property.

After clicking on the **OK** button, we can see our newly created message topic as follows:

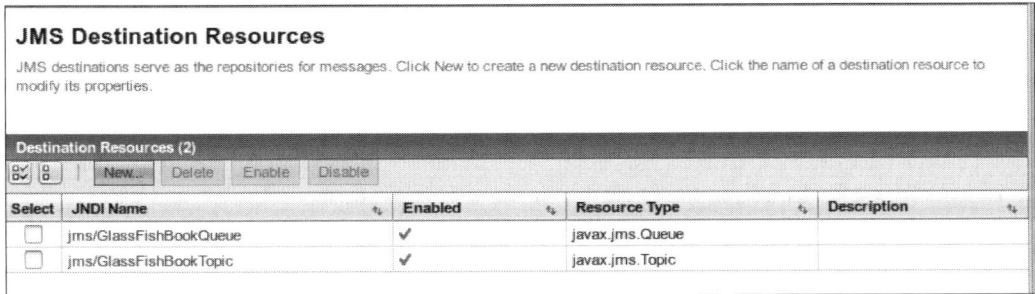

Now that we have set up a connection factory, a message queue, and a message topic, we are ready to start writing code using the JMS API.

Working with message queues

Like we mentioned earlier, message queues are used when our JMS code uses the **Point-To-Point** (**PTP**) messaging domain. For the PTP messaging domain, there is usually one message producer and one message consumer. The message producer and the message consumer don't need to be running concurrently in order to communicate. The messages placed in the message queue by the message producer will stay there until the message consumer executes and requests for the messages from the queue.

Sending messages to a message queue

Sending messages to a JMS queue consists of injecting a few resources to our code and making a few simple JMS API calls.

The following example illustrates how to add messages to a message queue:

```
package net.ensode.glassfishbook;

import javax.annotation.Resource;
import javax.jms.ConnectionFactory;
import javax.jms.JMSContext;
import javax.jms.JMSProducer;
import javax.jms.Queue;

public class MessageSender {
```

```java
    @Resource(mappedName = "jms/GlassFishBookConnectionFactory")
    private static ConnectionFactory connectionFactory;

    @Resource(mappedName = "jms/GlassFishBookQueue")
    private static Queue queue;

    public void produceMessages() {

        JMSContext jmsContext = connectionFactory.createContext();
        JMSProducer jmsProducer = jmsContext.createProducer();

        String msg1 = "Testing, 1, 2, 3. Can you hear me?";
        String msg2 = "Do you copy?";
        String msg3 = "Good bye!";

        System.out.println("Sending the following message: "
                + msg1);
        jmsProducer.send(queue, msg1);
        System.out.println("Sending the following message: "
                + msg2);
        jmsProducer.send(queue, msg2);
        System.out.println("Sending the following message: "
                + msg3);
        jmsProducer.send(queue, msg3);
    }

    public static void main(String[] args) {
        new MessageSender().produceMessages();
    }
}
```

Before delving into the details of our code, alert readers may have noticed that the `MessageSender` class is a standalone Java application, since it contains a main method. Since this class is standalone, it is executed outside of the application server; yet, we can see that some resources are injected into it, specifically the connection factory object and the queue. The reason we can inject resources into this code even though it runs outside the application server is because GlassFish includes a utility called `appclient`.

This utility allows us to "wrap" an executable JAR file and allow it to have access to the application server resources. To execute our code, assuming it is packaged in an executable JAR file called `jmsptpproducer.jar`, we would type the following in the command line:

`appclient -client jmsptpproducer.jar`

We would then see, after some GlassFish log entries, the following output on the console:

```
Sending the following message: Testing, 1, 2, 3. Can you hear me?
Sending the following message: Do you copy?
Sending the following message: Good bye!
```

The `appclient` executable script can be found under `[GlassFish installation directory]/glassfish/bin`; our example assumes that this directory is in the `PATH` variable and if it isn't, the complete path to the `appclient` script must be typed in the command line.

With that out of the way, we can now explain the code.

The `produceMessages()` method performs all the necessary steps to send messages to a message queue.

The first thing this method does is create an instance of `javax.jms.JMSContext` by invoking the `createContext()` method on the injected instance of `javax.jms.ConnectionFactory`. Notice that the `mappedName` attribute of the `@Resource` annotation decorating the connection factory object matches the JNDI name of the connection factory we set up in the GlassFish web console. Behind the scenes, a JNDI lookup is made using this name to obtain the connection factory object.

Next, we create an instance of `javax.jms.JMSProducer` by invoking the `createProducer()` method on the `JMSContext` instance we just created.

After obtaining an instance of `JMSProducer`, the code sends a series of text messages by invoking its `send()` method; this method takes the message destination as its first parameter, and a string containing the message text as its second parameter.

There are several overloaded versions of the `send()` method in `JMSProducer`; the one we used in our example is a convenience method that creates an instance of `javax.jms.TextMessage` and sets its text to the string we provide as the second parameter in the method invocation.

Although our example sends only text messages to the queue, we are not limited to sending only this type of message. The JMS API provides several types of messages that can be sent and received by JMS applications. All message types are defined as interfaces in the `javax.jms` package.

The following table lists all of the available message types:

Message Type	Description
`BytesMessage`	Allows sending an array of bytes as a message. `JMSProducer` has a convenience `send()` method that takes an array of bytes as one of its parameters; this method creates an instance of `javax.jms.BytesMessage` on the fly as the message is being sent.
`MapMessage`	Allows sending an implementation of `java.util.Map` as a message. `JMSProducer` has a convenience `send()` method that takes a `Map` as one of its parameters; this method creates an instance of `javax.jms.MapMessage` on the fly as the message is being sent.
`ObjectMessage`	Allows sending any Java object implementing `java.io.Serializable` as a message. `JMSProducer` has a convenience `send()` method that takes an instance of a class implementing `java.io.Serializable` as its second parameter; this method creates an instance of `javax.jms.ObjectMessage` on the fly as the message is being sent.
`StreamMessage`	Allows sending an array of bytes as a message. Differs from `BytesMessage` in that it stores the type of each primitive type added to the stream.
`TextMessage`	Allows sending `java.lang.String` as a message. As seen in our example, `JMSProducer` has a convenience `send()` method that takes `String` type as its second parameter; this method creates an instance of `javax.jms.TextMessage` on the fly as the message is being sent.

For more information on all JMS message types, consult their JavaDoc documentation at `http://docs.oracle.com/javaee/7/api/`.

Retrieving messages from a message queue

Of course, there is no point in sending messages from a queue if nothing is going to receive them. The following example illustrates how to retrieve messages from a JMS message queue:

```
package net.ensode.glassfishbook;

import javax.annotation.Resource;
import javax.jms.ConnectionFactory;
import javax.jms.JMSConsumer;
```

```java
import javax.jms.JMSContext;
import javax.jms.Queue;

public class MessageReceiver {

    @Resource(mappedName = "jms/GlassFishBookConnectionFactory")
    private static ConnectionFactory connectionFactory;
    @Resource(mappedName = "jms/GlassFishBookQueue")
    private static Queue queue;

    public void getMessages() {
        String message;
        boolean goodByeReceived = false;

        JMSContext jmsContext = connectionFactory.createContext();
        JMSConsumer jMSConsumer = jmsContext.createConsumer(queue);

        System.out.println("Waiting for messages...");
        while (!goodByeReceived) {
            message = jMSConsumer.receiveBody(String.class);

            if (message != null) {
                System.out.print("Received the following message: ");
                System.out.println(message);
                System.out.println();
                if (message.equals("Good bye!")) {
                    goodByeReceived = true;
                }
            }
        }
    }

    public static void main(String[] args) {
        new MessageReceiver().getMessages();
    }
}
```

Just like in the previous example, an instance of javax.jms.ConnectionFactory and an instance of javax.jms.Queue are injected using the @Resource annotation.

In our code, we get an instance of javax.jms.JMSContext by invoking the createContext() method of ConnectionFactory, just like in the previous example.

In this example, we obtain an instance of javax.jms.JMSConsumer by calling the createConsumer() method on our JMSContext instance.

Messages are received by invoking the `receiveBody()` method on our instance of `JMSConsumer`. This method takes the type of the message we are expecting as its sole parameter (`String.class` in our example). This method returns an object of the type specified in its parameter (an instance of `java.lang.String` in our example).

In this particular example, we placed this method call in a `while` loop since we are expecting a message that will let us know that no more messages are coming. Specifically, we are looking for a message containing the text `"Good bye!"`. Once we receive that message, we break out of the loop and continue with further processing. In this particular case, there is no more processing left to do, therefore, execution ends after we break out of the loop.

Just like in the previous example, using the `appclient` utility allows us to inject resources into the code and prevents us from having to add any libraries to the CLASSPATH. After executing the code through the `appclient` utility, we should see the following output in the command line:

```
appclient -client target/jmsptpconsumer.jar
Waiting for messages...
Received the following message: Testing, 1, 2, 3. Can you hear me?

Received the following message: Do you copy?

Received the following message: Good bye!
```

The previous example placed some messages on the queue. This example retrieves the messages. If the previous example has not been executed yet, then there are no messages to retrieve.

Asynchronously receiving messages from a message queue

The `JMSConsumer.receiveBody()` method has a disadvantage: it blocks execution until a message is received from the queue. We worked around this limitation in our previous example by breaking out of the loop once we received a specific message (`"Good bye!"`).

We can prevent our JMS consumer code from blocking execution by receiving messages asynchronously via an implementation of the `javax.jms.MessageListener` interface.

The `javax.jms.MessageListener` interface contains a single method called `onMessage`, it takes an instance of a class implementing the `javax.jms.Message` interface as its sole parameter. The following example illustrates a typical implementation of this interface:

```java
package net.ensode.glassfishbook;

import javax.jms.JMSException;
import javax.jms.Message;
import javax.jms.MessageListener;
import javax.jms.TextMessage;

public class ExampleMessageListener implements MessageListener {

  @Override
  public void onMessage(Message message) {
    TextMessage textMessage = (TextMessage) message;

    try {
      System.out.print("Received the following message: ");
      System.out.println(textMessage.getText());
      System.out.println();
    } catch (JMSException e) {
      e.printStackTrace();
    }
  }
}
```

In this case, the `onMessage()` method simply outputs the message text to the console. Recall that behind the scenes, the JMS API creates instances of `javax.jms.TextMessage` when we invoke `JMSProducer.send()` with a `String` as its second parameter; our `MessageListener` implementation casts the `Message` instance it receives as a parameter to `TextMessage`, and then gets the `String` message sent by the `JMSProducer` variable, invoking its `getText()` method.

Our main code can now delegate message retrieval to our custom `MessageListener` implementation:

```java
package net.ensode.glassfishbook;

import javax.annotation.Resource;
import javax.jms.ConnectionFactory;
import javax.jms.JMSConsumer;
import javax.jms.JMSContext;
```

```java
    import javax.jms.Queue;

public class AsynchMessReceiver {

    @Resource(mappedName = "jms/GlassFishBookConnectionFactory")
    private static ConnectionFactory connectionFactory;
    @Resource(mappedName = "jms/GlassFishBookQueue")
    private static Queue queue;

    public void getMessages() {
        try {
            JMSContext jmsContext = connectionFactory.createContext();
            JMSConsumer jMSConsumer = jmsContext.createConsumer(queue);

            jMSConsumer.setMessageListener(
                new ExampleMessageListener());

            System.out.println("The above line will allow the "
                    + "MessageListener implementation to "
                    + "receiving and processing messages"
                    + " from the queue.");
            Thread.sleep(1000);
            System.out.println("Our code does not have to block "
                    + "while messages are received.");
            Thread.sleep(1000);
            System.out.println("It can do other stuff "
                    + "(hopefully something more useful than sending "
                    + "silly output to the console. :)");
            Thread.sleep(1000);

        } catch (InterruptedException e) {
            e.printStackTrace();
        }
    }

    public static void main(String[] args) {
        new AsynchMessReceiver().getMessages();
    }
}
```

The only relevant difference between this example and the one in the previous section is that in this case, we are calling the `setMessageListener()` method on the instance of `javax.jms.JMSConsumer` obtained from the JMS context. We pass an instance of our custom implementation of `javax.jms.MessageListener` to this method; its `onMessage()` method is automatically called whenever there is a message waiting in the queue. Using this approach, the main code does not block execution while it is waiting to receive messages.

Executing the preceding example (using, of course, GlassFish's `appclient` utility), results in the following output:

```
appclient -client target/jmsptpasynchconsumer.jar
The above line will allow the MessageListener implementation to receive
and process messages from the queue.

Received the following message: Testing, 1, 2, 3. Can you hear me?

Received the following message: Do you copy?

Received the following message: Good bye!

Our code does not have to block while messages are received.

It can do other stuff (hopefully something more useful than sending silly
output to the console. :)
```

Notice how the messages were received and processed while the main thread was executing. We can tell that this is the case because the output of our `MessageListener` class' `onMessage()` method can be seen between calls to `System.out.println()` in the primary class.

Browsing message queues

JMS provides a way to browse message queues without actually removing the messages from the queue. The following example illustrates how to do this:

```
package net.ensode.glassfishbook;

import java.util.Enumeration;

import javax.annotation.Resource;
import javax.jms.ConnectionFactory;
```

```java
import javax.jms.JMSContext;
import javax.jms.JMSException;
import javax.jms.Queue;
import javax.jms.QueueBrowser;
import javax.jms.TextMessage;

public class MessageQueueBrowser {

    @Resource(mappedName = "jms/GlassFishBookConnectionFactory")
    private static ConnectionFactory connectionFactory;
    @Resource(mappedName = "jms/GlassFishBookQueue")
    private static Queue queue;

    public void browseMessages() {
        try {
            Enumeration messageEnumeration;
            TextMessage textMessage;
            JMSContext jmsContext = connectionFactory.createContext();
            QueueBrowser browser = jmsContext.createBrowser(queue);

            messageEnumeration = browser.getEnumeration();

            if (messageEnumeration != null) {
                if (!messageEnumeration.hasMoreElements()) {
                    System.out.println("There are no messages "
                            + "in the queue.");
                } else {
                    System.out.println(
                            "The following messages are "
                            + "in the queue");
                    while (messageEnumeration.hasMoreElements()) {
                        textMessage = (TextMessage)
                                messageEnumeration.nextElement();
                        System.out.println(textMessage.getText());
                    }
                }
            }
        } catch (JMSException e) {
            e.printStackTrace();
        }
    }

    public static void main(String[] args) {
        new MessageQueueBrowser().browseMessages();
    }
}
```

As we can see, the procedure to browse messages in a message queue is straightforward. We obtain a JMS connection factory, a JMS queue, and a JMS context in the usual way, and then invoke the `createBrowser()` method on the JMS context object. This method returns an implementation of the `javax.jms.QueueBrowser` interface, containing a `getEnumeration()` method that we can invoke to obtain an `Enumeration` containing all messages in the queue. To examine the messages in the queue, we simply traverse this enumeration and obtain the messages one by one. In our example, we simply invoked the `getText()` method of each message in the queue.

Working with message topics

Message topics are used when our JMS code uses the Publish/Subscribe (pub/sub) messaging domain. When using this messaging domain, the same message can be sent to all subscribers of a topic.

Sending messages to a message topic

Sending messages to a JMS topic is very similar to sending messages to a queue; simply inject the required resources and make some simple JMS API calls.

The following example illustrates how to send messages to a message topic:

```java
package net.ensode.glassfishbook;

import javax.annotation.Resource;
import javax.jms.ConnectionFactory;
import javax.jms.JMSContext;
import javax.jms.JMSProducer;
import javax.jms.Topic;

public class MessageSender {

    @Resource(mappedName = "jms/GlassFishBookConnectionFactory")
    private static ConnectionFactory connectionFactory;
    @Resource(mappedName = "jms/GlassFishBookTopic")
    private static Topic topic;

    public void produceMessages() {
        JMSContext jmsContext = connectionFactory.createContext();
        JMSProducer jmsProducer = jmsContext.createProducer();
```

```
            String msg1 = "Testing, 1, 2, 3. Can you hear me?";
            String msg2 = "Do you copy?";
            String msg3 = "Good bye!";

            System.out.println("Sending the following message: "
                    + msg1);
            jmsProducer.send(topic, msg1);
            System.out.println("Sending the following message: "
                    + msg2);
            jmsProducer.send(topic, msg2);
            System.out.println("Sending the following message: "
                    + msg3);
            jmsProducer.send(topic, msg3);

        }

        public static void main(String[] args) {
            new MessageSender().produceMessages();
        }
    }
```

As we can see, this example is nearly identical to the `MessageSender` class we saw when we discussed Point-To-Point messaging. As a matter of fact, the only lines of code that are different are those that are highlighted. The JMS API was designed this way so that application developers do not have to learn two different APIs for the PTP and pub/sub domains.

Since the code is nearly identical to the corresponding example in the *Working with message queues* section, we will only explain the differences between the two examples. In this example, instead of declaring an instance of a class implementing `javax.jms.Queue`, we declare an instance of a class implementing `javax.jms.Topic`. We will then pass this instance of `javax.jms.Topic` as the first parameter of the `send()` method of our `JMSProducer` object, along with the message we wish to send.

Receiving messages from a message topic

Just as sending messages to a message topic is nearly identical to sending messages to a message queue, receiving messages from a message topic is nearly identical to receiving messages from a message queue, as can be seen in the following example:

```
    package net.ensode.glassfishbook;

    import javax.annotation.Resource;
    import javax.jms.ConnectionFactory;
```

```java
import javax.jms.JMSConsumer;
import javax.jms.JMSContext;
import javax.jms.Topic;

public class MessageReceiver {

    @Resource(mappedName = "jms/GlassFishBookConnectionFactory")
    private static ConnectionFactory connectionFactory;
    @Resource(mappedName = "jms/GlassFishBookTopic")
    private static Topic topic;

    public void getMessages() {
        String message;
        boolean goodByeReceived = false;

        JMSContext jmsContext = connectionFactory.createContext();
        JMSConsumer jMSConsumer = jmsContext.createConsumer(topic);

        System.out.println("Waiting for messages...");
        while (!goodByeReceived) {
            message = jMSConsumer.receiveBody(String.class);

            if (message != null) {
                System.out.print("Received the following message: ");
                System.out.println(message);
                System.out.println();
                if (message.equals("Good bye!")) {
                    goodByeReceived = true;
                }
            }
        }
    }

    public static void main(String[] args) {
        new MessageReceiver().getMessages();
    }
}
```

Once again, the differences between this code and the corresponding code for PTP messaging are simple. Instead of declaring an instance of a class implementing `javax.jms.Queue`, we declare a class implementing `javax.jms.Topic`. We use the `@Resource` annotation to inject an instance of this class into our code using the JNDI name we used when creating it in the GlassFish web console. We then obtain an instance of `JMSContext` and `JMSConsumer` as we did before, and then receive the messages from the topic by invoking the `receiveBody()` method on `JMSConsumer`.

Using the pub/sub messaging domain as illustrated in this section has the advantage that messages can be sent to several message consumers. This can be easily tested by concurrently executing two instances of the `MessageReceiver` class we developed in this section, and then executing the `MessageSender` class we developed in the previous section. We should see the console output for each instance, indicating that both instances received all messages.

Just like with message queues, messages can be retrieved asynchronously from a message topic. The procedure to do so is so similar to the message queue version that we will not show an example. To convert the asynchronous example shown earlier in this chapter to use a message topic, simply replace the `javax.jms.Queue` variable with an instance of `javax.jms.Topic` and inject the appropriate instance using `"jms/GlassFishBookTopic"` as the value of the `mappedName` attribute of the `@Resource` annotation decorating the instance of `javax.jms.Topic`.

Creating durable subscribers

The disadvantage of using the pub/sub messaging domain is that message consumers must be running when the messages are sent to the topic. If the message consumer is not running at the time, it will not receive the messages; whereas, in PTP, messages are kept in the queue until the message consumer runs. Fortunately, the JMS API provides a way to use the pub/sub messaging domain and keep messages in the topic until all subscribed message consumers run and receive the message. This can be accomplished by creating durable subscribers for a JMS topic.

In order to be able to serve durable subscribers, we need to set the `ClientId` property of our JMS connection factory. Each durable subscriber must have a unique client ID; therefore, a unique connection factory must be declared for each potential durable subscriber.

InvalidClientIdException?

Only one JMS client can connect to a topic for a specific client ID. If more than one JMS client attempts to obtain a JMS connection using the same connection factory, a `JMSException` stating that the Client ID is already in use will be thrown. The solution is to create a connection factory for each potential client that will be receiving messages from the durable topic.

Like we mentioned before, the easiest way to add a connection factory is through the GlassFish web console, as shown in the following steps:

1. Expand the **Resources** node to the left-hand side of the web console.
2. Expand the **JMS Resources** node.
3. Click on the **Connection Factories** node.
4. Click on the **New...** button in the main area of the page.

Our next example will use the settings displayed in the following screenshot:

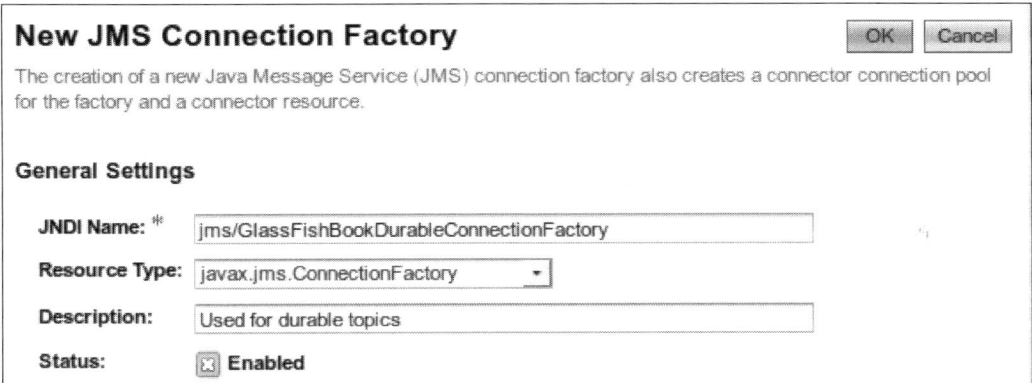

Before clicking on the **OK** button, we need to scroll to the bottom of the page, click on the **Add Property** button, and enter a new property named `ClientId`. Our example will use `ExampleId` as the value for this property, as shown in the following screenshot:

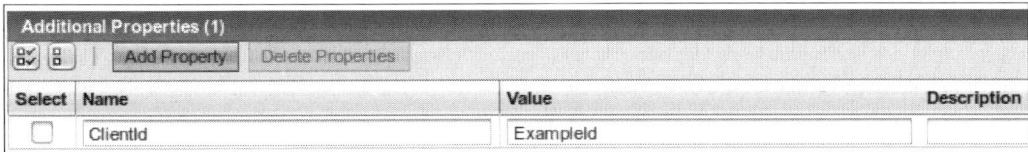

Now that we have set up GlassFish to be able to provide durable subscriptions, we are ready to write some code to take advantage of them:

```
package net.ensode.glassfishbook;

import javax.annotation.Resource;
import javax.jms.Connection;
```

```java
import javax.jms.ConnectionFactory;
import javax.jms.JMSConsumer;
import javax.jms.JMSContext;
import javax.jms.JMSException;
import javax.jms.MessageConsumer;
import javax.jms.Session;
import javax.jms.TextMessage;
import javax.jms.Topic;

public class MessageReceiver {

    @Resource(mappedName
            = "jms/GlassFishBookDurableConnectionFactory")
    private static ConnectionFactory connectionFactory;
    @Resource(mappedName = "jms/GlassFishBookTopic")
    private static Topic topic;

    public void getMessages() {
        String message;
        boolean goodByeReceived = false;

        JMSContext jmsContext = connectionFactory.createContext();
        JMSConsumer jMSConsumer =
            jmsContext.createDurableConsumer(topic, "Subscriber1");

        System.out.println("Waiting for messages...");
        while (!goodByeReceived) {
            message = jMSConsumer.receiveBody(String.class);

            if (message != null) {
                System.out.print("Received the following message: ");
                System.out.println(message);
                System.out.println();
                if (message.equals("Good bye!")) {
                    goodByeReceived = true;
                }
            }
        }
    }

    public static void main(String[] args) {
        new MessageReceiver().getMessages();
    }
}
```

As we can see, this code is not very different from the previous examples of code, the purpose of which was to retrieve messages. There are only two differences from previous examples: the instance of `ConnectionFactory` that we are injecting is the one we set up earlier in this section to handle durable subscriptions, and instead of calling the `createConsumer()` method on the JMS context object, we are calling `createDurableConsumer()`. The `createDurableConsumer()` method takes two arguments: a JMS topic object to retrieve messages from and a `String` designating a name for this subscription. This second parameter must be unique across all subscribers to that durable topic.

Summary

In this chapter, we covered how to set up JMS connection factories, JMS message queues, and JMS message topics in GlassFish using the GlassFish web console.

We also covered how to send messages to a message queue via the `javax.jms.JMSProducer` interface.

Additionally, we covered how to receive messages from a message queue via the `javax.jms.JMSConsumer` interface. We also covered how to asynchronously receive messages from a message queue by implementing the `javax.jms.MessageListener` interface.

We also saw how to use these interfaces to send and receive messages to and from a JMS message topic.

We also covered how to browse messages in a message queue without removing them from the queue via the `javax.jms.QueueBrowser` interface.

Finally, we saw how to set up and interact with durable subscriptions to JMS topics.

In the next chapter, we will cover how to secure Java EE applications.

Securing Java EE Applications

In this chapter, we will cover how to secure Java EE applications by taking advantage of GlassFish's built-in security features.

Java EE security relies on the **Java Authentication and Authorization Service (JAAS)** API. As we will see, securing Java EE applications requires very little coding for the most part. Securing an application is achieved by setting up users and security groups to a security realm in the application server and then configuring our applications to rely on a specific security realm for authentication and authorization.

Some of the topics we will cover in this chapter include:

- Admin realms
- File realms
- Certificate realms
- Creating self-signed security certificates
- JDBC realms
- Custom realms

Security realms

Security realms are, in essence, collections of users and related security groups. A user can belong to one or more security groups. The groups that the user belongs to define what actions the system will allow the user to perform. For example, an application can have regular users that can only use basic application functionality, and it can have administrators that, in addition to being able to use basic application functionality, can add additional users to the system.

Security realms store user information (user name, password, and security groups). Therefore, applications don't need to implement this functionality and can simply be configured to obtain this information from a security realm. A security realm can be used by more than one application.

Predefined security realms

GlassFish comes preconfigured with three predefined security realms: **admin-realm**, **file**, and **certificate**. The **admin-realm** is used to manage the user's access to the GlassFish web console and shouldn't be used for other applications. The **file** realm stores user information in a file. The **certificate** realm looks for a client-side certificate to authenticate the user.

The following screenshot shows the predefined realms in the GlassFish web console:

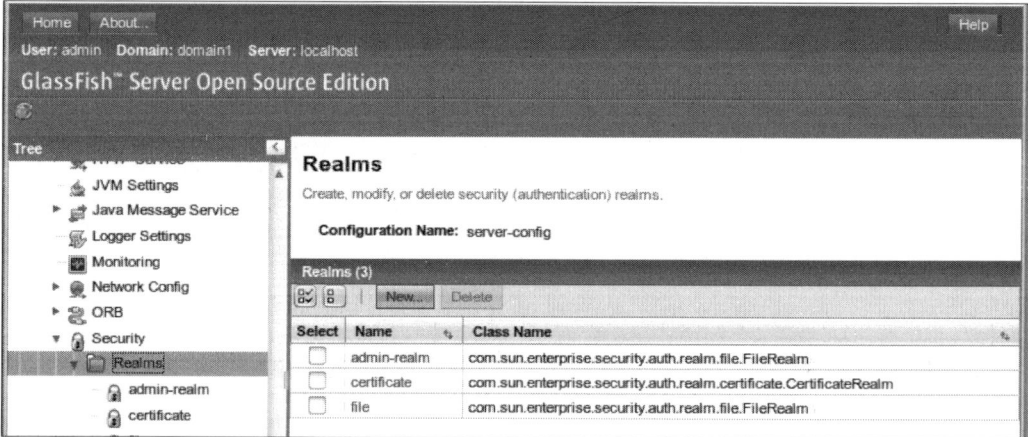

In addition to the predefined security realms, we can add additional realms with very little effort. We will cover how to do this later in this chapter, but first let's discuss GlassFish's predefined security realms.

The admin-realm

The admin-realm has a predefined user called **admin**, which belongs to a predefined group called **asadmin**.

To illustrate how to add users to a realm, let's add a new user to the admin-realm. This will allow an additional user to log in to the GlassFish web console. In order to add a user to admin-realm, log in to the GlassFish web console and expand the **Configurations** node on the left-hand side. Then expand the **server-config** node, followed by the **Security** node. Then expand the **Realms** node and click on **admin-realm**. The main area of the page should look like the following screenshot:

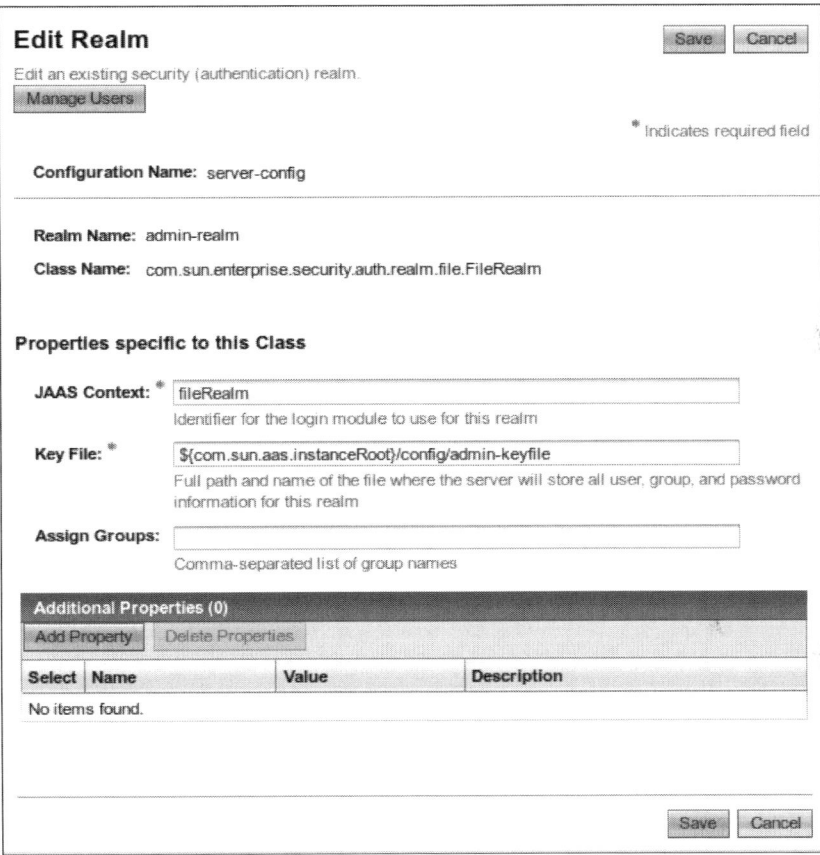

Securing Java EE Applications

To add a user to the realm, click on the button to the top-left labeled **Manage Users**. The main area of the page should now look like the following screenshot:

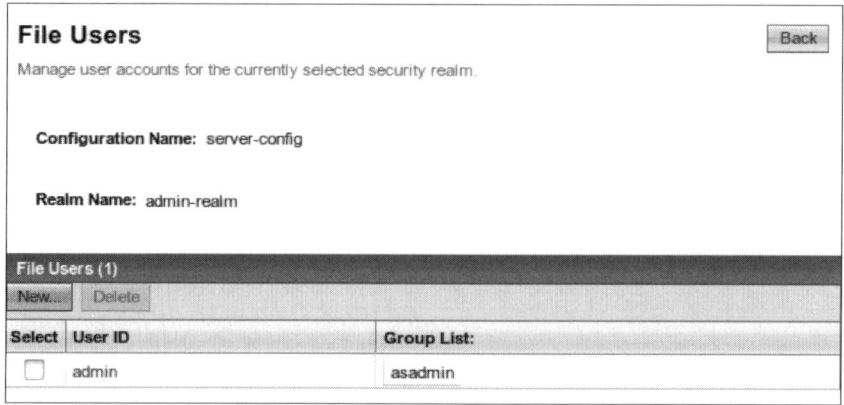

To add a new user to the realm, simply click on the **New...** button to the top-left of the screen and then enter the new user information as shown in the following screenshot:

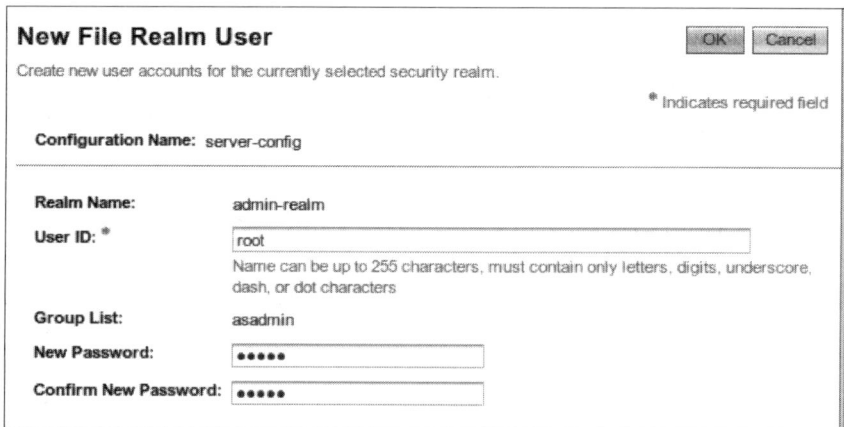

As shown in this screenshot, we added a new user named `root`, added this user to the `asadmin` group, and entered this user's password.

> The GlassFish web console will only allow users in the **asadmin** group to log in. Failing to add our user to this security group will prevent him/her from logging in to the console.

We can now see our newly created user in the list of admin-realm users, as can be seen in the following screenshot:

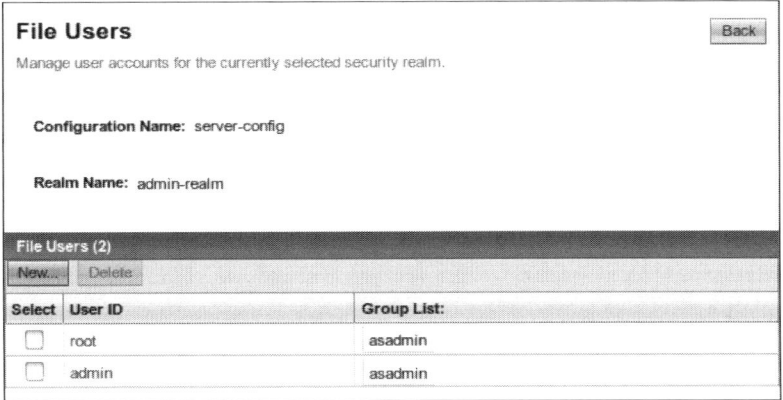

We have successfully added a new user for the GlassFish web console. We can test this new account by logging in to the console with this new user's credentials.

The file realm

The second predefined realm in GlassFish is the file realm. This realm stores user information encrypted in a text file. Adding users to this realm is very similar to adding users to **admin-realm**. We can add a user by navigating to **Configurations | server-config | Security | Realm**. Under the **Realm** node, click on **file**, then on the **Manage Users** button, and finally on the **New...** button. The main area of the page should look like the following screenshot:

Since this realm is meant to be used for our applications, we can come up with our own groups. Groups are useful to give the same permissions to several users. For example, all users requiring administrative permissions can be added to an admin group (the name of the group is, of course, arbitrary).

In this example, we added a user with the user ID `peter` to the groups `appuser` and `appadmin`.

Clicking on the **OK** button should save the new user and take us to the user list for this realm, as shown in the following screenshot:

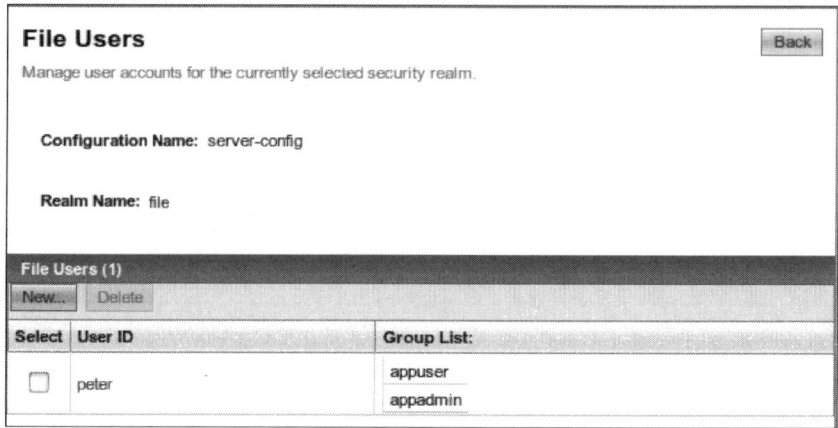

Clicking on the **New...** button allows us to add additional users to the realm. Let's add an additional user named `joe` belonging only to the `appuser` group, as shown in the following screenshot:

As we have seen in this section, adding users to the file realm is very simple. We will now illustrate how to authenticate and authorize users via the file realm.

Basic authentication via the file realm

In the previous section, we covered how to add users to the file realm and how to assign these users to groups. In this section, we will illustrate how to secure a web application so that only properly authenticated and authorized users can access it. This web application will use the file realm for user access control.

The application will consist of a few very simple JSF pages. All authentication logic is taken care of by the application server; therefore, the only place we need to make modifications in order to secure the application is in its deployment descriptors, web.xml and glassfish-web.xml. We will first discuss web.xml, which is as follows:

```xml
<?xml version="1.0" encoding="UTF-8"?>
<web-app version="3.0" xmlns="http://java.sun.com/xml/ns/javaee"
  xmlns:xsi="http://www.w3.org/2001/XMLSchema-instance"
  xsi:schemaLocation="http://java.sun.com/xml/ns/javaee
  http://java.sun.com/xml/ns/javaee/web-app_3_0.xsd">
  <context-param>
    <param-name>javax.faces.PROJECT_STAGE</param-name>
    <param-value>Development</param-value>
  </context-param>
  <servlet>
    <servlet-name>Faces Servlet</servlet-name>
    <servlet-class>javax.faces.webapp.FacesServlet</servlet-class>
    <load-on-startup>1</load-on-startup>
  </servlet>
  <servlet-mapping>
    <servlet-name>Faces Servlet</servlet-name>
    <url-pattern>*.jsf</url-pattern>
  </servlet-mapping>
  <welcome-file-list>
    <welcome-file>index.jsf</welcome-file>
  </welcome-file-list>
  <security-constraint>
    <web-resource-collection>
      <web-resource-name>Admin Pages</web-resource-name>
      <url-pattern>/admin/*</url-pattern>
    </web-resource-collection>
    <auth-constraint>
      <role-name>admin</role-name>
    </auth-constraint>
  </security-constraint>
```

```xml
<security-constraint>
  <web-resource-collection>
    <web-resource-name>AllPages</web-resource-name>
    <url-pattern>/*</url-pattern>
  </web-resource-collection>
  <auth-constraint>
    <role-name>user</role-name>
  </auth-constraint>
</security-constraint>
<login-config>
  <auth-method>BASIC</auth-method>
  <realm-name>file</realm-name>
</login-config>
</web-app>
```

The `<security-constraint>` element defines who can access pages matching a certain URL pattern. The URL pattern of the pages is defined inside the `<url-pattern>` element, which, as shown in the example, must be nested inside a `<web-resource-collection>` element. Roles allowed to access the pages are defined in the `<role-name>` element, which must be nested inside an `<auth-constraint>` element.

In our example, we define two sets of pages to be protected. The first set of pages are those whose URLs start with /admin. These pages can be accessed only by users belonging to the admin group. The second set of pages are the rest of the pages, defined by the URL pattern of /*. Only users with the role user can access these pages. It is worth noting that the second set of pages is a superset of the first set, that is, any page whose URL matches /admin/* also matches /*. In cases like these, the most specific case wins. In this particular case, users with the role user (and without the role admin) will not be able to access any page whose URL starts with /admin.

The next element we need to add to web.xml in order to protect our pages is the `<login-config>` element. This element must contain an `<auth-method>` element, which defines the authorization method for the application. Valid values for this element include BASIC, DIGEST, FORM, and CLIENT-CERT.

BASIC indicates that basic authentication will be used. This type of authentication will result in a browser-generated pop up prompting the user for a username and password to be displayed the first time a user tries to access a protected page. Unless using the HTTPS protocol, when using basic authentication, the user's credentials are Base64 encoded, not encrypted. It would be fairly easy for an attacker to decode these credentials; therefore, using basic authentication is not recommended.

The DIGEST authentication value is similar to basic authentication, except that it uses an MD5 digest to encrypt the user credentials instead of sending them Base64 encoded.

The FORM authentication value uses a custom HTML or JSP page containing an HTML form with the username and password fields. The values in the form are then checked against the security realm for user authentication and authorization. Unless using HTTPS, user credentials are sent in clear text when using form-based authentication; therefore, using HTTPS is recommended since it encrypts the data. We will cover setting up GlassFish to use HTTPS later in this chapter.

The CLIENT-CERT authentication value uses client-side certificates to authenticate and authorize the user.

The <realm-name> element of <login-config> indicates what security realm to use to authenticate and authorize the user. In this particular example, we are using the file realm.

All of the web.xml elements we have discussed in this section can be used with any security realm; they are not tied to the file realm. The only thing that ties our application to the file realm is the value of the <realm-name> element. Something else to keep in mind is that not all authentication methods are supported by all realms. The file realm supports only basic and form-based authentication.

Before we can successfully authenticate our users, we need to link the user roles defined in web.xml with the groups defined in the realm. We accomplish this in the glassfish-web.xml deployment descriptor as follows:

```
<?xml version="1.0" encoding="UTF-8"?>
<!DOCTYPE glassfish-web-app PUBLIC "-//GlassFish.org//DTD
  GlassFish Application Server 3.1 Servlet 3.0//EN"
  "http://glassfish.org/dtds/glassfish-web-app_3_0-1.dtd">
<glassfish-web-app error-url="">
  <context-root>/filerealmauth</context-root>
  <security-role-mapping>
    <role-name>admin</role-name>
    <group-name>appadmin</group-name>
  </security-role-mapping>
  <security-role-mapping>
    <role-name>user</role-name>
    <group-name>appuser</group-name>
  </security-role-mapping>
  <class-loader delegate="true"/>
</glassfish-web-app>
```

As can be seen in the preceding example, the `glassfish-web.xml` deployment descriptor can have one or more `<security-role-mapping>` elements. One of these elements is needed for each role defined in each `<auth-constraint>` tag in `web.xml`. The `<role-name>` subelement indicates the role to map. Its value must match the value of the corresponding `<role-name>` element in `web.xml`. The `<group-name>` subelement must match the value of a security group in the realm used to authenticate users in the application.

In this example, the first `<security-role-mapping>` element maps the `admin` role defined in the application's `web.xml` deployment descriptor to the `appadmin` group we created when adding users to the file realm earlier in the chapter. The second `<security-role-mapping>` element maps the `user` role in `web.xml` to the `appuser` group in the file realm.

As mentioned earlier, there is nothing we need to do in our code in order to authenticate and authorize users. All we need to do is modify the application's deployment descriptors as described in this section. Since our application is nothing but a few simple pages, we will not show the source code for them. The structure of our application is shown in the following screenshot:

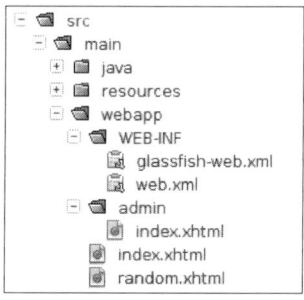

Based on the way we set up our application in the deployment descriptors, users with the role `user` will be able to access the two pages at the root of the application (`index.xhtml` and `random.xhtml`). Only users with the role `admin` will be able to access any pages under the `admin` folder, which in this particular case is a single page named `index.xhtml`.

After packaging and deploying our application and pointing the browser to the URL of any of its pages, we should see a pop up asking for a **User Name** and **Password**, as shown in the following screenshot:

Chapter 9

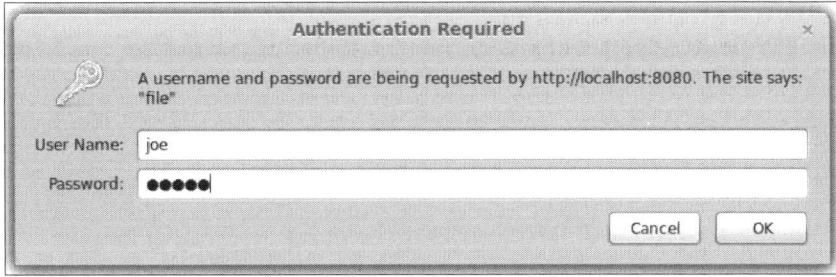

After entering the correct username and password, we are directed to the page we were attempting to see, as follows:

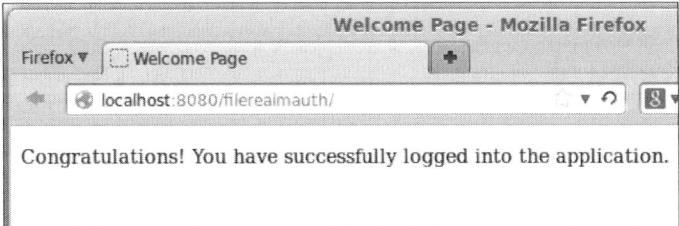

At this point, the user can navigate to any page he/she is allowed to access in the application, either by following links or by typing in the URL in the browser, without having to reenter his/her username and password.

Note that we logged in as the user `joe`; this user belongs only to the `user` role. Therefore, he does not have access to any page that starts with `/admin` as the URL. If `joe` tries to access one of these pages, he will get an HTTP error reporting **HTTP Status 403-Forbidden**, as shown in the following screenshot:

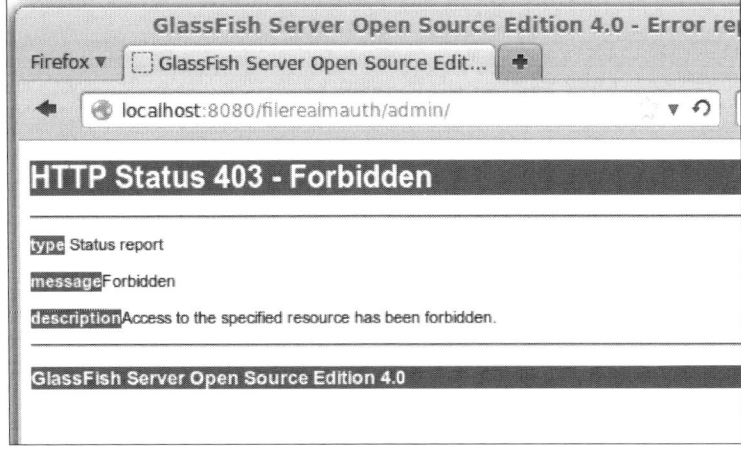

Only users belonging to the admin role can see pages that match the URL shown in the screenshot. When we were adding users to the file realm, we added a user named peter that had this role. If we log in as peter, we will be able to see the requested page. For basic authentication, the only possible way to log out of the application is to close the browser. Therefore, to log in as peter, we need to close and reopen the browser. Once logged in as Peter, we will see a window as shown in the following screenshot:

As mentioned before, one disadvantage of the basic authentication method we used in this example is that login information is not encrypted. One way to get around this is to use the HTTPS (HTTP over SSL) protocol. When using this protocol, all information between the browser and the server is encrypted.

The easiest way to use HTTPS is by modifying the application's web.xml deployment descriptor as follows:

```xml
<?xml version="1.0" encoding="UTF-8"?>
<web-app xmlns="http://java.sun.com/xml/ns/javaee"
  xmlns:xsi="http://www.w3.org/2001/XMLSchema-instance"
  xsi:schemaLocation="http://java.sun.com/xml/ns/javaee
  http://java.sun.com/xml/ns/javaee/web-app_3_0.xsd"
  version="3.0">
  <security-constraint>
    <web-resource-collection>
      <web-resource-name>Admin Pages</web-resource-name>
      <url-pattern>/admin/*</url-pattern>
    </web-resource-collection>
    <auth-constraint>
      <role-name>admin</role-name>
    </auth-constraint>
    <user-data-constraint>
      <transport-guarantee>CONFIDENTIAL</transport-guarantee>
    </user-data-constraint>
  </security-constraint>
  <security-constraint>
```

```xml
        <web-resource-collection>
          <web-resource-name>AllPages</web-resource-name>
          <url-pattern>/*</url-pattern>
        </web-resource-collection>
        <auth-constraint>
          <role-name>user</role-name>
        </auth-constraint>
        <user-data-constraint>
          <transport-guarantee>CONFIDENTIAL</transport-guarantee>
        </user-data-constraint>
      </security-constraint>
      <login-config>
        <auth-method>BASIC</auth-method>
        <realm-name>file</realm-name>
      </login-config>
    </web-app>
```

As we can see, all we need to do to have the application be accessed only through HTTPS is to add a `<user-data-constraint>` element containing a nested `<transport-guarantee>` element to each set of pages we want to encrypt. Sets of pages to be protected are declared in the `<security-constraint>` elements in the `web.xml` deployment descriptor.

Now, when we access the application through the (unsecure) HTTP port (by default, it is 8080), the request is automatically forwarded to the (secure) HTTPS port (by default, 8181).

In our example, we set the value of the `<transport-guarantee>` element to `CONFIDENTIAL`. This has the effect of encrypting all the data between the browser and the server. Also, if the request is made through the unsecured HTTP port, it is automatically forwarded to the secured HTTPS port.

Another valid value for the `<transport-guarantee>` element is `INTEGRAL`. When using this value, the integrity of the data between the browser and the server is guaranteed. In other words, the data cannot be changed in transit. When using this value, requests made over HTTP are not automatically forwarded to HTTPS. If a user attempts to access a secure page via HTTP when this value is used, the browser will deny the request and return a 403 (Access Denied) error.

The third and last valid value for the `<transport-guarantee>` element is `NONE`. When using this value, no guarantees are made about the integrity or confidentiality of the data. The `NONE` value is the default value used when the `<transport-guarantee>` element is not present in the application's `web.xml` deployment descriptor.

After making the preceding modifications to the `web.xml` deployment descriptor, redeploying the application, and pointing the browser to any of the pages in the application, we should see the following warning page when accessing our application on Firefox:

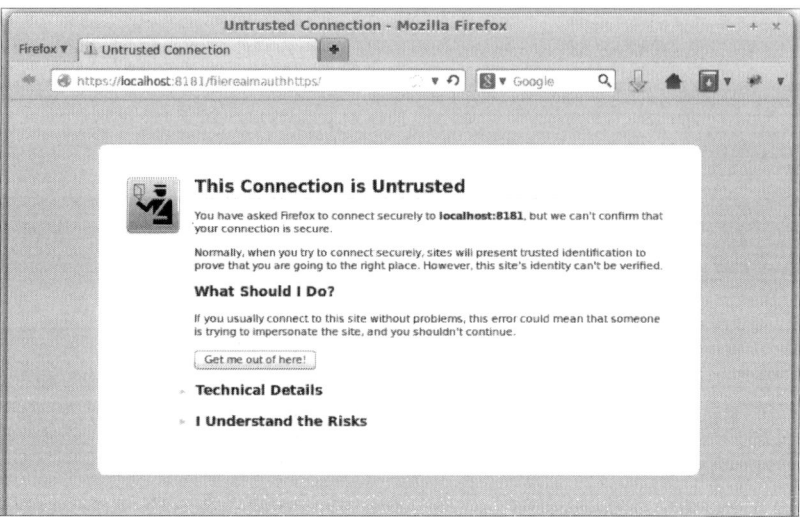

After expanding the **I Understand the Risks** node and clicking on the button labeled **Add Exception...**, we should see a window similar to the one shown in the following screenshot:

After clicking on the button labeled **Confirm Security Exception**, we are prompted for a username and password. After entering the appropriate credentials, we are allowed access to the requested page as shown in the following screenshot:

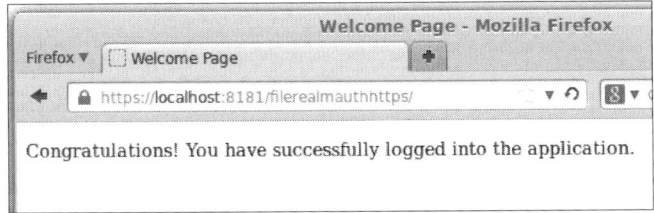

The reason we see this warning is that, in order for a server to use the HTTPS protocol, it must have an SSL certificate. Typically, SSL certificates are issued by **Certificate Authorities (CA)** such as Verisign or Thawte. These certificate authorities digitally sign the certificate. By doing this, they certify that the server belongs to the entity it claims it belongs to.

A digital certificate from one of these certificate authorities typically costs around USD 400 and expires after a year. Since the cost of these certificates may be prohibitive for development or testing purposes, GlassFish comes preconfigured with a self-signed SSL certificate. Since this certificate has not been signed by a certificate authority, the browser shows a warning window when we try to access a secured page via HTTPS.

Notice the URL in the screenshot. The protocol is set to HTTPS, and the port is 8181. The URL we pointed the browser to was `http://localhost:8080/filerealmauthhttps`, because of the modifications we made to the application's `web.xml` deployment descriptor, the request was automatically redirected to this URL. Of course, users may directly type in the secure URL and it will work without a problem.

Any data transferred over HTTPS is encrypted, including the username and password entered in the pop-up window generated by the browser. Using HTTPS allows us to safely use basic authentication. However, basic authentication has a disadvantage, which is that the only way that users can log out of the application is to close the browser. If we need to allow users to log out of the application without closing the browser, we need to use form-based authentication.

Form-based authentication

We need to make some modifications to the application's `web.xml` deployment descriptor to use form-based authentication, as follows:

```xml
<?xml version="1.0" encoding="UTF-8"?>
<web-app version="3.0" xmlns="http://java.sun.com/xml/ns/javaee"
  xmlns:xsi="http://www.w3.org/2001/XMLSchema-instance"
 xsi:schemaLocation="http://java.sun.com/xml/ns/javaee
   http://java.sun.com/xml/ns/javaee/web-app_3_0.xsd">
  <context-param>
    <param-name>javax.faces.PROJECT_STAGE</param-name>
    <param-value>Development</param-value>
  </context-param>
  <servlet>
    <servlet-name>Faces Servlet</servlet-name>
    <servlet-class>javax.faces.webapp.FacesServlet</servlet-class>
    <load-on-startup>1</load-on-startup>
  </servlet>
  <servlet-mapping>
    <servlet-name>Faces Servlet</servlet-name>
    <url-pattern>*.jsf</url-pattern>
  </servlet-mapping>
  <welcome-file-list>
    <welcome-file>index.jsf</welcome-file>
  </welcome-file-list>
  <security-constraint>
    <web-resource-collection>
      <web-resource-name>Admin Pages</web-resource-name>
      <url-pattern>/admin/*</url-pattern>
    </web-resource-collection>
    <auth-constraint>
      <role-name>admin</role-name>
    </auth-constraint>
    <user-data-constraint>
      <transport-guarantee>CONFIDENTIAL</transport-guarantee>
    </user-data-constraint>
  </security-constraint>
  <security-constraint>
    <web-resource-collection>
      <web-resource-name>AllPages</web-resource-name>
      <url-pattern>/*</url-pattern>
    </web-resource-collection>
    <auth-constraint>
      <role-name>user</role-name>
    </auth-constraint>
```

```
      <user-data-constraint>
        <description/>
        <transport-guarantee>CONFIDENTIAL</transport-guarantee>
      </user-data-constraint>
    </security-constraint>
    <login-config>
      <auth-method>FORM</auth-method>
      <realm-name>file</realm-name>
      <form-login-config>
        <form-login-page>/login.jsf</form-login-page>
        <form-error-page>/loginerror.jsf</form-error-page>
      </form-login-config>
    </login-config>
</web-app>
```

When using form-based authentication, we simply use FORM as the value of the `<auth-method>` element in `web.xml`. When using this authentication method, we need to provide a login page and a login error page. We indicate the URLs for the login and login error pages as the values of the `<form-login-page>` and `<form-error-page>` elements, respectively. As we can see in the example, these elements must be nested inside the `<form-login-config>` element.

The markup for the login page for our application is shown as follows:

```
<?xml version='1.0' encoding='UTF-8' ?>
<!DOCTYPE html PUBLIC "-//W3C//DTD XHTML 1.0 Transitional//EN"
   "http://www.w3.org/TR/xhtml1/DTD/xhtml1-transitional.dtd">
<html xmlns="http://www.w3.org/1999/xhtml"
  xmlns:h="http://xmlns.jcp.org/jsf/html">
  <h:head>
    <title>Login</title>
  </h:head>
  <h:body>
    <p>Please enter your username and password to access the
      application
    </p>
    <form method="POST" action="j_security_check">
      <table cellpadding="0" cellspacing="0" border="0">
        <tr>
          <td align="right">Username: </td>
          <td>
            <input type="text" name="j_username"/>
          </td>
        </tr>
        <tr>
```

```
            <td align="right">Password: </td>
            <td>
              <input type="password" name="j_password"/>
            </td>
          </tr>
          <tr>
            <td></td>
            <td>
              <input type="submit" value="Login"/>
            </td>
          </tr>
        </table>
      </form>
    </h:body>
</html>
```

Please note that even though our login page is a JSF page, it uses a standard `<form>` tag as opposed to the JSF-specific `<h:form>` tag. The reason for this is that the form's action attribute value must be `j_security_check` and it is not possible to set this attribute in the JSF `<h:form>` tag. Similarly, the input fields in the form are standard HTML fields, as opposed to their JSF-specific counterparts.

The login page for an application using form-based authentication must contain a form whose method is POST and whose action is `j_security_check`. We don't need to implement the authentication code as it is supplied by the application server.

The form in the login page must contain a text field named `j_username`. This text field is meant to hold the username. Additionally, the form must contain a password field named `j_password`, meant for the password. Of course, the form must contain a submit button to submit the data to the server.

The only requirement for a login page is for it to have a form whose attributes match those in our example, and the `j_username` and `j_password` input fields as described in the preceding paragraph.

There are no special requirements for the error page. Of course, it should show an error message telling the user that login was unsuccessful. However, it can contain anything we wish. The error page for our application simply tells the user that there was an error logging in and links back to the login page to give the user a chance to log back in.

In addition to a login page and a login error page, we added a CDI named bean to our application. This allows us to implement the logout functionality, something that wasn't possible when we were using basic authentication. The code to implement the logout functionality is as follows:

```
package net.ensode.glassfishbook;

import javax.enterprise.context.RequestScoped;
import javax.faces.context.ExternalContext;
import javax.faces.context.FacesContext;
import javax.inject.Named;
import javax.servlet.http.HttpSession;

@Named
@RequestScoped
public class LogoutManager {

  public String logout() {
    FacesContext facesContext = FacesContext.getCurrentInstance();
    ExternalContext externalContext =
      facesContext.getExternalContext();
    HttpSession session = (HttpSession)
      externalContext.getSession(true);

    session.invalidate();

    return "index?faces-redirect=true";
  }
}
```

The first few lines of the logout method are meant to get a reference to the `HttpSession` object. Once we obtain this object, all we need to do is invalidate the session by invoking its `invalidate()` method. In our code, we redirect the response to the index page. Since the session is invalid at this point, the security mechanism automatically directs the user to the login page.

We are now ready to test form-based authentication. After building our application, deploying it, and pointing the browser to any of its pages, we should see our login page rendered in the browser as shown in the following screenshot:

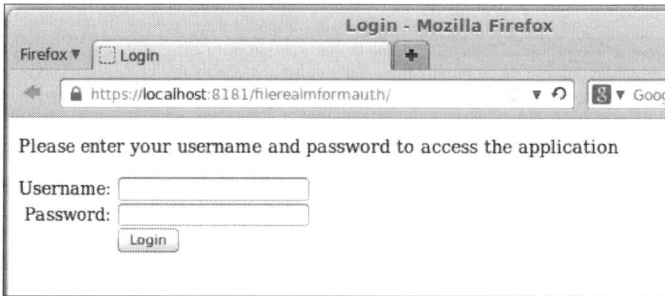

If we submit invalid credentials, we are automatically forwarded to the login error page, as shown in the following screenshot:

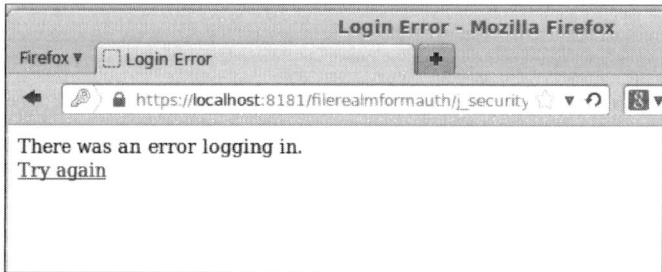

We can click on the **Try again** link to try again. After entering the valid credentials, we are allowed into the application. The following screenshot shows the screen after a successful login:

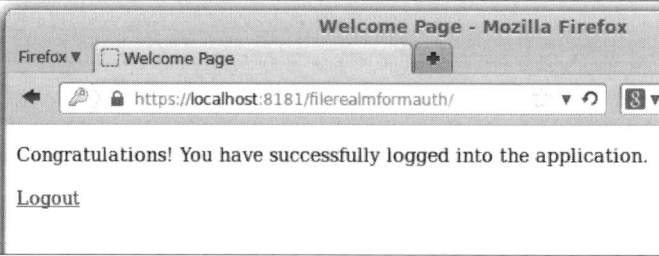

As we can see, we added a **Logout** link to the page. This link directs the user to the `logout()` method of our CDI named bean, which, as mentioned before, simply invalidates the session. From the user's point of view, this link will simply log them out and direct them to the login screen.

The certificate realm

The certificate realm uses client-side certificates for authentication. Just like server-side certificates, client-side certificates are typically obtained from a certificate authority such as Verisign or Thawte. These certificate authorities verify that the certificate really belongs to who it says it belongs to.

Obtaining a certificate from a certificate authority costs money and takes some time. It might not be practical to obtain a certificate from one of the certificate authorities when we are developing and/or testing our application. Fortunately, we can create self-signed certificates for testing purposes.

Creating self-signed certificates

We can create self-signed certificates with little effort with the **keytool** utility included with the **Java Development Kit (JDK)**.

> We will only briefly cover some of the keytool utility features, specifically the features that are necessary to create and import self-signed certificates into GlassFish and the browser. To learn more about the keytool utility, refer to http://docs.oracle.com/javase/7/docs/technotes/tools/solaris/keytool.html.

You can generate a self-signed certificate by typing in the following command in the command line:

```
keytool -genkey -v -alias selfsignedkey -keyalg RSA -storetype PKCS12
-keystore client_keystore.p12 -storepass wonttellyou -keypass wonttellyou
```

This command assumes that the keytool utility is in the system path. This tool can be found in the `bin` directory under the directory where JDK is installed.

Substitute the values for the `-storepass` and `-keypass` parameters with your own password. Both of these passwords must be the same in order to successfully use the certificate to authenticate the client. You may choose any value for the `-alias` parameter. You may also choose any value for the `-keystore` parameter. However, the value must end in `.p12`, since this command generates a file that needs to be imported into the web browser, and it won't be recognized unless it has the `.p12` extension.

After entering the above command from the command line, keytool will prompt for some information as follows:

```
What is your first and last name?
  [Unknown]:  David Heffelfinger
What is the name of your organizational unit?
  [Unknown]:  Book Writing Division
What is the name of your organization?
  [Unknown]:  Ensode Technology, LLC
What is the name of your City or Locality?
  [Unknown]:  Fairfax
What is the name of your State or Province?
  [Unknown]:  Virginia
What is the two-letter country code for this unit?
  [Unknown]:  US
Is CN=David Heffelfinger, OU=Book Writing Division, O="Ensode Technology, LLC", L=Fairfax, ST=Virginia, C=US correct?
  [no]:  y
```

After entering the data for each prompt, keytool will generate the certificate. It will be stored in the current directory, and the name of the file will be the value we used for the `-keystore` parameter (`client_keystore.p12` in the example).

To be able to use this certificate to authenticate ourselves, we need to import it into the browser. The procedure, although similar, varies from browser to browser. In Firefox, this can be accomplished by going to the **Preferences** menu, clicking on the **Advanced** icon at the top of the pop-up window that appears, and then clicking on the **Certificates** tab as shown in the following screenshot:

Chapter 9

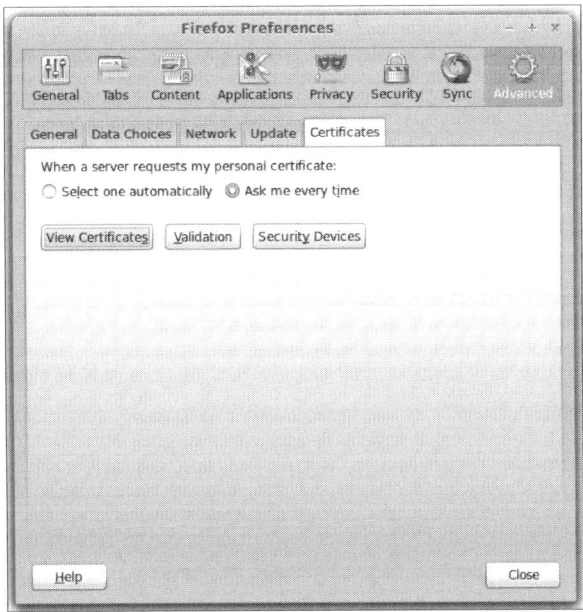

We then need to navigate to **View Certificates** | **Your Certificates** | **Import** on the window that appears. Then navigate and select our certificate from the directory in which it was created. At this point, Firefox will ask us for the password used to encrypt the certificate; in our example, we used `wonttellyou` as the password. After entering the password, we should see a pop-up window confirming that our certificate was successfully imported. We should then see it in the list of certificates, as shown in the following screenshot:

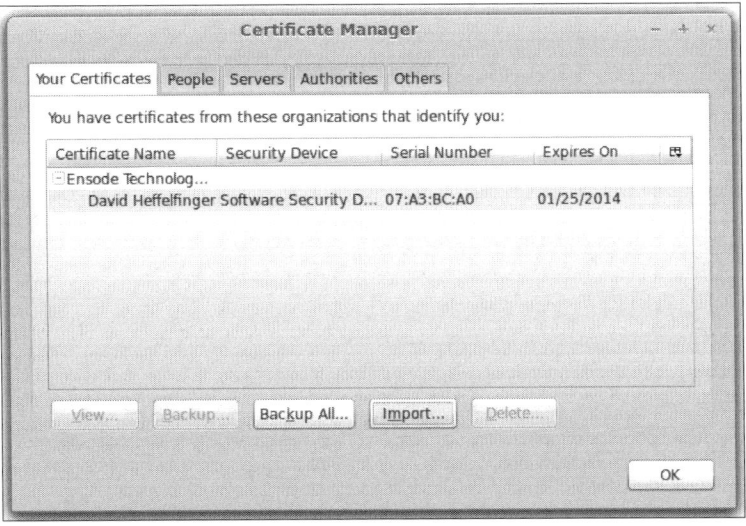

We have now added our certificate to Firefox so that it can be used to authenticate us. If you are using another browser, the procedure will be similar. Consult your browser's documentation for details.

The certificate we created in the previous step needs to be exported into a format that GlassFish can understand. We can accomplish this by running the following command:

```
keytool -export -alias selfsignedkey -keystore client_keystore.p12
-storetype PKCS12 -storepass wonttellyou -rfc -file selfsigned.cer
```

The value for the `-alias`, `-keystore`, and `-storepass` parameters must match the values used in the previous command. You may choose any value for the `-file` parameter, but it is recommended for the value to end in the `.cer` extension.

Since our certificate was not issued by a certificate authority, GlassFish by default will not recognize it as a valid certificate. GlassFish knows what certificates to trust based on the certificate authority that created them. This is implemented through the storing of certificates for these various authorities in a keystore named `cacerts.jks`. This keystore can be found at `[glassfish installation directory]/glassfish/domains/domain1/config/cacerts.jks`.

In order for GlassFish to accept our certificate, we need to import it into the `cacerts` keystore. This can be accomplished by issuing the following command from the command line:

```
keytool -import -file selfsigned.cer -keystore [glassfish installation
directory]/glassfish/domains/domain1/config/cacerts.jks -keypass changeit
-storepass changeit
```

At this point, keytool will display the following certificate information in the command line and ask us if we want to trust it:

```
Owner: CN=David Heffelfinger, OU=Book Writing Division, O="Ensode
Technology, LLC", L=Fairfax, ST=Virginia, C=US

Issuer: CN=David Heffelfinger, OU=Book Writing Division, O="Ensode
Technology, LLC", L=Fairfax, ST=Virginia, C=US

Serial number: 7a3bca0

Valid from: Sun Oct 27 17:00:18 EDT 2013 until: Sat Jan 25 16:00:18 EST
2014
```

```
Certificate fingerprints:

    MD5:    46:EA:41:ED:12:8A:EC:CE:8C:BE:F2:49:D5:71:00:ED

    SHA1:   32:C2:D4:20:87:22:95:25:5D:B0:AC:35:43:0D:60:35:94:27:44:58

    SHA256: 8C:2E:56:F4:98:45:AC:46:FD:20:27:38:D2:7D:BF:D8:2D:56:D3:91:B7
:78:AA:ED:FA:93:30:27:77:7F:F9:03

    Signature algorithm name: SHA256withRSA

    Version: 3

Extensions:

#1: ObjectId: 2.5.29.14 Criticality=false

SubjectKeyIdentifier [

KeyIdentifier [

0000: E8 75 1D 12 2F 18 D0 4B   E5 84 C4 79 B6 C0 98 80   .u../..K...y....

0010: 33 84 E7 C0                                         3...

]

]


Trust this certificate? [no]:  y

Certificate was added to keystore
```

Once we add the certificate to the `cacerts.jks` keystore, we need to restart the domain for the change to take effect.

What we are effectively doing here is adding ourselves as a certificate authority that GlassFish will trust. This, of course, should not be done in a production system.

Securing Java EE Applications

The value for the `-file` parameter must match the value we used for this same parameter when we exported the certificate.

>
> Note that `changeit` is the default password for the `-keypass` and `-storepass` parameters for the `cacerts.jks` keystore. This value can be changed by issuing the following command:
>
> `[glassfish installation directory]/glassfish/bin/asadmin change-master-password --savemasterpassword=true`
>
> This command will prompt for the existing as well as the new master password. The `-savemasterpassword=true` parameter is optional; it saves the master password into a file called `master-password` in the root directory of the domain. If we don't use this parameter when changing the master password, then we will need to enter the master password every time we want to start the domain.

Now that we have created a self-signed certificate, imported it into our browser, and established ourselves as a certificate authority that GlassFish will trust, we are ready to develop an application that will use client-side certificates for authentication.

Configuring applications to use the certificate realm

Since we are taking advantage of Java EE security features, we don't need to modify any code in order to use the security realm. All we need to do is modify the application's configuration on its deployment descriptors, `web.xml` and `glassfish-web.xml`, as follows:

```xml
<?xml version="1.0" encoding="UTF-8"?>
<web-app xmlns="http://java.sun.com/xml/ns/javaee"
  xmlns:xsi="http://www.w3.org/2001/XMLSchema-instance"
  xsi:schemaLocation="http://java.sun.com/xml/ns/javaee
  http://java.sun.com/xml/ns/javaee/web-app_3_0.xsd"
  version="3.0">
  <security-constraint>
    <web-resource-collection>
      <web-resource-name>AllPages</web-resource-name>
      <url-pattern>/*</url-pattern>
    </web-resource-collection>
    <auth-constraint>
      <role-name>users</role-name>
    </auth-constraint>
    <user-data-constraint>
      <transport-guarantee>CONFIDENTIAL</transport-guarantee>
    </user-data-constraint>
  </security-constraint>
```

```xml
    <login-config>
      <auth-method>CLIENT-CERT</auth-method>
      <realm-name>certificate</realm-name>
    </login-config>
</web-app>
```

The main difference between this `web.xml` deployment descriptor and the one we saw in the previous section is the contents of the `<login-config>` element. In this case, we declared `CLIENT-CERT` as the authorization method and `certificate` as the realm to use to authenticate. This will have the effect of GlassFish asking the browser for a client certificate before allowing a user into the application.

When using client certificate authentication, the request must always be made via HTTPS. Therefore, it is a good idea to add the `<transport-guarantee>` element with a value of `CONFIDENTIAL` to the `web.xml` deployment descriptor. Recall from the previous section that this has the effect of forwarding any requests through the HTTP port to the HTTPS port. If we don't add this value to the `web.xml` deployment descriptor, any requests through the HTTP port will fail, since client certificate authentication cannot be done through the HTTP protocol.

Notice that we declared that only users with the role `user` can access any page in the system. We did this by adding the role `user` to the `<role-name>` element nested inside the `<auth-constraint>` element of the `<security-constraint>` element in the `web.xml` deployment descriptor. In order to allow access to authorized users, we need to add them to this role. This is done in the `glassfish-web.xml` deployment descriptor as follows:

```xml
<?xml version="1.0" encoding="UTF-8"?>
<!DOCTYPE glassfish-web-app PUBLIC "-//GlassFish.org//DTD
  GlassFish Application Server 3.1 Servlet 3.0//EN"
   "http://glassfish.org/dtds/glassfish-web-app_3_0-1.dtd">
<glassfish-web-app error-url="">
  <context-root>/certificaterealm</context-root>
  <security-role-mapping>
    <role-name>user</role-name>
    <principal-name>CN=David Heffelfinger, OU=Book Writing
      Division, O="Ensode Technology, LLC", L=Fairfax,
      ST=Virginia, C=US</principal-name>
  </security-role-mapping>
  <class-loader delegate="true"/>
</glassfish-web-app>
```

This assignment is done by mapping the principal user to a role in a `<security-role-mapping>` element in the `glassfish-web.xml` deployment descriptor; its `<role-name>` subelement must contain the role name, and the `<principal-name>` subelement must contain the username. This username is taken from the certificate.

If you are not sure of the name to use, it can be obtained from the certificate with the keytool utility as follows:

```
keytool -printcert -file selfsigned.cer
Owner: CN=David Heffelfinger, OU=Book Writing Division, O="Ensode Technology, LLC", L=Fairfax, ST=Virginia, C=US


Issuer: CN=David Heffelfinger, OU=Book Writing Division, O="Ensode Technology, LLC", L=Fairfax, ST=Virginia, C=US


Serial number: 7a3bca0


Valid from: Sun Oct 27 17:00:18 EDT 2013 until: Sat Jan 25 16:00:18 EST 2014


Certificate fingerprints:

    MD5:   46:EA:41:ED:12:8A:EC:CE:8C:BE:F2:49:D5:71:00:ED

    SHA1:  32:C2:D4:20:87:22:95:25:5D:B0:AC:35:43:0D:60:35:94:27:44:58

    SHA256: 8C:2E:56:F4:98:45:AC:46:FD:20:27:38:D2:7D:BF:D8:2D:56:D3:91:B7:78:AA:ED:FA:93:30:27:77:7F:F9:03

    Signature algorithm name: SHA256withRSA

    Version: 3


Extensions:


#1: ObjectId: 2.5.29.14 Criticality=false

SubjectKeyIdentifier [

KeyIdentifier [
```

```
0000: E8 75 1D 12 2F 18 D0 4B    E5 84 C4 79 B6 C0 98 80    .u../..K...y....

0010: 33 84 E7 C0                                            3...
```

]

]

The value to use as `<principal-name>` is the line after `Owner:`. Please note that the value of `<principal-name>` must be in the same line as its open and closing elements (`<principal-name>` and `</principal-name>`). If there are newline or carriage return characters before or after the value, they are interpreted as being part of the value and validation will fail.

Since our application has a single user and a single role, we are ready to deploy it. If we had more users, we would have to add additional `<security-role-mapping>` elements to our `glassfish-web.xml` deployment descriptor, at least one per user. If we had users that belong to more than one role, then we would add a `<security-role-mapping>` element for each role the user belongs to, using the `<principal-name>` value corresponding to the user's certificate for each one of them.

We are now ready to test our application. After we deploy it and point the browser to any page in the application, we should see a screen like the following (assuming the browser hasn't been configured to provide a default certificate any time a server requests one):

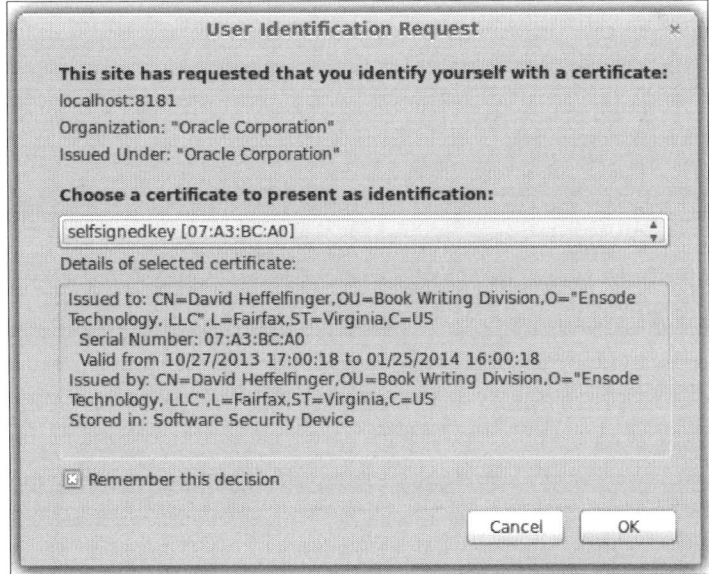

After clicking on the **OK** button, we are allowed to access the application, as shown in the following screenshot:

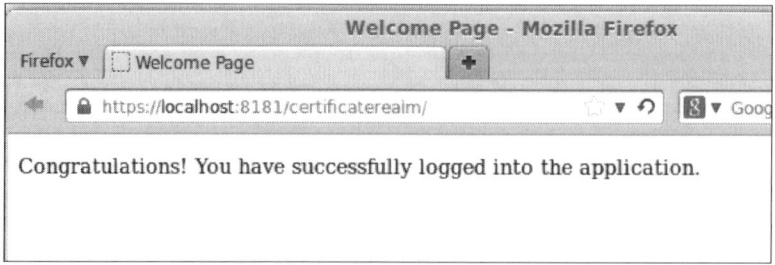

Before allowing access to the application, GlassFish checks the certificate authority that issued the certificate (since we self-signed the certificate, the owner of the certificate and the certificate authority are the same), checking against the list of trusted certificate authorities. Since we added ourselves as a trusted authority by importing our self-signed certificate into the `cacerts.jks` keystore, GlassFish recognizes the certificate authority as a valid one. It then gets the principal name from the certificate and compares it against entries in the application's `glassfish-web.xml` file. Since we added ourselves to this deployment descriptor and gave ourselves a valid role, we are allowed into the application.

Defining additional realms

In addition to the three preconfigured security realms we discussed in the previous section, we can create additional realms for application authentication. We can create realms that behave exactly like the file realm or admin-realm. We can also create realms that behave like the certificate realm. Additionally, we can create realms that use other methods of authentication. We can authenticate users against an LDAP database and against a relational database and, when GlassFish is installed on a Solaris server, use Solaris authentication within GlassFish. Also, if none of the predefined authentication mechanisms fit our needs, we can implement our own.

Defining additional file realms

In the administration console, expand the **Configurations** node, followed by the **server-config** node, and then the **Security** node. Click on the **Realms** node and then on the **New...** button on the resulting page in the main area of the web console.

We should now see a screen like the following:

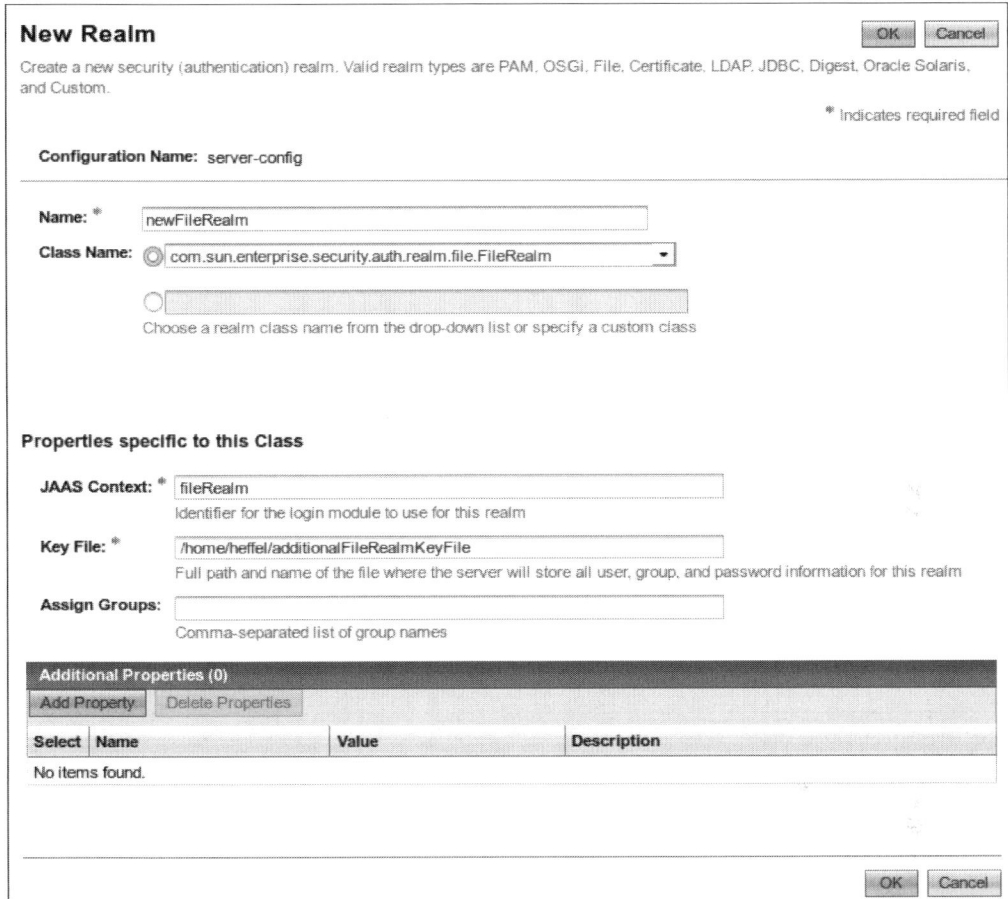

All we need to do to create an additional realm is enter a unique name for it in the **Name** field, pick `com.sun.enterprise.security.auth.realm.file.FileRealm` for the **Class Name** field, and enter a value for the **JAAS Context** and **Key File** fields; the value for the **Key File** field must be the absolute path to a file where user information will be stored and, for the file realm, the value for the **JAAS Context** field must always be `fileRealm`.

After entering all of the required information, we can click on the **OK** button and our new realm will be created. We can then use it just like the predefined file realm. Applications wanting to authenticate against this new realm must use its name as the value of the `<realm-name>` element in the application's `web.xml` deployment descriptor.

Alternatively, a custom file realm can be added from the command line via the `asadmin` utility by executing the following command:

```
asadmin create-auth-realm --classname com.sun.enterprise.
security.auth.realm.file.FileRealm --property file=/home/heffel/
additionalFileRealmKeyFile:jaas-context=fileRealm newFileRealm
```

The `create-auth-realm` argument tells `asadmin` that we want to create a new security realm. The value of the `--classname` parameter corresponds to the security realm class name. Notice that it matches the value we selected above in the web console. The `--property` parameter allows us to pass properties and their values; the value of this parameter must be a colon (`:`) separated list of properties and their values. The last argument of this command is the name we wish to give our security realm.

> Although it is easier to set up security realms via the web console, doing it through the `asadmin` command-line utility has the advantage that it is easily scriptable, allowing us to save this command in a script and easily configure several GlassFish instances.

Defining additional certificate realms

To define an additional certificate realm, we simply need to enter its name in the **Name** field and pick `com.sun.enterprise.security.auth.realm.certificate.CertificateRealm` as the value of the `Class Name` field and then click on **OK** to create our new realm, as shown in the following screenshot:

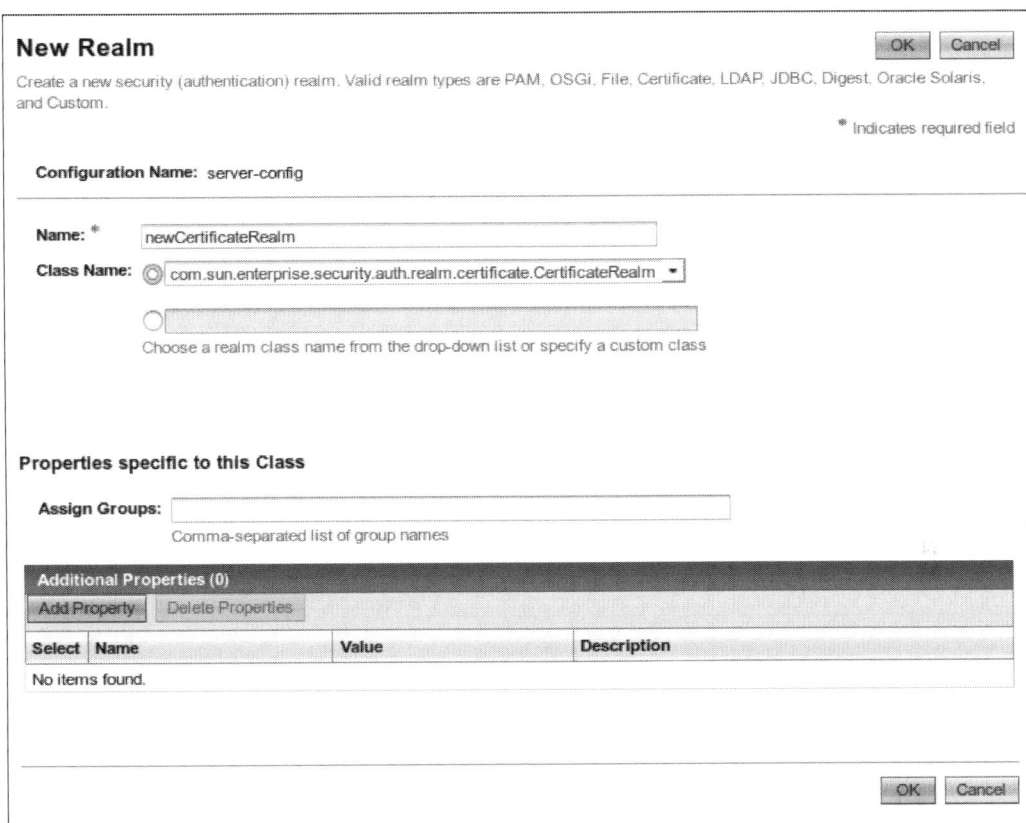

Applications wanting to use this new realm for authentication must use its name as the value of the `<realm-name>` element in the `web.xml` deployment descriptor and specify `CLIENT-CERT` as the value of its `<auth-method>` element. Of course, client certificates must be present and configured as explained in the *Configuring applications to use the certificate realm* section.

Alternatively, a custom certificate realm can be created on the command line via the `asadmin` utility by executing the following command:

`asadmin create-auth-realm --classname com.sun.enterprise.security.auth.realm.certificate.CertificateRealm newCertificateRealm`

In this case, we don't need to pass any properties as we had to when we created the custom file realm. Therefore, all we need to do is pass the appropriate value to the `--classname` parameter and specify the new security realm name.

Defining an LDAP realm

We can easily set up a realm to authenticate against an **LDAP (Lightweight Directory Access Protocol)** database. In order to do this, we need to, in addition to the obvious step of entering a name for the realm, select `com.sun.enterprise.security.auth.realm.ldap.LDAPRealm` as the **Class Name** value for a new realm. We then need to enter a URL for the directory server in the **Directory** field and the base distinguished name to be used to search user data as the value of the **Base DN** field, as shown in the following screenshot:

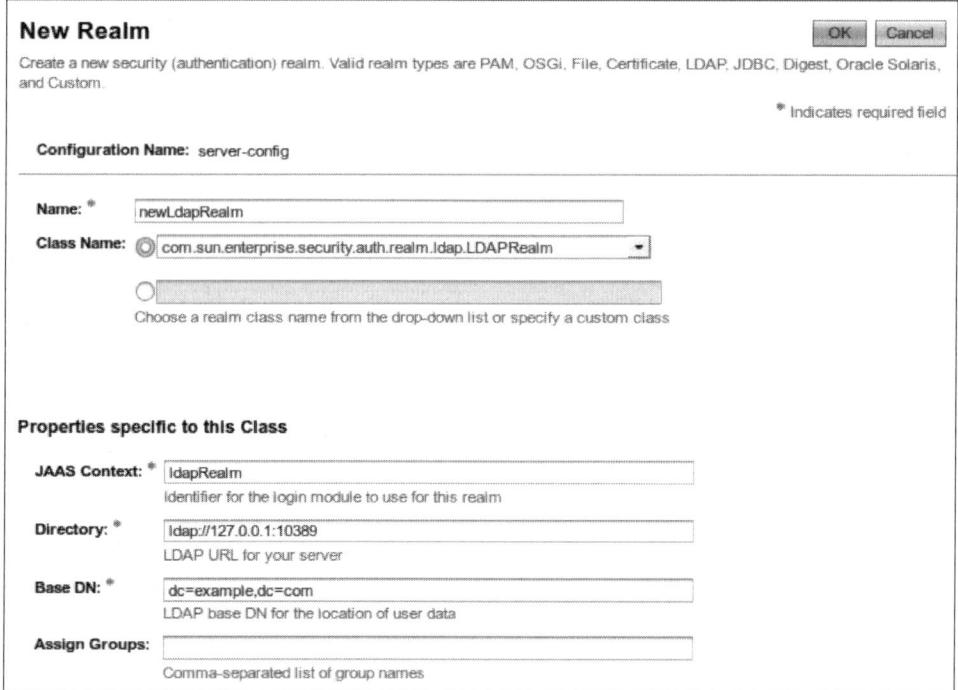

> At the time of this writing, GlassFish had a bug that prevents LDAP realms from being added successfully from the web admin console. In this section, we explain what should happen, not what actually happens. Hopefully, by the time you read this, the issue will be fixed.
>
> Adding an LDAP realm from the command line, as explained later in this section, works properly though.

After creating an LDAP realm, applications can use it to authenticate against the LDAP database. The name of the realm needs to be used as the value of the `<realm-name>` element in the application's `web.xml` deployment descriptor. The value of the `<auth-method>` element must be either `BASIC` or `FORM`.

Users and roles in the LDAP database can be mapped to groups in the application's `glassfish-web.xml` deployment descriptor using the `<principal-name>`, `<role-name>`, and `<group-name>` elements as discussed earlier in this chapter.

To create an LDAP realm from the command line, we need to use the following syntax:

```
asadmin create-auth-realm --classname com.sun.enterprise.security.auth.realm.ldap.LDAPRealm --property "jaas-context=ldapRealm:directory=ldap\://127.0.0.1\:1389:base-dn=dc\=ensode,dc\=com" newLdapRealm
```

Note that, in this case, the value of the `--property` parameter is between quotes. This is necessary because we need to escape some of the characters in its value, such as all the colons and equal signs. To escape these special characters, we simply prefix them with a backslash (\).

Defining a Solaris realm

When GlassFish is installed on a Solaris server, it can take advantage of the operating system authentication mechanism via a Solaris Realm. There are no special properties for this type of realm; all we need to do to create one is pick a name for it and select `com.sun.enterprise.security.auth.realm.solaris.SolarisRealm` as the value of the **Class Name** field and enter `solarisRealm` as the value of the **JAAS Context** field, as shown in the following screenshot:

The **JAAS Context** field must be set to `solarisRealm`. After adding the realm, applications can authenticate against it using basic or form-based authentication. Operating system groups and users can be mapped to application roles defined in the application's `web.xml` deployment descriptor via the `<principal-name>`, `<role-name>`, and `<group-name>` elements in its `glassfish-web.xml` deployment descriptor.

A Solaris realm can be created from the command line by executing the following command:

```
asadmin create-auth-realm --classname com.sun.enterprise.security.
auth.realm.solaris.SolarisRealm --property jaas-context=solarisRealm
newSolarisRealm
```

Defining a JDBC realm

Another type of realm we can create is a JDBC realm. This type of realm uses user information stored in database tables for user authentication.

In order to illustrate how to authenticate against a JDBC realm, we need to create a database to hold user information. The following entity-relationship diagram shows an example database we could use to authenticate against a JDBC realm:

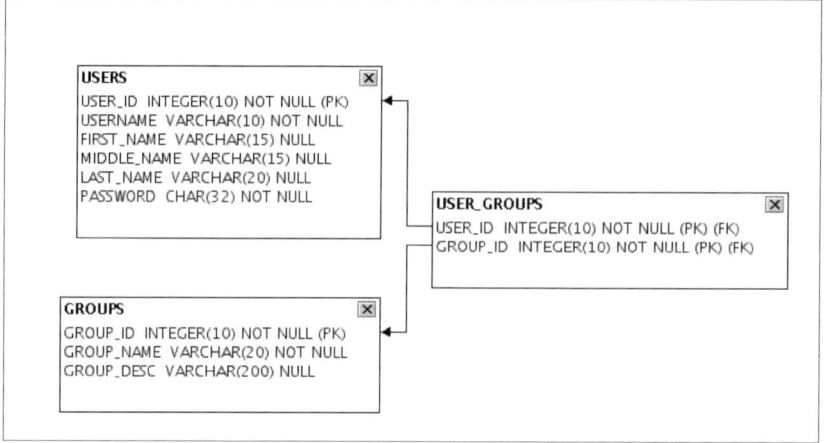

Our database consists of three tables. A `USERS` table holding user information and a `GROUPS` table holding group information are two of them. Since there is a many-to-many relationship between `USERS` and `GROUPS`, we need to add a join table to preserve data normalization. The name of this third table is `USER_GROUPS`.

Notice that the `PASSWORD` column of the `USERS` table is of type `CHAR(32)`. The reason we chose this type instead of `VARCHAR` is that we will be hashing passwords using the MD5 hashing algorithm, and these hashes are always 32 characters.

Passwords can be easily encrypted in the expected format by using the
`java.security.MessageDigest` class included with the JDK. The following
example code will accept a clear-text password and create an MD5 hash out of it:

```
package net.ensode.glassfishbook;

import java.security.MessageDigest;
import java.security.NoSuchAlgorithmException;

public class EncryptPassword {

  public static String encryptPassword(String password)
    throws NoSuchAlgorithmException {
    MessageDigest messageDigest =
      MessageDigest.getInstance("MD5");
    byte[] bs;

    messageDigest.reset();
    bs = messageDigest.digest(password.getBytes());

    StringBuilder stringBuilder = new StringBuilder();

    //hex encode the digest
    for (int i = 0; i < bs.length; i++) {
      String hexVal = Integer.toHexString(0xFF & bs[i]);
      if (hexVal.length() == 1) {
        stringBuilder.append("0");
      }
      stringBuilder.append(hexVal);
    }

    return stringBuilder.toString();
  }

  public static void main(String[] args) {
    String encryptedPassword = null;

    try {

      if (args.length == 0) {
        System.err.println("Usage: java "+
          "net.ensode.glassfishbook.EncryptPassword "+
          "cleartext");
      } else {
```

```
          encryptedPassword = encryptPassword(args[0]);
          System.out.println(encryptedPassword);
        }
      } catch (NoSuchAlgorithmException e) {
        e.printStackTrace();
      }
    }
  }
```

The main functionality of the preceding class is defined in its `encryptPassword()` method. It basically accepts a clear-text string and digests it using the MD5 algorithm using the `digest()` method of an instance of `java.security.MessageDigest`. It then encodes the digest as a series of hexadecimal numbers. This encoding is necessary because GlassFish by default expects MD5-digested passwords to be hex encoded.

When using JDBC realms, application users and groups are not added to the realm via the GlassFish console. Instead, they are added by inserting data into the appropriate tables.

Once we have the database that will hold user credentials in place, we are ready to create a new JDBC realm.

We can create a JDBC realm by entering its name in the **Name** field of the **New Realm** form in the GlassFish web console and then selecting `com.sun.enterprise.security.auth.realm.jdbc.JDBCRealm` as the value of the **Class Name** field, as shown in the following screenshot:

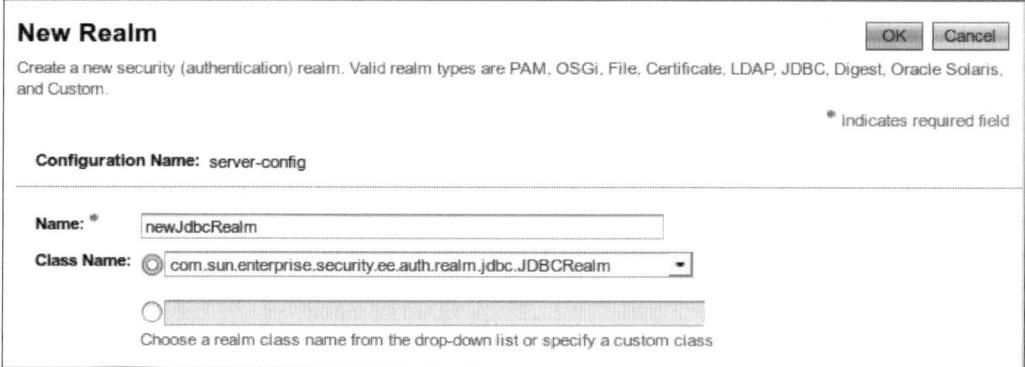

There are a number of other properties we need to set for our new JDBC realm, as shown in the following screenshot:

Properties specific to this Class

JAAS Context: *	jdbcRealm	Identifier for the login module to use for this realm
JNDI: *	jdbc/userauth	JNDI name of the JDBC resource used by this realm
User Table: *	V_USER_ROLE	Name of the database table that contains the list of authorized users for this realm
User Name Column: *	USERNAME	Name of the column in the user table that contains the list of user names
Password Column: *	PASSWORD	Name of the column in the user table that contains the user passwords
Group Table: *	V_USER_ROLE	Name of the database table that contains the list of groups for this realm
Group Table User Name Column:	USERNAME	Name of the column in the user group table that contains the list of groups for this realm
Group Name Column: *	GROUP_NAME	Name of the column in the group table that contains the list of group names
Password Encryption Algorithm: *	MD5	This denotes the algorithm for encrypting the passwords in the database. It is a security risk to leave this field empty.
Assign Groups:		Comma-separated list of group names
Database User:		Specify the database user name in the realm instead of the JDBC connection pool
Database Password:		Specify the database password in the realm instead of the JDBC connection pool
Digest Algorithm:	MD5	Digest algorithm (default is SHA-256); note that the default was MD5 in GlassFish versions prior to 3.1
Encoding:		Encoding (allowed values are Hex and Base64)
Charset:		Character set for the digest algorithm

The **JAAS Context** field must be set to `jdbcRealm` for JDBC realms. The value of the **JNDI** property must be the JNDI name of the data source corresponding to the database that contains the realm's user and group data. The value of the **User Table** property must be the name of the table that contains username and password information.

> Notice that, in the preceding screenshot, we used V_USER_ROLE as the value for the **User Table** property. V_USER_ROLE is a database view that contains both user and group information. We didn't use the USERS table directly because GlassFish assumes that both the user table and the group table contain a column containing the username. Doing this results in having duplicate data. To avoid this situation, we created a view that we could use as the value of both the **User Table** and **Group Table** (to be discussed shortly) properties.

The **User Name Column** property must contain the column in the **User Table** property that contains the usernames. The **Password Column** property value must be the name of the column in the **User Table** property that contains the user's password. The value of the **Group Table** property must be the name of the table containing user groups. The **Group Name Column** property must contain the name of the column in the **Group Table** property containing user group names.

All other properties are optional and, in most cases, left blank. Of special interest is the **Digest Algorithm** property. This property allows us to specify the message digest algorithm to use to hash the user's password. Valid values for this property include all algorithms supported by the JDK. These algorithms are MD2, MD5, SHA-1, SHA-256, SHA-384, and SHA-512. Additionally, if we wish to store user passwords in clear text, we can do so by using the value none for this property.

>  MD2, MD5, and SHA-1 are not very secure, and in most cases should not be used.

Once we have defined our JDBC realm, we need to configure our application via its web.xml and glassfish-web.xml deployment descriptors. Configuring an application to rely on a JDBC realm for authorization and authentication is done just like when using any other type of realm.

In addition to declaring that we will rely on the JDBC realm for authentication and authorization, just like with other types of realms, we need to map the roles defined in the web.xml deployment descriptor to security group names. This is accomplished in the glassfish-web.xml deployment descriptor.

Chapter 9

A JDBC realm can be created from the command line by executing the following command:

```
asadmin create-auth-realm --classname com.sun.enterprise.security.
ee.auth.realm.jdbc.JDBCRealm
--property jaas-context=jdbcRealm:datasource-jndi=jdbc/
UserAuthPool:user-table=V_USER_ROLE:user-name-column=USERNAME:password-
column=PASSWORD:group-table=V_USER_ROLE:group-name-column=GROUP_NAME
newJdbcRealm
```

Defining custom realms

Although the predefined realm types should cover the vast majority of cases, we can create custom realm types if the provided ones don't meet our needs. Doing so involves coding custom `Realm` and `LoginModule` classes. Let's first discuss the custom `Realm` class as follows:

```java
package net.ensode.glassfishbook;

import java.util.Enumeration;
import java.util.Vector;

import com.sun.enterprise.security.auth.realm.IASRealm;
import com.sun.enterprise.security.auth.realm.
  InvalidOperationException;
import com.sun.enterprise.security.auth.realm.NoSuchUserException;

public class SimpleRealm extends IASRealm {

  @Override
  public Enumeration getGroupNames(String userName)
    throws InvalidOperationException, NoSuchUserException {
    Vector vector = new Vector();

    vector.add("appuser");
    vector.add("appadmin");

    return vector.elements();
  }

  @Override
  public String getAuthType() {
    return "simple";
  }
```

```
    @Override
    public String getJAASContext() {
      return "simpleRealm";
    }

    public boolean loginUser(String userName, String password) {
      boolean loginSuccessful = false;

      if ("glassfish".equals(userName) && "secret".equals(
        password)) {
        loginSuccessful = true;
      }

      return loginSuccessful;
    }
}
```

Our custom `Realm` class must extend `com.sun.enterprise.security.auth.realm.IASRealm`. This class can be found inside the `security.jar` file, and therefore this JAR file must be added to the CLASSPATH before our `Realm` class can be successfully compiled.

> The `security.jar` file can be found under [glassfish installation directory]/glassfish/modules.
>
> When using Maven or Ivy dependency management, this JAR file can be found in the following repository:
>
> `http://download.java.net/maven/glassfish`
>
> The group ID is `org.glassfish.security` and the artifact ID is `security`.

Our class must override a method called `getGroupNames()`. This method takes a single string as a parameter and returns an `Enumeration` parameter. The `String` parameter is for the username of the user that is attempting to log in to the realm. The `Enumeration` parameter must contain a collection of strings indicating what groups the user belongs to. In our simple example, we simply hardcoded the groups. In a real application, these groups would be obtained from some kind of persistent storage (database, file, and so on).

The next method our `Realm` class must override is the `getAuthType()` method. This method must return a `String` containing a description of the type of authentication used by this realm.

The `getGroupNames()` and `getAuthType()` methods are declared as abstract in the `IASRealm` (parent) class. Although the `getJAASContext()` method is not abstract, we should nevertheless override it, since the value it returns is used to determine the type of authentication to use from the application server's `login.conf` file. The return value of this method is used to map the realm to the corresponding login module.

Finally, our `Realm` class must contain a method to authenticate the user. We are free to call it anything we want. Additionally, we can use as many parameters of any type as we wish. Our simple example has the values for a single username and password hardcoded. Again, a real application would obtain valid credentials from some kind of persistent storage. This method is meant to be called from the corresponding login module class as follows:

```java
package net.ensode.glassfishbook;

import java.util.Enumeration;

import javax.security.auth.login.LoginException;

import com.sun.appserv.security.AppservPasswordLoginModule;
import com.sun.enterprise.security.auth.realm
  .InvalidOperationException;
import com.sun.enterprise.security.auth.realm.NoSuchUserException;

public class SimpleLoginModule extends AppservPasswordLoginModule {

  @Override
  protected void authenticateUser() throws LoginException {
    Enumeration userGroupsEnum = null;
    String[] userGroupsArray = null;
    SimpleRealm simpleRealm;

    if (!(_currentRealm instanceof SimpleRealm)) {
      throw new LoginException();
    } else {
      simpleRealm = (SimpleRealm) _currentRealm;
    }

    if (simpleRealm.loginUser(_username, _password)) {
      try {
        userGroupsEnum = simpleRealm.getGroupNames(_username);
      } catch (InvalidOperationException e) {
        throw new LoginException(e.getMessage());
      } catch (NoSuchUserException e) {
```

```
            throw new LoginException(e.getMessage());
          }

          userGroupsArray = new String[2];
          int i = 0;

          while (userGroupsEnum.hasMoreElements()) {
            userGroupsArray[i++] = ((String)
              userGroupsEnum.nextElement());
          }
        } else {
          throw new LoginException();
        }
        commitUserAuthentication(userGroupsArray);
      }
    }
```

Our login module class must extend com.sun.appserv.security.AppservPasswordLoginModule. This class is also inside the security.jar file. Our login module class only needs to override a single method, namely authenticateUser(). This method takes no parameters and must throw a LoginException if user authentication is unsuccessful. The _currentRealm variable is defined in the parent class and is of type com.sun.enterprise.security.auth.realm. The Realm class is the parent of all Realm classes. This variable is initialized before the authenticateUser() method is executed. The LoginModule class must verify that this class is of the expected type (SimpleRealm in our example). If it is not, a LoginException must be thrown.

Two other variables that are defined in the parent class and initialized before the authenticateUser() method is executed are _username and _password. These variables contain the credentials the user entered in the login form (for form-based authentication) or pop-up window (for basic authentication). Our example simply passes these values to the Realm class so that it can verify the user credentials.

The authenticateUser() method must call the parent class's commitUserAuthentication() method upon successful authentication. This method takes an array of string objects containing the group the user belongs to. Our example simply invokes the getGroupNames() method defined in the Realm class and adds the elements of the Enumeration parameter it returns to an array; it then passes that array to commitUserAuthentication().

GlassFish is unaware of the existence of our custom realm and login module classes. We need to add these classes to GlassFish's CLASSPATH. The easiest way to do this is to copy the JAR file containing our custom realm and login module at [glassfish installation directory]/glassfish/domains/domain1/lib.

The last step we need to follow before we can authenticate applications against our custom realm is to add our new custom realm to the domain's `login.conf` file as follows:

```
fileRealm {
  com.sun.enterprise.security.auth.login.FileLoginModule required;
};

ldapRealm {
  com.sun.enterprise.security.auth.login.LDAPLoginModule required;
};

solarisRealm {
  com.sun.enterprise.security.auth.login.SolarisLoginModule
    required;
};

jdbcRealm {
  com.sun.enterprise.security.auth.login.JDBCLoginModule required;
};

jdbcDigestRealm {
  com.sun.enterprise.security.auth.login.JDBCDigestLoginModule
    required;
};

pamRealm {

  com.sun.enterprise.security.ee.auth.login.PamLoginModule
    required;

};

simpleRealm {
  net.ensode.glassfishbook.SimpleLoginModule required;
};
```

The value before the opening brace must match the return value of the `getJAASContext()` method defined in the `Realm` class. It is in this file that the `Realm` and `LoginModule` classes are linked to each other. The GlassFish domain needs to be restarted for this change to take effect.

Securing Java EE Applications

We are now ready to use our custom realm to authenticate users in our applications. We need to add a new realm of the type we created via GlassFish's admin console as shown in the following screenshot:

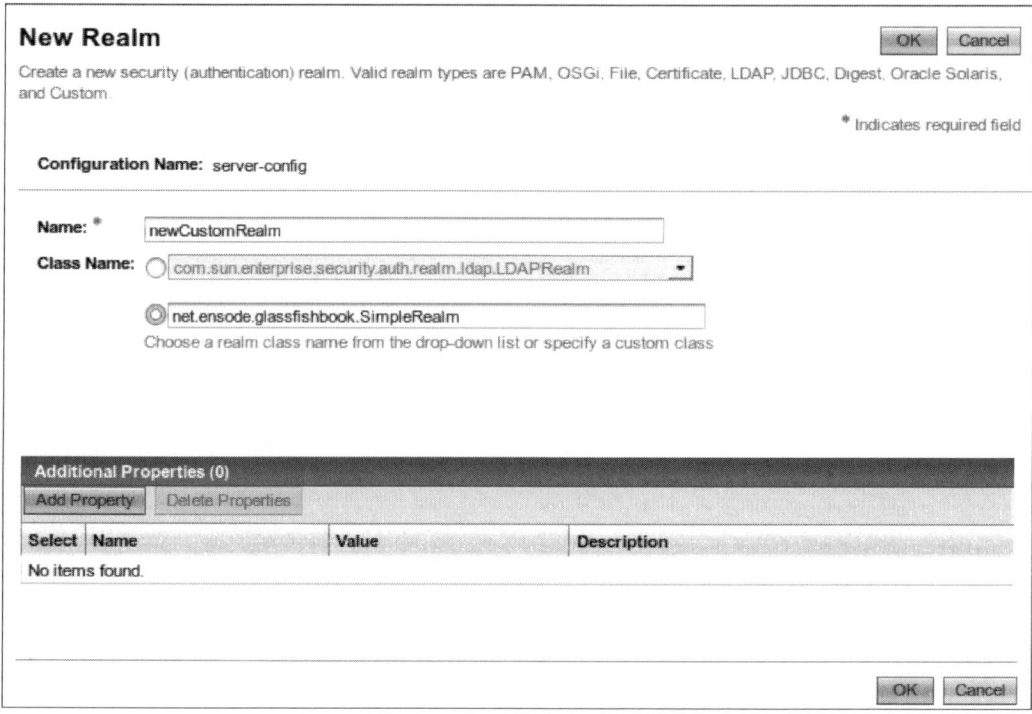

To create our realm, as usual, we need to give it a name. Instead of selecting a class name from the dropdown, we need to type it into the text field. Our custom realm didn't have any properties; therefore, we don't have to add any in this example. If it did, they would be added by clicking on the **Add Property** button and entering the property name and corresponding value. Our realm would then get the properties by overriding the `init()` method from its parent class. This method has the following signature:

```
protected void init(Properties arg0) throws BadRealmException,
    NoSuchRealmException
```

The instance of `java.util.Properties` it takes as a parameter would be prepopulated with the properties entered in the page shown in the screenshot (our custom realm doesn't have any properties, but for those that do, properties are entered the page shown in the screenshot).

Once we have added the pertinent information for our new custom realm, we can use it just like we use any of the predefined realms. Applications need to specify its name as the value of the `<realm-name>` element of the application's `web.xml` deployment descriptor. Nothing extraordinary needs to be done at the application level.

Just like with standard realms, custom realms can be added via the `asadmin` command-line utility, for example, for our custom realm, we would execute the following command:

```
asadmin create-auth-realm --classname net.ensode.glassfishbook.SimpleRealm newCustomRealm
```

Summary

In this chapter, we covered how to use GlassFish's default realms to authenticate our web applications. We covered the file realm, which stores user information in a flat file, and the certificate realm, which requires client-side certificates for user authentication.

We then covered how to create additional realms that behave just like the default realms by using the realm classes included with GlassFish.

We also covered how to use additional `Realm` classes included in GlassFish to create realms that authenticate against an LDAP database, against a relational database, and how to create realms that integrate with a Solaris server's authentication mechanism.

Finally, we covered how to create custom `Realm` classes for cases where the included ones don't fit our needs.

In the next chapter, we will cover SOAP web services with JAX-WS.

10
Web Services with JAX-WS

The Java EE specification includes the JAX-WS API as one of its technologies. JAX-WS is the standard way to develop **Simple Object Access Protocol (SOAP)** web services on the Java platform. It stands for **Java API for XML Web Services**. JAX-WS is a high-level API; invoking web services via JAX-WS is done via remote procedure calls. JAX-WS is a very natural API for Java developers.

Web services are application programming interfaces that can be invoked remotely. Web services can be invoked from clients written in any programming language.

Some of the topics we will cover include:

- Developing web services with the JAX-WS API
- Developing web service clients with the JAX-WS API
- Adding attachments to web service calls
- Exposing EJBs as web services
- Securing web services

Developing web services with the JAX-WS API

JAX-WS is a high-level API that simplifies development of SOAP-based web services. Developing a web service via JAX-WS consists of writing a class with public methods to be exposed as web services. The class needs to be decorated with the `@WebService` annotation. All public methods in the class are automatically exposed as web services, they can optionally be decorated with the `@WebMethod` annotation. The following example illustrates this process:

```
package net.ensode.glassfishbook;

import javax.jws.WebMethod;
```

```java
import javax.jws.WebService;

@WebService
public class Calculator {

    @WebMethod
    public int add(int first, int second) {
        return first + second;
    }

    @WebMethod
    public int subtract(int first, int second) {
        return first - second;
    }
}
```

The preceding class exposes its two methods as web services. The `add()` method simply adds the two `int` primitives it receives as parameters and returns the result. The `subtract()` method subtracts its two parameters and returns the result.

We indicate that the class implements a web service by decorating it with the `@WebService` annotation. Any methods that we would like exposed as web services can be decorated with the `@WebMethod` annotation; however, this isn't necessary, as all public methods are automatically exposed as web services.

To deploy our web service, we need to package it in a `.war` file. Before Java EE 6, all valid `.war` files were required to contain a `web.xml` deployment descriptor in their `WEB-INF` directory. As we have already covered in previous chapters, this deployment descriptor is optional when working with Java EE 6 (and later) and is not required to deploy a web service under this environment.

If we choose to add a `web.xml` deployment descriptor, nothing needs to be added to the `.war` file's `web.xml` in order to successfully deploy our web service. Simply having an empty `<web-app>` element in the deployment descriptor will be enough to successfully deploy our WAR file, as shown in the following code:

```xml
<?xml version="1.0" encoding="UTF-8"?>
<web-app xmlns="http://java.sun.com/xml/ns/javaee" version="2.5"
   xmlns:xsi="http://www.w3.org/2001/XMLSchema"
   xsi:schemaLocation="http://java.sun.com/xml/ns/javaee http://java.sun.com/xml/ns/javaee/web-app_2_5.xsd">
</web-app>
```

After compiling, packaging, and deploying the code, we can verify that it was successfully deployed by logging into the GlassFish admin web console and expanding the **Applications** node on the left-hand side. We should see our newly deployed web service listed under this node, as shown in the following screenshot:

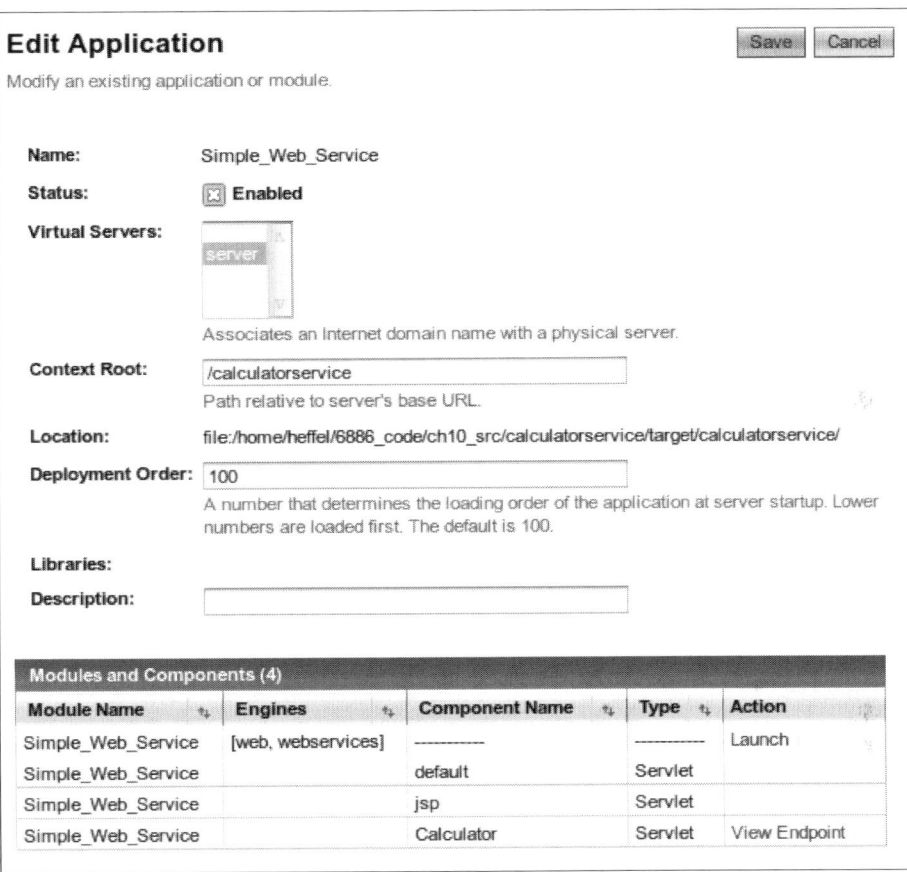

Web Services with JAX-WS

In the preceding screenshot, notice that there is a **View Endpoint** link at the bottom right of the page. Clicking on that button takes us to the **Web Service Endpoint Information** page shown in the following screenshot, which has some information about our web service:

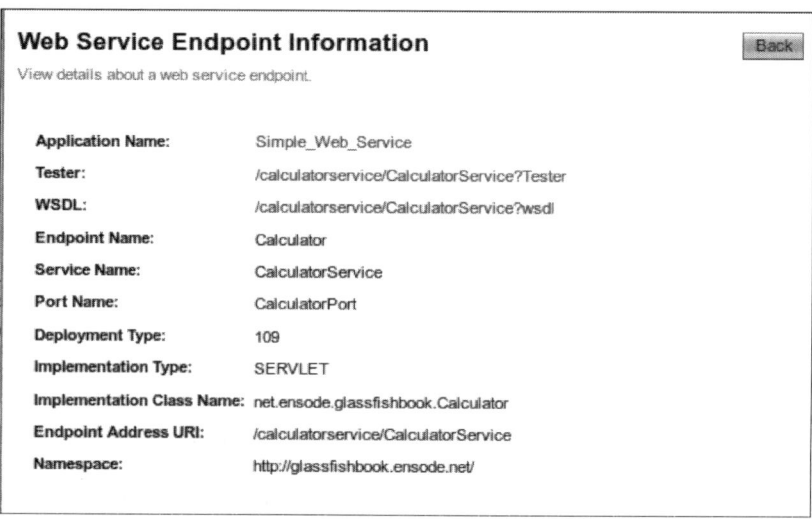

Notice that there is a link labeled **Tester:** in the preceding screenshot; clicking on this link takes us to an automatically generated page that allows us to test our web service. This page looks like the following screenshot:

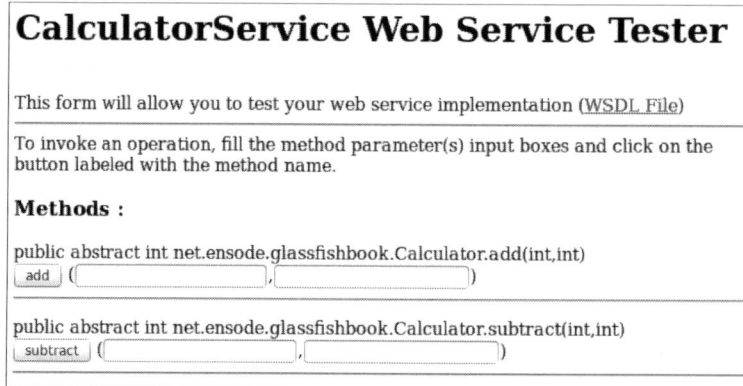

To test methods, we can simply enter some parameters in the text fields and click on the appropriate button. For example, entering the values 2 and 3 in the text fields corresponding to the add method and clicking on the **add** button would result in the following output:

add Method invocation

Method parameter(s)

Type	Value
int	2
int	3

Method returned

int : "**5**"

JAX-WS uses the SOAP protocol behind the scenes to exchange information between web service clients and servers. By scrolling down the preceding page, we can see the SOAP request and response generated by our test, as shown in the following screenshot:

SOAP Request

```
<?xml version="1.0" encoding="UTF-8"?><S:Envelope xmlns:S="http://schemas.xmlsoap.org/soap/envelope/" xml
    <SOAP-ENV:Header/>
    <S:Body>
        <ns2:add xmlns:ns2="http://glassfishbook.ensode.net/">
            <arg0>2</arg0>
            <arg1>3</arg1>
        </ns2:add>
    </S:Body>
</S:Envelope>
```

SOAP Response

```
<?xml version="1.0" encoding="UTF-8"?><S:Envelope xmlns:S="http://schemas.xmlsoap.org/soap/envelope/" xml
    <SOAP-ENV:Header/>
    <S:Body>
        <ns2:addResponse xmlns:ns2="http://glassfishbook.ensode.net/">
            <return>5</return>
        </ns2:addResponse>
    </S:Body>
</S:Envelope>
```

As application developers, we don't need to concern ourselves too much with these SOAP requests, since they are automatically taken care of by the JAX-WS API.

Web service clients need a **Web Services Definition Language (WSDL)** file in order to generate executable code that they can use to invoke the web service. WSDL is a standard XML-based interface definition language that defines the functionality of a web service.

WSDL files are typically placed in a web server and accessed by the client via its URL. When deploying web services developed using JAX-WS, a WSDL file is automatically generated for us. We can see it, along with its URL, by clicking on the **View WSDL** link on the **Web Service Endpoint Information** page, as shown in the following screenshot:

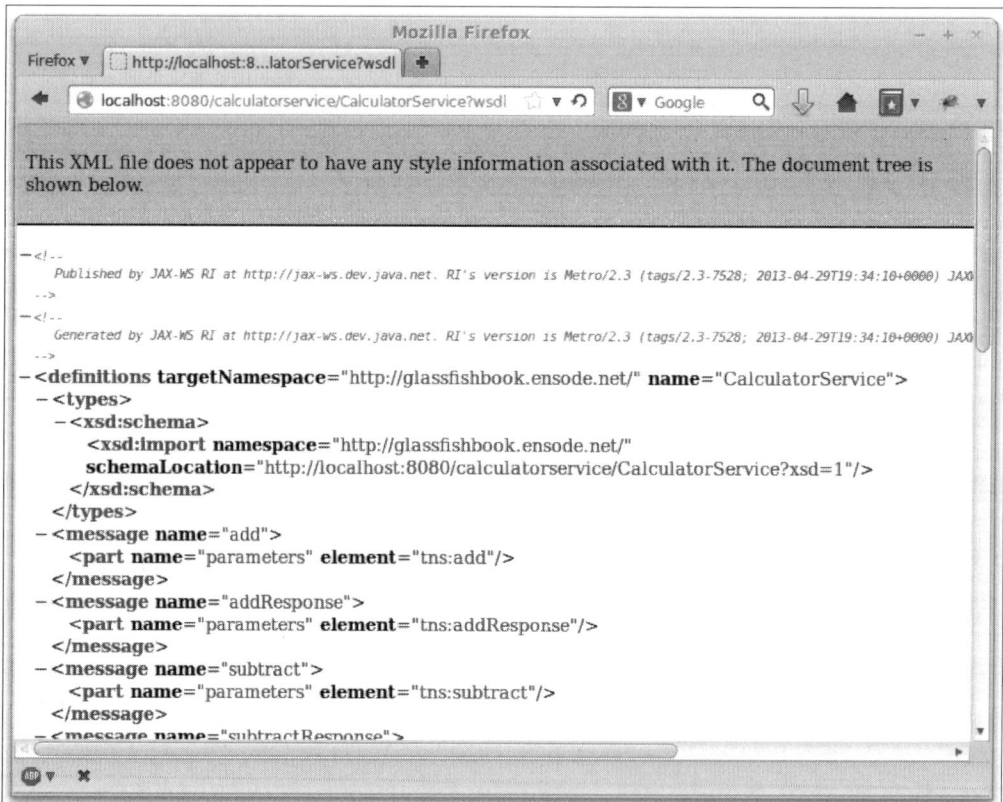

Notice the WSDL URL in the browser's location text field. We will need this URL when developing a client for our web service.

Developing a web service client

As mentioned earlier, executable code needs to be generated from the WSDL of a web service. A web service client will then invoke this executable code to access the web service.

GlassFish includes a utility to generate Java code from a WSDL. The name of the utility is wsimport. It can be found under [glassfish installation directory]/glassfish/bin/. The only required argument for wsimport is the URL of the WSDL, which corresponds to the web service, for example, wsimport http://localhost:8080/calculatorservice/CalculatorService?wsdl.

The command in the preceding screenshot will generate the following compiled Java classes that allow client applications to access our web service:

- Add.class
- AddResponse.class
- Calculator.class
- CalculatorService.class
- ObjectFactory.class
- package-info.class
- Subtract.class
- SubtractResponse.class

> **Keeping the Generated Source Code**
>
> By default, the source code for the generated class files is automatically deleted; it can be kept by passing the -keep parameter to wsimport.

These classes need to be added to the client's CLASSPATH in order for them to be accessible to the client's code.

In addition to the command-line tool, GlassFish includes a custom ANT task to generate code from a WSDL. The following ANT build script illustrates its usage:

```
<project name="calculatorserviceclient" default="wsimport"
  basedir=".">
  <target name="wsimport">
    <taskdef name="wsimport"
      classname="com.sun.tools.ws.ant.WsImport">
      <classpath path="/opt/glassfish-4.0/glassfish/
        modules/webservices-osgi.jar"/>
      <classpath path="/opt/glassfish-4.0/glassfish/modules/jaxb-
```

```
          osgi.jar"/>
        <classpath path="/opt/glassfish-
          4.0/glassfish/lib/javaee.jar"/>
      </taskdef>
       <wsimport wsdl=" HYPERLINK "http://localhost:8080/
          calculatorservice/CalculatorService?wsdl
          "http://localhost:8080/calculatorservice/
          CalculatorService?wsdl"xendorsed="true"/>
    </target>
  </project>
```

The preceding example is a very minimal ANT build script that only illustrates how to set up the custom `<wsimport>` ANT target. In reality, the ANT build script for the project would have several other targets for compilation, building a `.war` file, and so on.

Since `<wsimport>` is a custom ANT target and it is not standard, we need to add a `<taskdef>` element to our ANT build script. We need to set the `name` and `classname` attributes as illustrated in the example. Additionally, we need to add the following `.jar` files to the task's CLASSPATH via nested `<classpath>` elements:

- `webservices-osgi.jar`
- `jaxb-osgi.jar`
- `javaee.jar`

The `webservices-osgi.jar` and `jaxb-osgi.jar` files can be found under the `[glassfish installation directory]/glassfish/modules` directory. The `javaee.jar` file contains all the Java EE APIs and can be found under `[glassfish installation directory]/glassfish/lib`.

Once we set up the custom `<wsimport>` task via the `<taskdef>` element, we are ready to use it. We need to indicate the WSDL location via its `wsdl` attribute. Once this task executes, the Java code that is required to access the web service defined by the WSDL is generated.

JDK 1.6 comes bundled with JAX-WS 2.1. If we are using this version of the JDK, we need to tell ANT to use the JAX-WS 2.2 API included with GlassFish. This can be done easily by setting the `xendorsed` attribute of the custom `wsimport` ANT task to `true`.

Readers using Maven to build their projects can take advantage of Maven's `AntRun` plugin to execute the `wsimport` ANT target when building their code. This approach is illustrated in the following `pom.xml` file.

```
<?xml version="1.0" encoding="UTF-8" ?>
<project xmlns="http://maven.apache.org/POM/4.0.0"
```

```xml
xmlns:xsi="http://www.w3.org/2001/XMLSchema-instance"
xsi:schemaLocation="http://maven.apache.org/POM/4.0.0
http://maven.apache.org/maven-v4_0_0.xsd">
<modelVersion>4.0.0</modelVersion>
<groupId>net.ensode.glassfishbook</groupId>
<artifactId>calculatorserviceclient</artifactId>
<packaging>jar</packaging>
<name>Simple Web Service Client</name>
<version>1.0</version>
<url>http://maven.apache.org</url>
<repositories>
  <repository>
    <id>maven2-repository.dev.java.net</id>
    <name>Java.net Repository for Maven 2</name>
    <url>http://download.java.net/maven/2/</url>
  </repository>
</repositories>
<dependencies>
  <dependency>
    <groupId>javax</groupId>
    <artifactId>javaee-api</artifactId>
    <version>6.0</version>
    <scope>provided</scope>
  </dependency>
</dependencies>
<build>
  <finalName>calculatorserviceclient</finalName>
  <plugins>
    <plugin>
      <groupId>org.apache.maven.plugins</groupId>
      <artifactId>maven-antrun-plugin</artifactId>
      <executions>
        <execution>
          <phase>generate-sources</phase>
          <configuration>
            <tasks>
              <property name="target.dir" value="target" />
              <delete dir="${target.dir}/classes/com/
                testapp/ws/client" />
              <delete dir="${target.dir}/generated-
                sources/main/java/com/testapp/ws/client" />
              <mkdir dir="${target.dir}/classes" />
              <mkdir dir="${target.dir}/generated-
                sources/main/java" />
              <taskdef name="wsimport"
```

```xml
                        classname="com.sun.tools.ws.ant.WsImport">
                        <classpath path="/home/heffel/sges-
                          v3/glassfish/modules/webservices-osgi.jar" />
                        <classpath path="/home/heffel/sges-
                          v3/glassfish/modules/jaxb-osgi.jar" />
                        <classpath path="/home/heffel/sges-
                          v3/glassfish/lib/javaee.jar" />
                      </taskdef>
                      <wsimport wsdl="http://localhost:8080/
                        calculatorservice/CalculatorService?wsdl"
                        destdir="${target.dir}/classes" verbose="true"
                        keep="true" sourceDestDir="${target.dir}/
                        generated-sources/main/java" xendorsed="true" />
                    </tasks>
                    <sourceRoot>${project.build.directory}/generated-
                      sources/main/java</sourceRoot>
                  </configuration>
                  <goals>
                    <goal>run</goal>
                  </goals>
                </execution>
              </executions>
            </plugin>
            <plugin>
              <groupId>org.apache.maven.plugins</groupId>
              <artifactId>maven-jar-plugin</artifactId>
              <configuration>
                <archive>
                  <manifest>
                    <mainClass>net.ensode.glassfishbook
                      .CalculatorServiceClient</mainClass>
                    <addClasspath>true</addClasspath>
                  </manifest>
                </archive>
              </configuration>
            </plugin>
            <plugin>
              <groupId>org.apache.maven.plugins</groupId>
              <artifactId>maven-compiler-plugin</artifactId>
              <configuration>
                <source>1.6</source>
                <target>1.6</target>
              </configuration>
            </plugin>
          </plugins>
       </build>
</project>
```

Nested in the pom.xml file's <configuration> tag, corresponding to the AntRun plugin, we place any ANT tasks we need to execute. Unsurprisingly, the body of this tag in our example looks nearly identical to the ANT build file we just discussed.

Now that we know how to build our code with ANT or Maven, we can develop a simple client to access our web service, using the following code:

```
package net.ensode.glassfishbook;

import javax.xml.ws.WebServiceRef;

public class CalculatorServiceClient {

    @WebServiceRef(wsdlLocation = "http://localhost:8080/
calculatorservice/CalculatorService?wsdl")
    private static CalculatorService calculatorService;

    public void calculate() {
        Calculator calculator =
          calculatorService.getCalculatorPort();

        System.out.println("1 + 2 = "
                + calculator.add(1, 2));
        System.out.println("1 - 2 = "
                + calculator.subtract(1, 2));
    }

    public static void main(String[] args) {
        new CalculatorServiceClient().calculate();
    }
}
```

The @WebServiceRef annotation injects an instance of the web service into our client application. Its wsdlLocation attribute contains the URL of the WSDL that corresponds to the web service we are invoking.

Notice that the web service class is an instance of a class called CalculatorService. This class was created when we invoked the wsimport utility. The wsimport utility always generates a class whose name is the name of the class we implemented plus the Service suffix. We use this service class to obtain an instance of the web service class we developed. In our example, we do this by invoking the getCalculatorPort() method on the CalculatorService instance. In general, the method invoked to get an instance of our web service class follows the pattern getNamePort(), where Name is the name of the class we wrote to implement the web service. Once we get an instance of our web service class, we can simply invoke its methods like with any regular Java object.

> Strictly speaking, the getNamePort() method of the service class returns an instance of a class that implements an interface generated by wsimport. This interface is given the name of our web service class and declares all of the methods we declared to be web services. For all practical purposes, the object returned is equivalent to our web service class.

Recall from our previous discussion that in order for resource injection to work in a standalone client (that does not get deployed to GlassFish), we need to execute it through the appclient utility. Assuming we packaged our client in a .jar file called calculatorserviceclient.jar, the command to execute would be the following:

appclient -client calculatorserviceclient.jar

After entering the preceding command in the command line, we should see the following output of our client on the console:

```
1 + 2 = 3
1 - 2 = -1
```

In this example, we passed primitive types as parameters and return values. Of course, it is also possible to pass objects both as parameters and as return values. Unfortunately, not all standard Java classes or primitive types can be used as method parameters or return values when invoking web services. The reason for this is that behind the scenes, method parameters and return types get mapped to XML definitions, and not all types can be properly mapped.

Valid types that can be used in JAX-WS web service calls are listed as follows:

- java.awt.Image
- java.lang.Object
- Java.lang.String
- java.math.BigDecimal
- java.math.BigInteger
- java.net.URI
- java.util.Calendar
- java.util.Date
- java.util.UUID
- javax.activation.DataHandler
- javax.xml.datatype.Duration
- javax.xml.datatype.XMLGregorianCalendar
- javax.xml.namespace.QName
- javax.xml.transform.Source

Additionally, the following primitive types can be used:

- `boolean`
- `byte`
- `byte[]`
- `double`
- `float`
- `int`
- `long`
- `short`

We can also use our own custom classes as method parameters and/or return values for web service methods, but member variables of our classes must be one of the types listed in the preceding list.

Additionally, arrays can be used both as method parameters or return values, however, when executing `wsimport`, these arrays get converted to `List`s, generating a mismatch between the method signature in the web service and the method call invoked in the client. For this reason, it is preferred to use `List`s as method parameters and/or return values, since this is also valid and does not create a mismatch between the client and the server.

> JAX-WS internally uses the **Java Architecture for XML Binding (JAXB)** to create SOAP messages from method calls. The types we are allowed to use for method calls and return values are the ones that JAXB supports. You can get more information on JAXB at https://jaxb.dev.java.net/.

Sending attachments to web services

In addition to sending and accepting the data types discussed in the previous sections, web service methods can send and accept file attachments. The following example illustrates how to do this:

```
package net.ensode.glassfishbook;

import java.io.FileOutputStream;
import java.io.IOException;

import javax.activation.DataHandler;
```

```java
import javax.jws.WebMethod;
import javax.jws.WebService;

@WebService
public class FileAttachment {

  @WebMethod
  public void attachFile(DataHandler dataHandler) {
    FileOutputStream fileOutputStream;
    try {

      // substitute "/tmp/attachment.gif" with
      // a valid path, if necessary.
      fileOutputStream = new FileOutputStream(
          "/tmp/attachment.gif");

      dataHandler.writeTo(fileOutputStream);

      fileOutputStream.flush();
      fileOutputStream.close();
    } catch (IOException e) {
      e.printStackTrace();
    }

  }
}
```

In order to write a web service method that receives one or more attachments, all we need to do is to add a parameter of type `javax.activation.DataHandler` for each attachment the method will receive. In the preceding example code, the `attachFile()` method takes a single parameter of this type and simply writes it to the filesystem.

Just like with any standard web service, the preceding code needs to be packaged in a WAR file and deployed. Once deployed, a WSDL will automatically be generated. We then need to execute the `wsimport` utility to generate the code that our web service client can use to access the web service. As previously discussed, the `wsimport` utility can be invoked directly from the command line or via a custom ANT target.

Once we have executed `wsimport` to generate code to access the web service, we can write and compile our client code as follows:

```java
package net.ensode.glassfishbook;

import java.io.File;
import java.io.FileInputStream;
import java.io.IOException;
import java.nio.ByteBuffer;
import java.nio.channels.FileChannel;

import javax.xml.ws.WebServiceRef;

public class FileAttachmentServiceClient {

  @WebServiceRef(wsdlLocation =
    "http://localhost:8080/fileattachmentservice/"
      + "FileAttachmentService?wsdl")
  private static FileAttachmentService fileAttachmentService;

  public static void main(String[] args) {
    FileAttachment fileAttachment = fileAttachmentService.
        getFileAttachmentPort();
    File fileToAttach = new File("src/main/resources/logo.gif");

    byte[] fileBytes = fileToByteArray(fileToAttach);

    fileAttachment.attachFile(fileBytes);
    System.out.println("Successfully sent attachment.");
  }

  static byte[] fileToByteArray(File file) {
    byte[] fileBytes = null;

    try {
      FileInputStream fileInputStream;
      fileInputStream = new FileInputStream(file);

      FileChannel fileChannel = fileInputStream.getChannel();
      fileBytes = new byte[(int) fileChannel.size()];
      ByteBuffer byteBuffer = ByteBuffer.wrap(fileBytes);
      fileChannel.read(byteBuffer);
    } catch (IOException e) {
      e.printStackTrace();
    }
    return fileBytes;
  }
}
```

A web service client that needs to send one or more attachments to the web service first obtains an instance of the web service as usual. It then creates an instance of `java.io.File`, passing the location of the file to attach as its constructor's parameter.

Once we have an instance of `java.io.File` containing the file we wish to attach, we then need to convert the file to a byte array and pass this byte array to the web service method that expects an attachment.

Notice that the parameter type used when the client invokes a method expecting an attachment is different from the parameter type of the method in the web server code. The method in the web server code expects an instance of `javax.activation.DataHandler` for each attachment. However, the code generated by `wsimport` expects an array of bytes for each attachment. These arrays of bytes are converted to the right type (`javax.activation.DataHandler`) behind the scenes by the code generated by `wsimport`. We as application developers don't need to concern ourselves with the details of why this happens. We just need to keep in mind that when sending attachments to a web service method, the parameter types will be different in the web service code and in the client invocation.

Exposing EJBs as web services

In addition to creating web services as described in the previous section, public methods of stateless session beans can easily be exposed as web services. The following example illustrates how to do this:

```java
package net.ensode.glassfishbook;

import javax.ejb.Stateless;
import javax.jws.WebService;

@Stateless
@WebService
public class DecToHexBean {

  public String convertDecToHex(int i) {
    return Integer.toHexString(i);
  }
}
```

As we can see, the only thing we need to do to expose a stateless session bean's public methods is decorate its class declaration with the `@WebService` annotation. Since the class is a stateless session bean, it also needs to be decorated with the `@Stateless` annotation.

Just like regular stateless session beans, the ones whose methods are exposed as web services need to be deployed in a `.jar` file. Once deployed, we can see the new web service under the **Applications** node in the GlassFish administration web console. Clicking on the application's node, we can see some details in the GlassFish console, as shown in the following screenshot:

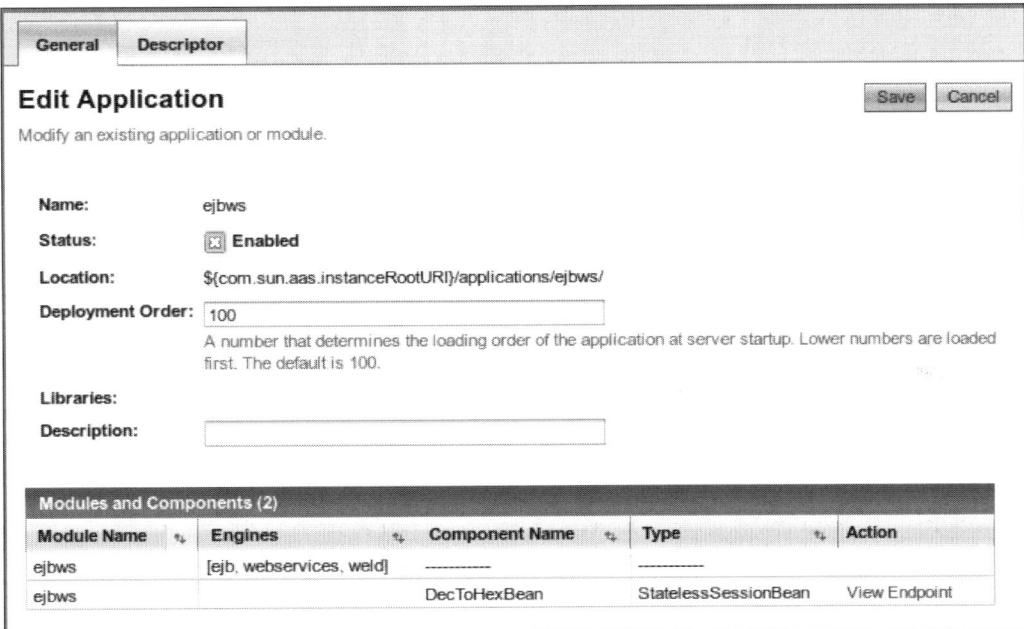

Notice that the value in the **Type** column for our new web service is **StatelessSessionBean**. This allows us to see at a glance that the web service is implemented as an **Enterprise JavaBean** (**EJB**).

Just like standard web services, EJB web services automatically generate a WSDL to be used by its clients upon deployment; it can be accessed the same way by clicking on the **View EndPoint** link.

EJB web service clients

The following class illustrates the procedure to be followed to access EJB web service methods from a client application:

```
package net.ensode.glassfishbook;

import javax.xml.ws.WebServiceRef;
```

```java
public class DecToHexClient {

  @WebServiceRef(wsdlLocation = 
    "http://localhost:8080/DecToHexBeanService/DecToHexBean?wsdl")
  private static DecToHexBeanService decToHexBeanService;

  public void convert() {
    DecToHexBean decToHexBean = 
      decToHexBeanService.getDecToHexBeanPort();

    System.out.println("decimal 4013 in hex is: "
        + decToHexBean.convertDecToHex(4013));
  }
  public static void main(String[] args) {
    new DecToHexClient().convert();
  }
}
```

As we can see, nothing special needs to be done when accessing an EJB web service from a client. The procedure is the same as with standard web services.

Since the preceding example is a standalone application, it needs to be executed via the `appclient` application as follows:

`appclient -client ejbwsclient.jar`

The preceding command results in the following output:

`decimal 4013 in hex is: fad`

Securing web services

Just like with regular web applications, web services can be secured so that only authorized users can access them. This can be accomplished by modifying the web service's `web.xml` deployment descriptor, as shown in the following code:

```xml
<?xml version="1.0" encoding="UTF-8"?>
<web-app xmlns="http://java.sun.com/xml/ns/javaee" version="2.5"
         xmlns:xsi="http://www.w3.org/2001/XMLSchema"
         xsi:schemaLocation="http://java.sun.com/xml/ns/javaee
         http://java.sun.com/xml/ns/javaee/web-app_2_5.xsd">
  <security-constraint>
    <web-resource-collection>
      <web-resource-name>Calculator Web Service</web-resource-name>
```

```
            <url-pattern>/CalculatorService/*</url-pattern>
            <http-method>POST</http-method>
        </web-resource-collection>
        <auth-constraint>
            <role-name>user</role-name>
        </auth-constraint>
    </security-constraint>
    <login-config>
        <auth-method>BASIC</auth-method>
        <realm-name>file</realm-name>
    </login-config>
</web-app>
```

In this example, we modify our calculator service so that only authorized users can access it. Notice that the modifications needed to secure the web service are no different from the modifications needed to secure any regular web application. The URL pattern to be used for the `<url-pattern>` element can be obtained by clicking on the **View WSDL** link corresponding to our service. In our example, the URL for the link is:

`http://localhost:8080/calculatorservice/CalculatorService?wsdl`

The value to be used for `<url-pattern>` is the value right after the context root (`/CalculatorService` in our example) and before the question mark, followed by a slash and an asterisk.

> Notice that the preceding web.xml deployment descriptor only secures HTTP POST requests. The reason for this is that wsimport uses a GET request to obtain the WSDL and generate the appropriate code. If GET requests are secured, wsimport will fail, since it will be denied access to the WSDL.

The following code illustrates how a standalone client can access a secured web service:

```
package net.ensode.glassfishbook;

import javax.xml.ws.BindingProvider;
import javax.xml.ws.WebServiceRef;

public class CalculatorServiceClient {

  @WebServiceRef(
```

```
    wsdlLocation =
      "http://localhost:8080/securecalculatorservice/CalculatorService?w
    sdl")
    private static CalculatorService calculatorService;

    public void calculate() {
      //add a user named "joe" with a password of "password"
      //to the file realm to successfuly execute the web service.
      //"joe" must belong to the group "appuser".
      Calculator calculator = calculatorService.getCalculatorPort();
      ((BindingProvider) calculator).getRequestContext().put(
          BindingProvider.USERNAME_PROPERTY, "joe");
      ((BindingProvider) calculator).getRequestContext().put(
          BindingProvider.PASSWORD_PROPERTY, "password");

      System.out.println("1 + 2 = " + calculator.add(1, 2));
      System.out.println("1 - 2 = " + calculator.subtract(1, 2));
    }

    public static void main(String[] args) {
      new CalculatorServiceClient().calculate();
    }
  }
```

The preceding code is a modified version of the `Calculator` service standalone client we saw earlier in the chapter. This version was modified to access the secure version of the service. As can be seen in the code, all we need to do to access the secured version of the server is put a username and a password in the request context. The username and password must be valid for the realm used to authenticate the web service.

We can add the username and password to the request context by casting our web service endpoint class to `javax.xml.ws.BindingProvider` and calling its `getRequestContext()` method. This method returns a `java.util.Map` instance. We can then simply add the username and password by calling the `put` method of `Map` and using the constants USERNAME_PROPERTY and PASSWORD_PROPERTY defined in `BindingProvider` as keys, and the corresponding `String` objects as values.

Securing EJB web services

Just like standard web services, EJBs exposed as web services can be secured so that only authorized clients can access them. This can be accomplished by configuring the EJB via the `glassfish-ejb-jar.xml` file as follows:

```xml
<?xml version="1.0" encoding="UTF-8"?>
<!DOCTYPE glassfish-ejb-jar PUBLIC "-//GlassFish.org//DTD
   GlassFish Application Server 3.1 EJB 3.1//EN"
     "http://glassfish.org/dtds/glassfish-ejb-jar_3_1-1.dtd">
<glassfish-ejb-jar>
    <ejb>
        <ejb-name>SecureDecToHexBean</ejb-name>
        <webservice-endpoint>
            <port-component-name>
              SecureDecToHexBean
            </port-component-name>
            <login-config>
                <auth-method>BASIC</auth-method>
                <realm>file</realm>
            </login-config>
        </webservice-endpoint>
    </ejb>
</glassfish-ejb-jar>
```

As seen in the preceding deployment descriptor, security is set up differently for EJBs exposed as web services rather than with standard EJBs. For EJBs exposed as web services, the security configuration is done inside the `<webservice-endpoint>` element of the `glassfish-ejb-jar.xml` file.

The `<port-component-name>` element must be set to the name of the EJB we are exposing as a web service. This name is defined in the `<ejb-name>` element for the EJB.

The `<login-config>` element is very similar to the corresponding element in a web application's `web.xml` deployment descriptor. The `<login-config>` element must contain an authorization method, defined by its `<auth-method>` subelement, and a realm to use for authentication. The realm is defined by the `<realm>` subelement.

Do not use the `@RolesAllowed` annotation for EJBs intended to be exposed as web services. This annotation is intended for when the EJB methods are accessed through its remote or local interface. If an EJB or one or more of its methods are decorated with this annotation, then invoking the method will fail with a security exception.

Once we configure an EJB web service for authentication, we package it in a .jar file, and then deploy it as usual. The EJB web service is now ready to be accessed by clients.

The following code example illustrates how an EJB web service client can access a secure EJB web service:

```
package net.ensode.glassfishbook;

import javax.xml.ws.BindingProvider;
import javax.xml.ws.WebServiceRef;

public class DecToHexClient {

  @WebServiceRef(
  wsdlLocation =
  "http://localhost:8080/SecureDecToHexBeanService/SecureDecToHexBean?wsdl")
  private static SecureDecToHexBeanService
    secureDecToHexBeanService;

  public void convert() {
    SecureDecToHexBean secureDecToHexBean =
      secureDecToHexBeanService.
        getSecureDecToHexBeanPort();
    ((BindingProvider) secureDecToHexBean).getRequestContext().put(
        BindingProvider.USERNAME_PROPERTY, "joe");
    ((BindingProvider) secureDecToHexBean).getRequestContext().put(
        BindingProvider.PASSWORD_PROPERTY, "password");

    System.out.println("decimal 4013 in hex is: "
        + secureDecToHexBean.convertDecToHex(4013));
  }

  public static void main(String[] args) {
    new DecToHexClient().convert();
  }
}
```

As we can see in the previous example, the procedure for accessing an EJB exposed as a web service is identical to accessing a standard web service. The implementation of the web service is irrelevant to the client.

Summary

In this chapter, we covered how to develop web services and web service clients via the JAX-WS API. We explained how to incorporate web service code generation for web service clients when using ANT or Maven as a build tool. We also covered the valid types that can be used for remote method calls via JAX-WS. Additionally, we discussed how to send attachments to a web service. We also covered how to expose EJB methods as web services. Lastly, we covered how to secure web services so that they are not accessible to unauthorized clients.

In the next chapter, we will cover RESTful web services with JAX-RS.

11
Developing RESTful Web Services with JAX-RS

Representational State Transfer (REST) is an architectural style in which web services are viewed as resources and can be identified by Uniform Resource Identifiers (URIs).

Web services developed using REST are known as RESTful web services.

Java EE 6 added support to RESTful web services through the addition of the Java API for RESTful Web Services (JAX-RS). JAX-RS had been available as a standalone API for a while, it became part of Java EE in Version 6 of the specification. In this chapter, we will cover how to develop RESTful web services through the JAX-RS.API.

The following topics will be covered in this chapter:

- Introduction to RESTful web services and JAX-RS
- Developing a simple RESTful web service
- Developing a RESTful web service client
- Path parameters
- Query parameters

Introducing RESTful web services and JAX-RS

RESTful web services are very flexible. RESTful web services can consume several different kinds of MIME types, although they are typically written to consume and/or produce XML or JSON (JavaScript Object Notation).

Web services must support one or more of the following four HTTP methods:

- `GET`: By convention, a `GET` request is used to retrieve an existing resource
- `POST`: By convention, a `POST` request is used to update an existing resource
- `PUT`: By convention, a `PUT` request is used to create a new resource
- `DELETE`: By convention, a `DELETE` request is used to delete an existing resource

We develop a RESTful web service with JAX-RS by creating a class with annotated methods that are invoked when our web service receives one of the above HTTP request methods. Once we have developed and deployed our RESTful web service, we need to develop a client that will send requests to our service. JAX-RS 2.0 introduces a standard client-side API that we can use to develop RESTful web service clients.

Developing a simple RESTful web service

In this section, we will develop a simple web service to illustrate how to make methods in our service respond to the different HTTP request methods.

Developing a RESTful web service using JAX-RS is simple and straightforward. Each of our RESTful web services needs to be invoked via its Unique Resource Identifier (URI). This URI is specified by the `@Path` annotation, which we need to use to decorate our RESTful web service resource class.

When developing RESTful web services, we need to develop methods that will be invoked when our web service receives an HTTP request. We need to implement methods to handle one or more of the four types of request that RESTful web services handle: `GET`, `POST`, `PUT`, and/or `DELETE`.

The JAX-RS API provides four annotations that we can use to decorate methods in our web service; the annotations are appropriately named `@GET`, `@POST`, `@PUT`, and `@DELETE`. Decorating a method in our web service with one of these annotations will make it respond to the corresponding HTTP method.

Additionally, each method in our service must produce and/or consume a specific MIME type.

 **Multipurpose Internet Mail Extensions (MIME)** is a standard for transferring nonASCII text over the Internet. MIME was originally developed to send nontextual data over e-mail, but later, its use was expanded to include other forms of data transfer such as RESTful web services.

The MIME type that is going to be produced needs to be specified with the
@Produces annotation; similarly, the MIME type that is going to be consumed
must be specified with the @Consumes annotation.

 Please note that this example does not really do anything; its
purpose is to illustrate how to make different methods in our
RESTful web service resource class respond to the different
HTTP methods.

The following example illustrates the concepts we have just explained:

```
package com.ensode.jaxrsintro.service;

import javax.ws.rs.Consumes;
import javax.ws.rs.DELETE;
import javax.ws.rs.GET;
import javax.ws.rs.POST;
import javax.ws.rs.PUT;
import javax.ws.rs.Path;
import javax.ws.rs.Produces;

@Path("customer")
public class CustomerResource {

  @GET
  @Produces("text/xml")
  public String getCustomer() {
    //in a "real" RESTful service, we would retrieve data from a
      database
    //then return an XML representation of the data.

    System.out.println("--- " + this.getClass().getCanonicalName()
        + ".getCustomer() invoked");

    return "<customer>\n"
        + "<id>123</id>\n"
        + "<firstName>Joseph</firstName>\n"
        + "<middleName>William</middleName>\n"
        + "<lastName>Graystone</lastName>\n"
        + "</customer>\n";
  }
```

```java
/**
 * Create a new customer
 * @param customer XML representation of the customer to create
 */
@PUT
@Consumes("text/xml")
public void createCustomer(String customerXML) {
  //in a "real" RESTful service, we would parse the XML
  //received in the customer XML parameter, then insert
  //a new row into the database.

  System.out.println("--- " + this.getClass().getCanonicalName()
      + ".createCustomer() invoked");

  System.out.println("customerXML = " + customerXML);
}


@POST
@Consumes("text/xml")
public void updateCustomer(String customerXML) {
  //in a "real" RESTful service, we would parse the XML
  //received in the customer XML parameter, then update
  //a row in the database.

  System.out.println("--- " + this.getClass().getCanonicalName()
      + ".updateCustomer() invoked");

  System.out.println("customerXML = " + customerXML);
}

@DELETE
@Consumes("text/xml")
public void deleteCustomer(String customerXML) {
  //in a "real" RESTful service, we would parse the XML
  //received in the customer XML parameter, then delete
  //a row in the database.

  System.out.println("--- " + this.getClass().getCanonicalName()
      + ".deleteCustomer() invoked");

  System.out.println("customerXML = " + customerXML);
}
}
```

Notice that this class is annotated with the @Path annotation; this annotation designates the Uniform Resource Identifier (URI) for our RESTful web service. The complete URI for our service will include the protocol, server name, port, context root, the REST resources path (see the next subsection), and the value passed to this annotation.

Assuming our web service was deployed to a server called example.com using the HTTP protocol on port 8080, and has a context root called "jaxrsintro" and a REST resources path called resources, then the complete URI for our service would be http://example.com:8080/jaxrsintro/resources/customer.

> Since web browsers generate a GET request when pointed to a URL, we can test the GET method of our service by simply pointing the browser to our service's URI.

Notice that each of the methods in our class is annotated with one of the @GET, @POST, @PUT, or @DELETE annotations. These annotations make our methods respond to their corresponding HTTP method.

Additionally, if our method returns data to the client, we declare that the MIME type of the data should be returned in the @Produces annotation. In our example, only the getCustomer() method returns data to the client; we wish to return data in an XML format, therefore, we set the value of the @Produces annotation to text/xml. Similarly, if our method needs to consume data from the client, we need to specify the MIME type of the data to be consumed; this is done via the @Consumes annotation. All methods in our service except getCustomer() consume data; in all cases, we expect the data to be in XML, therefore, we again specify text/xml as the MIME type to be consumed.

Configuring the REST resources path for our application

As briefly mentioned in the previous section, before successfully deploying a RESTful web service developed using JAX-RS, we need to configure the REST resources path for our application. We can do this by developing a class that extends javax.ws.rs.core.Application and decorating it with the @ApplicationPath annotation.

Configuring via the @ApplicationPath annotation

As mentioned in previous chapters, Java EE 6 added several new features to the Java EE specification so that in many cases it isn't necessary to write a `web.xml` deployment descriptor. JAX-RS is no different. We can configure the REST resources path in Java code via an annotation.

To configure our REST resources path without having to rely on a `web.xml` deployment descriptor, all we need to do is write a class that extends `javax.ws.ApplicationPath` and decorate it with the `@ApplicationPath` annotation; the value passed to this annotation is the REST resources path for our services.

The following code sample illustrates this process:

```
package com.ensode.jaxrsintro.service.config;

import javax.ws.rs.ApplicationPath;
import javax.ws.rs.core.Application;

@ApplicationPath("resources")
public class JaxRsConfig extends Application {
}
```

Notice that the class does not have to implement any methods. It simply needs to extend `javax.ws.rs.Application` and be decorated with the `@ApplicationPath` annotation. The class must be public, may have any name, and may be placed in any package.

Testing our web service

As we mentioned earlier, web browsers send a GET request to any URLs we point them to; therefore, the easiest way to test GET requests to our service is by simply pointing the browser to our service's URI, as shown in the following screenshot:

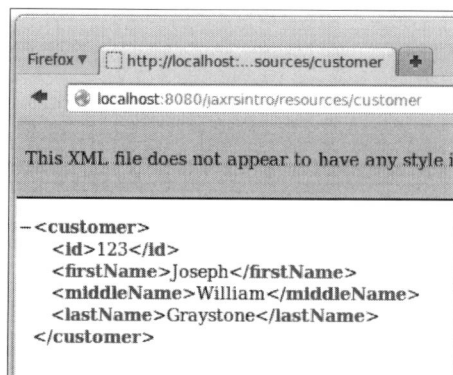

Web browsers only support GET and POST requests. To test a POST request through the browser, we would have to write a web application containing an HTML form that has an action attribute value of our service's URI. Although this is simple to do for a single service, it can become cumbersome to do this for every RESTful web service we develop.

Thankfully, there is an open source command-line utility called curl that we can use to test our web services. The curl command is included with most Linux distributions and can be easily downloaded for Windows, Mac OS X, and several other platforms. The curl utility can be downloaded at http://curl.haxx.se/.

curl can send all four request method types (GET, POST, PUT and DELETE) to our service. Our server's response will simply be displayed on the command-line console. curl takes the -X command-line option, which allows us to specify what request method to send; to send a GET request, we simply need to type the following into the command line:

`curl -XGET http://localhost:8080/jaxrsintro/resources/customer`

This results in the following output:

```
<customer>
<id>123</id>
<firstName>Joseph</firstName>
<middleName>William</middleName>
<lastName>Graystone</lastName>
</customer>
```

This, unsurprisingly, is the same output we saw when we pointed our browser to our service's URI.

The default request method for curl is GET, therefore, the -X parameter in our previous example is redundant; we could have achieved the same result by invoking the following command from the command line:

`curl  HYPERLINK "http://localhost:8080/jaxrsintro/resources/customer"http://localhost:8080/jaxrsintro/resources/customer`

After submitting any of the two previous commands and examining the GlassFish log, we should see the output of the System.out.println() statements we added to the getCustomer() method.

```
INFO: --- com.ensode.jaxrsintro.service.CustomerResource.getCustomer() invoked
```

For all other request method types, we need to send some data to our service. This can be accomplished by the `--data` command-line argument to the `curl` command, as shown in the following code:

```
curl -XPUT -HContent-type:text/xml --data "<customer><id>321</id><firstName>Amanda</firstName><middleName>Zoe</middleName><lastName>Adams</lastName></customer>" http://localhost:8080/jaxrsintro/resources/customer
```

As shown in this example, we need to specify the MIME type via the curl's `-H` command-line argument using the format shown in the example.

We can verify that the previous command worked as expected by inspecting the GlassFish log by executing the following code:

```
INFO: --- com.ensode.jaxrsintro.service.CustomerResource.createCustomer() invoked
INFO: customerXML = <customer><id>321</id><firstName>Amanda</firstName><middleName>Zoe</middleName><lastName>Adams</lastName></customer>
```

We can test other request method types just as easily by executing the following code:

```
curl -XPOST -HContent-type:text/xml --data "<customer><id>321</id><firstName>Amanda</firstName><middleName>Tamara</middleName><lastName>Adams</lastName></customer>" http://localhost:8080/jaxrsintro/resources/customer
```

The GlassFish log shows the corresponding output:

```
INFO: --- com.ensode.jaxrsintro.service.CustomerResource.updateCustomer() invoked
INFO: customerXML = <customer><id>321</id><firstName>Amanda</firstName><middleName>Tamara</middleName><lastName>Adams</lastName></customer>
```

We can test the `delete` method by executing the following command:

```
curl -XDELETE -HContent-type:text/xml --data "<customer><id>321</id><firstName>Amanda</firstName><middleName>Tamara</middleName><lastName>Adams</lastName></customer>" http://localhost:8080/jaxrsintro/resources/customer
```

Again the GlassFish log shows the corresponding output:

```
INFO: --- com.ensode.jaxrsintro.service.CustomerResource.deleteCustomer()
invoked
INFO: customerXML = <customer><id>321</id><firstName>Amanda</
firstName><middleName>Tamara</middleName><lastName>Adams</lastName></
customer>
```

Converting data between Java and XML with JAXB

In our previous example, we processed raw XML data. In a real application, we would more than likely parse the XML data received from the client and use it to populate a Java object. Additionally, any XML data that we need to return to the client would have to be constructed from a Java object.

Converting data from Java to XML and back is such a common use case that the Java EE specification provides an API to do it. This API is the **Java API for XML Binding (JAXB)**.

JAXB makes converting data from Java to XML transparent and simple. All we need to do is decorate the class that we wish to convert to XML with the `@XmlRootElement` annotation. The following code example illustrates how to do this:

```java
package com.ensode.jaxrstest.entity;

import java.io.Serializable;
import javax.xml.bind.annotation.XmlRootElement;

@XmlRootElement
public class Customer implements Serializable {

  private Long id;
  private String firstName;
  private String middleName;
  private String lastName;

  public Customer() {
  }

  public Customer(Long id, String firstName,
      String middleInitial, String lastName) {
    this.id = id;
```

```java
      this.firstName = firstName;
      this.middleName = middleInitial;
      this.lastName = lastName;
    }

    public String getFirstName() {
      return firstName;
    }

    public void setFirstName(String firstName) {
      this.firstName = firstName;
    }

    public Long getId() {
      return id;
    }

    public void setId(Long id) {
      this.id = id;
    }

    public String getLastName() {
      return lastName;
    }

    public void setLastName(String lastName) {
      this.lastName = lastName;
    }

    public String getMiddleName() {
      return middleName;
    }

    public void setMiddleName(String middleName) {
      this.middleName = middleName;
    }

    @Override
    public String toString() {
      return "id = " + getId() + "\nfirstName = " + getFirstName()
          + "\nmiddleName = " + getMiddleName() + "\nlastName = "
          + getLastName();
    }
}
```

As shown in this example, other than the @XmlRootElement annotation at the class level, there is nothing unusual about the above Java class.

Once we have a class that we have decorated with the @XmlRootElement annotation, we need to change the parameter type of our web service from String to our custom class, as shown in the following code:

```
package com.ensode.jaxbxmlconversion.service;

import com.ensode.jaxbxmlconversion.entity.Customer;
import javax.ws.rs.Consumes;
import javax.ws.rs.DELETE;
import javax.ws.rs.GET;
import javax.ws.rs.POST;
import javax.ws.rs.PUT;
import javax.ws.rs.Path;
import javax.ws.rs.Produces;

@Path("customer")
public class CustomerResource {

  private Customer customer;

  public CustomerResource() {
    //"fake" the data, in a real application the data
    //would come from a database.
    customer = new Customer(1L, "David",
        "Raymond", "Heffelfinger");
  }

  @GET
  @Produces("text/xml")
  public Customer getCustomer() {
    //in a "real" RESTful service, we would retrieve data from a
      database
    //then return an XML representation of the data.

    System.out.println("--- " + this.getClass().getCanonicalName()
        + ".getCustomer() invoked");

    return customer;
  }

  @POST
  @Consumes("text/xml")
```

```java
    public void updateCustomer(Customer customer) {
      //in a "real" RESTful service, JAXB would parse the XML
      //received in the customer XML parameter, then update
      //a row in the database.

      System.out.println("--- " + this.getClass().getCanonicalName()
          + ".updateCustomer() invoked");

      System.out.println("---- got the following customer: "
          + customer);
    }

    @PUT
    @Consumes("text/xml")
    public void createCustomer(Customer customer) {
      //in a "real" RESTful service, we would insert
      //a new row into the database with the data in the
      //customer parameter

      System.out.println("--- " + this.getClass().getCanonicalName()
          + ".createCustomer() invoked");

      System.out.println("customer = " + customer);

    }

    @DELETE
    @Consumes("text/xml")
    public void deleteCustomer(Customer customer) {
      //in a "real" RESTful service, we would delete a row
      //from the database corresponding to the customer parameter
      System.out.println("--- " + this.getClass().getCanonicalName()
          + ".deleteCustomer() invoked");

      System.out.println("customer = " + customer);
    }
}
```

As we can see, the difference between this version of our RESTful web service and the previous one is that all parameter types and return values have been changed from `String` to `Customer`. JAXB takes care of converting our parameters and return types to and from XML as appropriate. When using JAXB, an object of our custom class is automatically populated with data from the XML data sent from the client, return values are similarly transparently converted to XML.

Developing a RESTful web service client

Although `curl` allows us to quickly test our RESTful web services and is a developer friendly tool, it is not exactly user friendly; we shouldn't expect to have our user enter `curl` commands in their command line to use our web service. For this reason, we need to develop a client for our services. JAX-RS 2.0 introduces a standard client-side API that we can use to easily develop RESTful web service clients.

The following example illustrates how to use the JAX-RS client API:

```java
package com.ensode.jaxrsintroclient;

import com.ensode.jaxbxmlconversion.entity.Customer;
import javax.ws.rs.client.Client;
import javax.ws.rs.client.ClientBuilder;
import javax.ws.rs.client.Entity;

public class App {

    public static void main(String[] args) {
        App app = new App();
        app.insertCustomer();
    }

    public void insertCustomer() {
        Customer customer = new Customer(234L, "Tamara", "A",
                "Graystone");
        Client client = ClientBuilder.newClient();
        client.target(
        "http://localhost:8080/jaxbxmlconversion/resources/customer").
                request().put(
                        Entity.entity(customer, "text/xml"),
                        Customer.class);
    }
}
```

The first thing we need to do is create an instance of `javax.ws.rs.client.Client` by invoking the static `newClient()` method on the `javax.ws.rs.client.ClientBuilder` class.

We then invoke the `target()` method on our `Client` instance, passing the URI of our RESTful web service as the parameter. The `target()` method returns an instance of a class implementing the `javax.ws.rs.client.WebTarget` interface.

At this point, we invoke the `request()` method on our `WebTarget` instance; this method returns an implementation of the `javax.ws.rs.client.Invocation.Builder` interface.

In this particular example, we are sending an HTTP PUT request to our RESTful web service; therefore, at this point, we invoke the `put()` method of our `Invocation.Builder` implementation. The first parameter of the `put()` method is an instance of `javax.ws.rs.client.Entity`. We can create an instance of `javax.ws.rs.client.Entity` on the fly by invoking the static `entity()` method on the `Entity` class. The first parameter for this method is the object we wish to pass to our RESTful web service and the second parameter is the String representation of the MIME type of the data we will be passing to the RESTful web service. The second parameter of the `put()` method is the type of response the client expects from the service. After we invoke the `put()` method, an HTTP PUT request is sent to our RESTful web service and the method we decorated with the `@Put` annotation (`createCustomer()` in our example) is invoked. There are similar `get()`, `post()`, and `delete()` methods we can invoke to send the corresponding HTTP requests to our RESTful web service.

Working with query and path parameters

In our previous examples, we have been working with a RESTful web service to manage a single `customer` object. In real life, this would obviously not be very helpful. The common case is to develop a RESTful web service to handle a collection of objects (customers, in our example). To determine which specific object in the collection we are working with, we can pass parameters to our RESTful web services. There are two types of parameters we can use: query and path.

Query parameters

We can add parameters to methods that will handle HTTP requests in our web service. Parameters decorated with the `@QueryParam` annotation will be retrieved from the request URL.

The following example illustrates how to use query parameters in our JAX-RS RESTful web services:

```
package com.ensode.queryparams.service;

import com.ensode.queryparams.entity.Customer;
import javax.ws.rs.Consumes;
import javax.ws.rs.DELETE;
import javax.ws.rs.GET;
import javax.ws.rs.POST;
```

```java
import javax.ws.rs.PUT;
import javax.ws.rs.Path;
import javax.ws.rs.Produces;
import javax.ws.rs.QueryParam;

@Path("customer")
public class CustomerResource {

  private Customer customer;

  public CustomerResource() {
    customer = new Customer(1L, "Samuel",
        "Joseph", "Willow");
  }

  @GET
  @Produces("text/xml")
  public Customer getCustomer(@QueryParam("id") Long id) {
    //in a "real" RESTful service, we would retrieve data from a
database
    //using the supplied id.

    System.out.println("--- " + this.getClass().getCanonicalName()
        + ".getCustomer() invoked, id = " + id);

    return customer;
  }

  /**
   * Create a new customer
   * @param customer XML representation of the customer to create
   */
  @PUT
  @Consumes("text/xml")
  public void createCustomer(Customer customer) {
    //in a "real" RESTful service, we would parse the XML
    //received in the customer XML parameter, then insert
    //a new row into the database.

    System.out.println("--- " + this.getClass().getCanonicalName()
        + ".createCustomer() invoked");

    System.out.println("customer = " + customer);
```

```
    }

    @POST
    @Consumes("text/xml")
    public void updateCustomer(Customer customer) {
      //in a "real" RESTful service, we would parse the XML
      //received in the customer XML parameter, then update
      //a row in the database.

      System.out.println("--- " + this.getClass().getCanonicalName()
          + ".updateCustomer() invoked");

      System.out.println("customer = " + customer);

      System.out.println("customer= " + customer);
    }

    @DELETE
    @Consumes("text/xml")
    public void deleteCustomer(@QueryParam("id") Long id) {
      //in a "real" RESTful service, we would invoke
      //a DAO and delete the row in the database with the
      //primary key passed as the "id" parameter.

      System.out.println("--- " + this.getClass().getCanonicalName()
          + ".deleteCustomer() invoked, id = " + id);

      System.out.println("customer = " + customer);
    }
}
```

Notice that all we had to do was decorate the parameters with the `@QueryParam` annotation. This annotation allows JAX-RS to retrieve any query parameters matching the value of the annotation and assign its value to the parameter variable.

We can add a parameter to the web service's URL just like we pass parameters to any URL:

```
curl -XGET -HContent-type:text/xml http://localhost:8080/queryparams/
resources/customer?id=1
```

Sending query parameters via the JAX-RS client API

The JAX-RS client API provides an easy and straightforward way of sending query parameters to RESTful web services. The following example illustrates how to do this:

```java
package com.ensode.queryparamsclient;

import com.ensode.queryparamsclient.entity.Customer;
import javax.ws.rs.client.Client;
import javax.ws.rs.client.ClientBuilder;

public class App {

    public static void main(String[] args) {
        App app = new App();
        app.getCustomer();
    }

    public void getCustomer() {
        Client client = ClientBuilder.newClient();
        Customer customer = client.target(
            "http://localhost:8080/queryparams/resources/customer").
              queryParam("id", 1L).
                request().get(Customer.class);

        System.out.println(
          "Received the following customer information:");
        System.out.println("Id: " + customer.getId());
        System.out.println("First Name: " + customer.getFirstName());
        System.out.println("Middle Name: " +
          customer.getMiddleName());
        System.out.println("Last Name: " + customer.getLastName());
    }
}
```

As we can see, all we need to do to pass a parameter is invoke the `queryParam()` method on the instance of `javax.ws.rs.client.WebTarget` returned by invoking the `target()` method on our `Client` instance. The first argument to this method is the parameter name and it must match the value of the `@QueryParam` annotation in the web service. The second parameter is the value that we need to pass to the web service. If our web service accepts multiple parameters, we can chain `queryParam()` method invocations, using one for each parameter that our RESTful web service expects.

Path parameters

Another way we can pass parameters to our RESTful web services is via path parameters. The following example illustrates how to develop a JAX-RS RESTful web service that accepts path parameters:

```java
package com.ensode.pathparams.service;

import com.ensode.pathparams.entity.Customer;
import javax.ws.rs.Consumes;
import javax.ws.rs.DELETE;
import javax.ws.rs.GET;
import javax.ws.rs.POST;
import javax.ws.rs.PUT;
import javax.ws.rs.Path;
import javax.ws.rs.PathParam;
import javax.ws.rs.Produces;

@Path("/customer/")
public class CustomerResource {

  private Customer customer;

  public CustomerResource() {
    customer = new Customer(1L, "William",
        "Daniel", "Graystone");
  }

  @GET
  @Produces("text/xml")
  @Path("{id}/")
  public Customer getCustomer(@PathParam("id") Long id) {
    //in a "real" RESTful service, we would retrieve data from a
      database
    //using the supplied id.

    System.out.println("--- " + this.getClass().getCanonicalName()
        + ".getCustomer() invoked, id = " + id);

    return customer;
  }

  @PUT
  @Consumes("text/xml")
  public void createCustomer(Customer customer) {
```

```
        //in a "real" RESTful service, we would parse the XML
        //received in the customer XML parameter, then insert
        //a new row into the database.
        System.out.println("--- " + this.getClass().getCanonicalName()
            + ".createCustomer() invoked");
        System.out.println("customer = " + customer);
    }

    @POST
    @Consumes("text/xml")
    public void updateCustomer(Customer customer) {
        //in a "real" RESTful service, we would parse the XML
        //received in the customer XML parameter, then update
        //a row in the database.
        System.out.println("--- " + this.getClass().getCanonicalName()
            + ".updateCustomer() invoked");
        System.out.println("customer = " + customer);
        System.out.println("customer= " + customer);
    }

    @DELETE
    @Consumes("text/xml")
    @Path("{id}/")
    public void deleteCustomer(@PathParam("id") Long id) {
        //in a "real" RESTful service, we would invoke
        //a DAO and delete the row in the database with the
        //primary key passed as the "id" parameter.
        System.out.println("--- " + this.getClass().getCanonicalName()
            + ".deleteCustomer() invoked, id = " + id);
        System.out.println("customer = " + customer);
    }
}
```

Any method that accepts a path parameter must be decorated with the @Path annotation. The value attribute of this annotation must be formatted as "{paramName}/", where paramName is the parameter the method expects to receive. Additionally, method parameters must be decorated with the @PathParam annotation. The value of the @PathParam annotation must match the parameter name declared in the @Path annotation for the method.

We can pass path parameters from the command line by adjusting our web service's URI as appropriate; for example, to pass an `"id"` parameter of 1 to the `getCustomer()` method (which handles `HTTP GET` requests), we could do it from the command line as follows:

```
curl -XGET -HContent-type:text/xml http://localhost:8080/pathparams/resources/customer/1
```

This returns the expected output of an XML representation of the `Customer` object returned by the `getCustomer()` method, as follows:

```
<?xml version="1.0" encoding="UTF-8" standalone="yes"?><customer><firstName>William</firstName><id>1</id><lastName>Graystone</lastName><middleName>Daniel</middleName></customer>
```

Sending path parameters via the JAX-RS Client API

Sending path parameters to a web service via the JAX-RS client API is easy and straightforward; all we need to do is add a couple of method invocations to specify the path parameter and its value. The following example illustrates how to do this:

```
package com.ensode.pathparamsclient;

import com.ensode.pathparamsclient.entity.Customer;
import javax.ws.rs.client.Client;
import javax.ws.rs.client.ClientBuilder;

public class App {

    public static void main(String[] args) {
        App app = new App();
        app.getCustomer();
    }

    public void getCustomer() {
        Client client = ClientBuilder.newClient();
        Customer customer = client.target(
                "http://localhost:8080/pathparams/resources/customer").
                path("{id}").
                resolveTemplate("id", 1L).
                request().get(Customer.class);
```

```
            System.out.println("Received the following customer
              information:");
            System.out.println("Id: " + customer.getId());
            System.out.println("First Name: " +
              customer.getFirstName());
            System.out.println("Middle Name: " +
              customer.getMiddleName());
            System.out.println("Last Name: " +
              customer.getLastName());
    }
}
```

In this example, we invoke the `path()` method on the instance of `WebTarget` returned by `client.target()`. This method appends the specified path to our `WebTarget` instance; the value of this method must match the value of the `@Path` annotation in our RESTful web service.

After invoking the `path()` method on our `WebTarget` instance, we need to invoke `resolveTemplate()`; the first parameter for this method is the name of the parameter (without the curly braces) and the second parameter is the value we wish to pass as a parameter to our RESTful web service.

If we need to pass more than one parameter to one of our web services, we simply need to use the following format for the `@Path` parameter at the method level:

```
@Path("/{paramName1}/{paramName2}/")
```

Then annotate the corresponding method arguments with the `@PathParam` annotation, as follows:

```
public String someMethod(@PathParam("paramName1") String param1,
    @PathParam("paramName2") String param2)
```

The web service can then be invoked by modifying the web service's URI to pass the parameters in the order specified in the `@Path` annotation. For example, the following URI would pass the values 1 and 2 for `paramName1` and `paramName2`:

`http://localhost:8080/contextroot/resources/customer/1/2`

The previous URI will work both from the command line and through a web service client we have developed with the JAX-RS client API.

Summary

In this chapter, we discussed how to develop RESTful web services using JAX-RS, a new addition to the Java EE specification.

We covered how to develop a RESTful web service by adding a few simple annotations to our code. We also explained how to automatically convert data between Java and XML by taking advantage of the Java API for XML Binding (JAXB).

We also discussed how to develop RESTful web service clients via the JAX-RS client API.

Finally, we covered how to pass parameters to our RESTful web services via the `@PathParam` and `@QueryParam` annotations.

Index

Symbols

@ApplicationPath annotation 304
@ApplicationScoped annotation 48, 170
@Asynchronous annotation 134
@ClientEndPoint annotation 199
@Column annotation 78
@ConversationScoped annotation 48, 169, 171
_currentRealm variable 270
@Dependent annotation 48, 170
@EJB annotation 159
@FacesValidator annotation 51
<f:ajax> attribute 63
<f:ajax> tag 61, 64
@FlowScoped annotation 71
<f:validateBean> tag 44
<f:validateDoubleRange> tag 44
<f:validateLength> tag 44, 60
<f:validateLongRange> tag 45
<f:validateRegex> tag 45
<f:validateRequired> tag 45
<f:validator> tag 52
<f:validator> tags 56
<h:commandButton> tag 46
 <h:form> tag 244
<h:form> tag 37
<h:messages> tag 58
<h:outputLabel> tag 40
<h:outputStylesheet> tag 37
<h:outputText> component 63
<h:outputText> tag 49
<h:panelGrid> tag 38
<h:panelGroup> tag 45
@Id annotation 78
@IdClass annotation 106
@JoinColumn annotation 98
@JoinTable annotation 100
-keep parameter 281
-keystore parameter 247
<login-config> element 295
@ManyToMany annotation 100
<message-bundle> element 60
@Named annotation 46
@Named class annotation 47
@NamedQuery annotation 110
:name parameter 109
@NotNull annotation 121
@OnClose annotation 200
@OnError annotation 200
@OneToMany annotation 93
@OneToOne annotation 85
@OnMessage annotation 191
@OnMessage method 200
@OnOpen annotation 200
< operator 110
<= operator 110
= operator 110
> operator 110
>= operator 110
@Path annotation 303, 319
@PathParam annotation 317
--portbase parameter 24
<port-component-name> element 295
@PostActivate annotations 146
@PostConstruct method 149
@PreDestroy annotation 149
@PrePassivate annotations 146
--property parameter 261
@QueryParam annotation 314
<realm-name> element 273
@Remove annotations 146

@RequestScoped annotation 47, 48, 169
@RequestScoped annotations 47
@Resource annotation 221
@RolesAllowed annotation 157, 295
-savemasterpassword=true parameter 252
@Schedule annotation
  dayOfMonth attribute 153
  dayOfWeek attribute 153
  hour attribute 154
  minute attribute 154
  month attribute 154
  second attribute 154
  timezone attribute 154
  year attribute 154
@ServerEndpoint annotation 191
@SessionScoped annotation 48, 169
@Stateless annotation 290
@TransactionAttribute annotation
  TransactionAttributeType.MANDATORY 138
  TransactionAttributeType.NEVER 138
  TransactionAttributeType.NOT_SUPPORTED 138
  TransactionAttributeType.REQUIRED 138
  TransactionAttributeType.REQUIRES_NEW 138
  TransactionAttributeType.SUPPORTS 138
@TransactionManagement annotation 142
@WebMethod annotation 276
@WebService annotation 275, 290
@WebServiceRef annotation 285
@XmlRootElement annotation 309

A

actionListener attribute 64
add button 279
additional certificate realms
  defining 258, 259
additional file realms
  defining 262, 267
additional realms
  defining 256-261
addMessageHandler() method 192
addMessage() method 38
add() method 178, 276
Add Property button 223, 272

ADDRESS_TYPES table 76
admin 228
admin group 232
admin-realm
  users, adding to 229-231
Advanced icon 248
Ajax-enabling JSF applications
  about 61-63
  supported JavaScript events 64-66
annotated WebSocket server endpoint
  developing 190-192
AntRun plugin 282
Apache Commons Validator 51
appclient utility 159, 214
application
  structure 236
Applications node 277
Applications window 19
asadmin 228
asadmin command-line utility 22, 23
asadmin group 230
Aspect Oriented Programming (AOP) 9
asynchronous methods
  about 133-135
  cancel(boolean mayInterruptIfRunning) 135
  get() 135
  get(long timeout, TimeUnit unit) 135
  isCancelled() 135
  isDone() 135
attachFile() method 288
authenticateUser() method 270
autodeploy directory 21, 22

B

bean-managed transactions 140-143
Bean Validation support 119, 121
begin() method 170, 173
blur event 64
build() method 179
BytesMessage 212

C

Calendar-based EJB timer expressions
  @Schedule annotation 153
  about 152

cancel() method 150
Cascading Style Sheets. *See* CSS
CDI
  about 34, 161
  dependency injection 164, 165
  Named beans 161-163
  Qualifiers 165
CDI Qualifiers
  about 165
  named bean scopes 169-175
  working with 165-168
Certificate Authorities (CA) 241
certificate realm
  about 247
  self-signed certificates, creating 247-251
  using, by configuring application 252-256
change event 64
classname parameter 259
click event 64
CLIENT-CERT authentication 235
client-side JavaScript code
  developing 193-196
closeConnection() JavaScript function 196
commitUserAuthentication() method 270
Common Development and Distribution License (CDDL) 8
composite primary keys
  about 102, 106, 107
  conditions 104
connection pools
  setting up 26-29
connectToServer() method 199
container-managed transactions
  @TransactionAttribute annotation 138
  about 137-140
Contexts and Dependency Injection. *See* CDI
Converters 9
createBrowser() method 219
createConsumer() method 213, 225
createContext() method 211, 213
createCriteriaDelete() method 118
createDurableConsumer() method 225
createJsonParser() method 186
createNamedQuery() method 110
createProducer() method 211
createReader() method 182

Create, Read, Update, Delete. *See* CRUD
createTimer() method 150
createWriter() method 179
Criteria API
  about 111
  data, deleting with 117, 118
  data, updating with 115-117
  using 111-115
CRUD 75
CSS 57
curl command 305
CustomerDB database
  about 75, 76
  ADDRESS_TYPES table 76
  TELEPHONE_TYPES table 76
  US_STATES table 76
customerinfo.xhtml 71
custom realms
  defining 267-272
custom validators, JSF
  about 50
  creating 50-53
  methods 53-56

D

data
  deleting, with Criteria API 117, 118
  updating, with Criteria API 115-117
Data Access Objects (DAOs) 121, 128
Database Connectivity
  connection pools, setting up 26-29
  data sources, setting up 30
  setting up 26
data sources
  setting up 30
dblclick event 64
default messages, JSF
  about 56
  styles, customizing 57, 58
  text, customizing 59-61
delete() methods 312
dependency injection, CDI Qualifiers 164, 165
Digest Algorithm property 266
digest() method 264
Does Not Exist state 146

durable subscribers
   creating 222-225

E

ejbActivate() method 146
ejbRemove() method 146
EJBs
   exposing, as web services 290, 291
   life cycle 143
   web service clients 291, 292
EJB Security
   about 155-157
   client authentication 158, 159
EJB Timer Service
   about 149-152
   calendar-based 152-154
EJB web services
   securing 295, 296
encryptPassword() method 264
end() method 170
Enterprise JavaBean. *See* EJBs
Enterprise JavaBean life cycle
   message-driven bean life cycle 148, 149
   stateful session bean life cycle 143-146
   stateless session bean life cycle 146-148
Enterprise JavaBeans
   about 123
   transactions 137
EntityManager.createQuery() method 109
EntityManager.find() method 107
entity() method 312
entity relationships
   about 82
   many-to-many relationships 95-102
   one-to-many relationships 89-95
   one-to-one relationships 83-88
Enumeration parameter 268
Event.END_ARRAY event 187
Event.END_OBJECT event 187
Event.KEY_NAME event 187
Event.START_ARRAY event 187
Event.START_OBJECT event 187
Event.VALUE_FALSE event 187
Event.VALUE_NULL event 187
Event.VALUE_NUMBER event 187

Event.VALUE_STRING event 187
Event.VALUE_TRUE event 187

F

facelets, first JSF application 35-41
facelets, JSF 34
faces-config.xml, JSF
   about 34
   standard resource locations 34, 35
Faces Flows, JSF 2.2
   about 70-74
   confirmation page 73
file realm
   about 231-233
   basic authentication 233-246
findByPrimaryKey() method 81
first JSF application
   developing 35
first JSF application development
   components, grouping 45
   facelets 35-40
   form submission 46
   named beans 46-48
   navigation 48, 49
   project stages 41-43
   validation 44, 45
focus event 64

G

getAuthType() method 268
getBasicRemote() method 192, 200
getBigDecimal() method 187
getBoolean(String name) method 182
getCalculatorPort() method 285
getCriteriaBuilder() method 113, 116
getCustomer() method 128, 303, 318
getDeclaredSingularAttribute() method 114
getEnumeration() method 219
getGroupNames() method 268, 270
getInfo() method 150
getInt() method 187
getInt(String name) method 182
getJAASContext() method 269, 271
getJsonNumber(String name) method 182

getJsonObject(String name) method 182
getJsonString(String name) method 182
getLabel() method 51
getLong() method 187
getNamePort() method 286
get(Object key) method 182
getOpenSessions() method 192
getOrders() method 95
getReasonPhrase() method 200
getRequestContext() method 294
getResultList() method 109
getSingleResult() method 110
getString() method 182
getString(String Name) method 182
getText() method 215, 219
getTimers() method 150
GlassFish
  about 8
  advantages 10
  installing 13, 14
  obtaining 11, 12
  predefined security realms 228
  starting, from command line 14, 15
  URL 11
GlassFish domains
  about 23
  creating 23-25
  deleting 25
  stopping 25
GlassFish installation
  dependencies 13
GlassFish setup, for JMS
  JMS connection factory, setting up 204-206
  JMS queue, setting up 207
  JMS topic, setting up 208, 209
GlassFish, starting
  Java EE application, deploying 16-23

H

hasNext() method 186
HTML5 pass-through elements 68, 69

I

ICEfaces
  URL 74
init() method 196, 272

invalidate() method 245
isIntegralNumber() method 187
isOpen() method 192

J

JAAS 227
JAAS Context field 265
Java
  WebSocket clients, developing in 197-200
Java API
  for WebSocket 201
Java API for JSON Processing. *See* JSON-P 1.0
Java API for RESTful Web Services 2.0. *See* JAX-RS 2.0
Java API for WebSocket 1.0 10
Java API for XML Binding. *See* JAXB
Java API for XML Web Services. *See* JAX-WS
Java Authentication and Authorization Service. *See* JAAS
Java Development Kit. *See* JDK
Java EE
  overview 7
Java EE 5 34
Java EE 7 189, 204
Java EE 7 improvements
  Java API for WebSocket 1.0 10
  JAX-RS 2.0 9
  JMS 2.0 9
  JPA 2.1 9
  JSF 2.2 8
  JSON-P 10
Java EE application
  deploying 16
  deploying, through command line 20
  deploying, through Web Console 16-19
  undeploying, through GlassFish Admin Console 19
Java EE application deployment, command line
  asadmin command-line utility, using 22, 23
  autodeploy directory, using 21, 22
Java Enterprise Edition. *See* Java EE
Java Message API. *See* JMS
Java Message Service 2.0. *See* JMS 2.0

Java Messaging Service. *See* JMS
Java Persistence API. *See* JPA
Java Persistence API 2.1. *See* JPA 2.1
Java Persistence Query Language. *See* JPQL
JavaScript Object Notation. *See* JSON
java.security.MessageDigest class 263
JavaServer Faces. *See* JSF 2.2
Java Specification Request. *See* JSR
javax.jms.ConnectionFactory option 206
javax.jms.QueueConnectionFactory option 206
javax.jms.TopicConnectionFactory option 206
JAXB
  about 287
  used, for data conversion between Java-XML 307
JAX-RS 2.0
  about 9
  features 9
JAX-RS client API
  query parameters, sending via 315
JAX-RS Client API
  query path parameters, sending via 318, 319
JAX-WS 275
JAX-WS API
  used, for web service development 275-280
JAX-WS web service calls
  valid types 286
JDBC realm
  defining 262-266
JDK
  about 13, 247
  URL 13
JMS
  about 136, 137, 203
  GlassFish, setting up for 203
JMS 2.0 9
JMS connection factory
  setting up 204-206
JMSConsumer.receiveBody() method 214
JMS queue
  setting up 207
JMS topic
  setting up 208, 209

JPA
  about 75-82
  Bean Validation support 119, 121
  composite primary keys 102
  Criteria API 111
  entity relationships 82
  JPQL 108
JPA 2.1
  about 8
  features 9
JPQL 108, 109, 110
JSF
  about 33
  custom validators 50
  default messages 56
  facelets 33, 34
  faces-config.xml 34
JSF 2.0
  faces-config.xml 34
  standard resource locations 34
JSF 2.2
  Faces Flows 70
  features 8
JSF 2.2 HTML5
  markup 66, 67
  pass-through elements 68, 69
JSF component libraries
  ICEfaces 74
  Primefaces 74
  RichFaces 74
JSON
  about 177
  Model API 177
  Streaming API 177
JSON data
  generating, with Model API 178-180
  generating, with Streaming API 183-185
  parsing with Model API 181, 182
JsonGenerator class 183
JsonGenerator write() methods
  write(String name, BigDecimal value) 184
  write(String name, BigInteger value) 184
  write(String name, boolean value) 184
  write(String name, double value) 185
  write(String name, int value) 185
  write(String name, JsonValue value) 184

write(String name, long value) 185
write(String name, String value) 184
JSON (JavaScript Object Notation) 10
JsonObjectBuilder methods
  add(String name, BigDecimal value) 180
  add(String name, BigInteger value) 180
  add(String name, boolean value) 180
  add(String name, double value) 180
  add(String name, int value) 180
  add(String name, JsonArrayBuilder value) 180
  add(String name, JsonObjectBuilder value) 180
  add(String name, JsonValue value) 180
  add(String name, long value) 180
  add(String name, String value) 180
JsonObject methods
  getBoolean(String name) 182
  getInt(String name) 182
  getJsonArray(String name) 182
  getJsonObject(String name) 182
  getJsonString(String name) 182
  get(Object key) 182
  getString(String Name) 182
JSON-P 1.0 10
JsonParser Event constants
  Event.END_ARRAY 187
  Event.END_OBJECT 187
  Event.KEY_NAME 187
  Event.START_ARRAY 187
  Event.START_OBJECT 187
  Event.VALUE_FALSE 187
  Event.VALUE_NULL 187
  Event.VALUE_NUMBER 187
  Event.VALUE_STRING 187
  Event.VALUE_TRUE 187
JsonParser methods
  getBigDecimal() 187
  getInt() 187
  getLong() 187
JsonParser.next() method 187
JSON-P Model API 178
JSON-P Streaming API 183
JSR 177

K

keydown event 64
keypress event 64
keytool 250
keytool utility 247
keyup event 64

L

LDAP 260
LDAP realm
  defining 260, 261
Lightweight Directory Access Protocol. *See* LDAP
like() method 114
LoginInfo field 87
LoginModule class 270
LoginModule classes 267
logout() method 246

M

managed bean scope
  @ApplicationScoped 48
  @ConversationScoped 48
  @Dependent 48
  @RequestScoped 48
  @SessionScoped 48
  about 48
many-to-many relationships 95-102
MapMessage 212
mappedName attribute 136, 211
message-driven bean life cycle 148
message queues
  messages, retrieving from 212, 213
  working with 209-219
MessageReceiver class 222
messages
  receiving, asynchronously from message queue 214-217
  receiving, from message topic 220-222
  retrieving, from message queue 212-214
  sending, to message queue 209-212
  sending, to message topic 219, 220
MessageSender class 210, 220

message topics
    durable subscribers, creating 222-225
    messages, receiving from 220-222
    messages, sending to 219, 220
    working with 219-225
Metamodel API 113
method binding expression 46
Model API
    used, for JSON data generation 178-180
    used, for JSON data parsing 181, 182
mousedown event 64
mousemove event 64
mouseout event 64
mouseover event 64
mouseup event 64
Multipurpose Internet Mail Extensions (MIME) 300

N

named bean, CDI Qualifiers 161-163
named bean scopes
    about 169
    Application 170
    Conversation 169
    Dependent 170
    Request 169
    Session 169
newClient() method 311

O

ObjectMessage 212
Object Relational Mapping. *See* ORM
onClose() method 192
onError() method 192
one-to-many relationships 89-95
one-to-one relationships 83-89
onMessage() method 215, 217
OrderItemPK class 105
ORM 75

P

Passive state 144
path() method 319
Physical Destination Name property 208
Plain Old Java Objects (POJOs) 80, 190

Point-to-Point (PTP) messaging 203
predefined security realms
    about 228
    admin-realm 228-231
    file realm 231
Primefaces
    URL 74
processMessage() method 191
produceMessages() method 211
project stages, JSF 2
    development 41
    production 41
    SystemTest 41
    UnitTest 41
Publish/Subscribe (pub/sub) messaging 203
put method 294

Q

query parameters
    sending, via JAX-RS client API 315
    working with 312, 314
queryParam() method 315
query path parameters
    sending, via JAX-RS Client API 318, 319
    working with 316-318

R

readObject() method 182
Ready state 146
receiveBody() method 214, 221
Relational Database Management System (RDBMS) 26, 75
Representational State Transfer. *See* REST
request() method 312
REST 9, 299
RESTful web service client
    developing 311, 312
RESTful web services
    about 299
    data conversion between Java-XML, with JAXB 307-310
    DELETE methods 300
    GET methods 300
    POST methods 300
    PUT methods 300

REST resources path, configuring 303
  testing 304-306
REST resources path
  configuring, via @ApplicationPath
    annotation 304
RichFaces
  URL 74
rollback() method 143

S

saveCustomer() method 128, 140
saveMultipleNewCustomers() method 142, 143
saveNewCustomer() method 140
security realms
  about 227
  additional realms 256
  predefined security realms 228
select event 64
sendMessage() function 196
sendMessage() method 200
send() method 212, 220
sendText() method 192, 200
server-config node 256
SessionBeanClient class 127
session beans
  about 124
  asynchronous method calls 133, 135
  example 128, 130
  invoking, from web applications 130, 132
  simple session bean, developing 124-127
  singleton session beans 132
setCustomerId() method 80
setCustomer() method 95
setItems() method 102
setMessageListener() method 217
set() method 117
setParameter() method 109
setRollBackOnly() method 140
setups
  JMS connection factory 204-207
  JMS topic 208, 209
  message queues 209
Simple Object Access Protocol (SOAP) 275

simple RESTful web service
  developing 300-303
singleton session beans 132
SOAP request 279
socket 189
Solaris realm
  defining 261, 262
standard resource locations, JSF 34, 35
stateful session bean life cycle
  about 143-146
  default, modifying 144
  Does Not Exist state 144
  Passive state 144
  Ready state 144
  SessionBean interface, methods 143
stateless session bean life cycle
  about 147
  controlling 147, 148
  Does Not Exist state 146
  Ready state 146
Streaming API
  used, for JSON data generation 183-185
  used, for JSON data parsing 185-187
StreamMessage 212
StringReader class 185
styleClass attribute 57, 58
subtract() method 276

T

target() method 311
TELEPHONE_TYPES table 76
TextMessage 212
Throwable parameter 200
TimerService.createTimer() method 150
toString() method 171, 179
TransactionAttributeType.MANDATORY value 138
TransactionAttributeType.NEVER value 138
TransactionAttributeType.NOT_SUPPORTED value 138
TransactionAttributeType.REQUIRED value 138
TransactionAttributeType.REQUIRES_NEW value 138

TransactionAttributeType.SUPPORTS
    value 138
transactions, Enterprise JavaBeans
    about 137
    bean-managed transactions 140-142
    container-managed transactions 137-140

U

Undeploy button 20
updateCustomer() method 140
URI (Uniform Resource Identifier) 191
User Name Column property 266
User Table property 265, 266

V

validate() method 54
value-binding expression 40
valueChange event 64

W

WAR (Web ARchive) file 16
web applications
    session beans, invoking from 130-132
web service client
    developing 281-286
web service development, JAX-WS API used
    about 275-280
    attachments, sending to web services 287-290
    web service client, developing 281-287
Web Service Endpoint Information page 278
web services
    EJBs, exposing as 290-292
    securing 292-294

Web Services Definition Language. *See* WSDL
WebSocket
    about 189
    Java API 189, 201
WebSocket clients
    developing 193
    developing, in Java 197-200
websocketError() function 196
webSocketMessage() function 196
websocketOpen() function 196
WebSocket server endpoint
    developing, by annotating Java class 190-192
    development 189, 190
writeEnd() method 185
write() method 184, 185
writeObject() method 179
writeStartObject() method 184
write(String name, BigDecimal value) method 184
write(String name, BigInteger value) method 184
write(String name, boolean value) method 184
write(String name, double value) method 185
write(String name, int value) method 185
write(String name, JsonValue value) method 184
write(String name, long value) method 185
write(String name, String value) method 184
WSDL 280
wsimport utility 288

Thank you for buying
Java EE 7 with GlassFish 4 Application Server

About Packt Publishing

Packt, pronounced 'packed', published its first book "*Mastering phpMyAdmin for Effective MySQL Management*" in April 2004 and subsequently continued to specialize in publishing highly focused books on specific technologies and solutions.

Our books and publications share the experiences of your fellow IT professionals in adapting and customizing today's systems, applications, and frameworks. Our solution based books give you the knowledge and power to customize the software and technologies you're using to get the job done. Packt books are more specific and less general than the IT books you have seen in the past. Our unique business model allows us to bring you more focused information, giving you more of what you need to know, and less of what you don't.

Packt is a modern, yet unique publishing company, which focuses on producing quality, cutting-edge books for communities of developers, administrators, and newbies alike. For more information, please visit our website: www.packtpub.com.

About Packt Open Source

In 2010, Packt launched two new brands, Packt Open Source and Packt Enterprise, in order to continue its focus on specialization. This book is part of the Packt Open Source brand, home to books published on software built around Open Source licences, and offering information to anybody from advanced developers to budding web designers. The Open Source brand also runs Packt's Open Source Royalty Scheme, by which Packt gives a royalty to each Open Source project about whose software a book is sold.

Writing for Packt

We welcome all inquiries from people who are interested in authoring. Book proposals should be sent to author@packtpub.com. If your book idea is still at an early stage and you would like to discuss it first before writing a formal book proposal, contact us; one of our commissioning editors will get in touch with you.

We're not just looking for published authors; if you have strong technical skills but no writing experience, our experienced editors can help you develop a writing career, or simply get some additional reward for your expertise.

Java EE 6 with GlassFish 3 Application Server

ISBN: 978-1-84951-036-3 Paperback: 488 pages

A practical guide to install and configure the GlassFish 3 Application Server and develop Java EE 6 applications to be deployed to this server

1. Install and configure the GlassFish 3 Application Server and develop Java EE 6 applications to be deployed to this server.

2. Specialize in all major Java EE 6 APIs, including new additions to the specification such as CDI and JAX-RS.

3. Use GlassFish v3 application server and gain enterprise reliability and performance with less complexity.

Java EE 7 First Look

ISBN: 978-1-84969-923-5 Paperback: 188 pages

Discover the new features of Java EE 7 and learn to put them together to build a large-scale application

1. Explore changes brought in by the Java EE 7 platform.

2. Master the new specifications that have been added in Java EE to develop applications without any hassle.

3. Quick guide on the new features introduced in Java EE7.

Please check **www.PacktPub.com** for information on our titles

Java EE 7 Developer Handbook

ISBN: 978-1-84968-794-2   Paperback: 634 pages

Develop professional applications in Java EE 7 with this essential reference guide

1. Learn about local and remote service endpoints, containers, architecture, synchronous and asynchronous invocations, and remote communications in a concise reference.

2. Understand the architecture of the Java EE platform and then apply the new Java EE 7 enhancements to benefit your own business-critical applications.

3. Learn about integration test development on Java EE with Arquillian Framework and the Gradle build system.

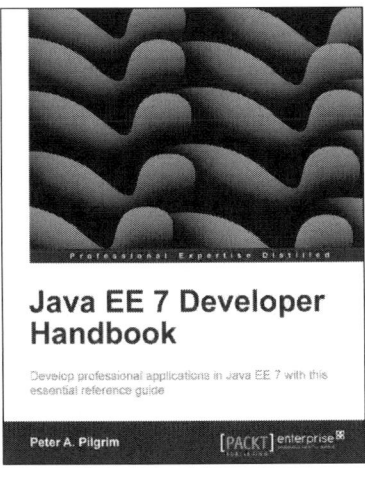

Developing RESTful Services with JAX-RS 2.0, WebSockets, and JSON

ISBN: 978-1-78217-812-5   Paperback: 128 pages

A complete and practical guide to building RESTful Web Services with the latest Java EE7 API

1. Learning about different client/server communication models including but not limited to client polling, Server-Sent Events and WebSockets.

2. Efficiently use WebSockets, Server-Sent Events, and JSON in Java EE applications.

3. Learn about JAX-RS 2.0 new features and enhancements.

Please check **www.PacktPub.com** for information on our titles

Printed in Great Britain
by Amazon.co.uk, Ltd.,
Marston Gate.